YES!

DANIEL BRYAN

WITH CRAIG TELLO

YES!

MY IMPROBABLE JOURNEY TO THE
MAIN EVENT OF WRESTLEMANIA

ST. MARTIN'S PRESS ⪪ NEW YORK

YES!. Copyright © 2015 by WWE. All rights reserved. Printed in the United States of America. For information, address St. Martin's Press, 175 Fifth Avenue, New York, N.Y. 10010.

Cover and design by Franco Malagisi

www.stmartins.com

Design by Jonathan Bennett

The Library of Congress Cataloging-in-Publication Data is available upon request.

ISBN 978-1-250-06788-3
ISBN 978-1-4668-7662-0 (e-book)

St. Martin's Press books may be purchased for educational, business, or promotional use. For information on bulk purchases, please contact the Macmillan Corporate and Premium Sales Department at 1-800-221-7945, extension 5442, or write to specialmarkets@macmillan.com.

First Edition: July 2015

10 9 8 7 6 5 4 3 2 1

CRAIG'S ACKNOWLEDGMENTS

I wish to extend my sincerest gratitude to Bryan for welcoming me into your WrestleMania journey and three decades of very personal detail. This has been an incredible experience, a true pleasure, and a dream of my own fulfilled. I raise my reusable water bottle to you and your abilities, humility, and beliefs. Thank you to Bri as well for your openness and enthusiasm for this project.

Very special thanks to photographer Rich Freeda, WWE books aficionado Steve Pantaleo, and the St. Martin's Press team, most notably, Michael Homler.

To Bret Hart, whose Sharpshooter on Curt Hennig at Summer-Slam '91 widened my eight-year-old eyes to what would become a career with WWE.

To every WWE talent who ever entertained a pitch or responded to an interview question of mine: thank you for your collaboration and the inspiration you evoke.

To the ever-diligent WWE.com staff—past and present—who consistently prove to be wildly talented, often underestimated story-tellers. Hat tip to all WWE employees, who've helped power the machine daily. Thank you to Vince McMahon and, most especially, Stephanie McMahon for giving me my first opportunity in this world ten years ago.

I thank my loving mom for her sacrifice and always demonstrating the powerful combo of heart and hard work. Thanks to Stacey, John, and Anthony for their boundless support and love. Thank you to my entire family—Jersey side and Poland side. To Chris, who believed so much in me and made me know that I could accomplish anything.

At last . . . my deepest love and appreciation to my marvelous wife, Monika, who inspires me to be the best me, every minute of every day. And to our beaming baby girl, Ruby, who I hope to see chase and realize her own vivid dreams one day long from now. Kocham cie, my boos.

YES!

1 THE BEGINNING
TUESDAY, APRIL 1, 2014—10:06 A.M.

This is a sight no one was supposed to see. Be it by fortune or the bureaucratic design of WWE brass, all signs suggested WWE Superstar Daniel Bryan would surface at WrestleMania 30 in a memorably competitive match yet in a far less marquee position than the main event bout for the WWE World Heavyweight Championship. He'd have been a contender for show-stealer but not positioned to make history, just a midshow blip on the radar of fans around the world during the thirtieth edition of WWE's grandest event.

Instead, Bryan is emerging from a private car parked at the mouth of New York City's Hard Rock Cafe. He's about to make a grand entrance into not just this morning's press event but what will be the most significant week in his career.

That signature beard is unmistakable, though the crisp suit he's wearing—a rarity—feels only slightly "Bryanized" by the shade of his shimmering maroon tie. Cameras flash, and members of the press squeeze in tight to capture a modest, five-foot-eight former vegan who quite quickly stirs a supportive reaction from a notoriously opinionated Big Apple crowd.

"Yes! Yes! Yes!" A simple, direct, and infectious string of words serves as entrance music for Bryan as he crosses the red carpet and pauses beneath a telltale marquee beaming WRESTLEMANIA 30 *in its LED glow. The synchronized*

"Yes!" chants drown out the late-morning Manhattan traffic in Times Square, and Bryan joins the throng for a brief, impromptu rally of sorts.

At this moment, Bryan stands a mere dozen blocks from the site of the inaugural WrestleMania, which emanated from world-famous Madison Square Garden almost three decades ago. Then, Vince McMahon's first major event was the symbolic underdog looking to sink its teeth into pop culture and create a worldwide phenomenon. It's fitting that Daniel Bryan's own fifteen-year journey to the main event of the "Show of Shows," WrestleMania, makes this all-important stop in the heart of New York City.

Bryan's forged his share of memories in this metropolis, yet this day is different. This is the beginning of a week even he perhaps never believed he'd live. On his Road to WrestleMania, this moment marks the final steps toward his ultimate destination: the WWE World Heavyweight Championship match at the biggest WrestleMania ever.

There's the ring within which he'll compete, and then there are the lingering visions of the ring he'll slide onto his fiancée's finger in eleven days. Bryan's experiencing the most significant moment in his professional career, but in his personal life, he's in the middle of wedding-day preparations with WWE Diva Brie Bella. A beloved couple in the eyes of adoring fans around the globe, "Braniel" is still negotiating table assignments for their nuptial celebration while readying themselves to compete at WWE's Show of Shows. There can be no more meaningful month—week, really—than this if you're Aberdeen, Washington's bearded son.

In Bryan's case, in mere days, thirty years of WrestleMania culminate simultaneously with a squared-circle Manifest Destiny, a "Yes!" Movement. On that day, a fairy tale unfolds for Daniel Bryan, and the so-called Face of WWE stands to become a bit more bewhiskered.

WWE recently asked many of their successful Superstars to take a personality inventory. In theory, these tests are able to assess personal qualities, such as sociability, prudence, and interpersonal sensitivity. The idea is that different professions require different personal characteristics, but these sorts of analytics had never been done with professional wrestlers. If WWE could find out the personality traits of their most successful Superstars, perhaps when they were recruiting, it would give them more information about the likelihood of a new signee being successful. I was one of the many people chosen to take the test.

The test involved reading many different statements and then indicating if the statement was true or false. For example, one statement would be: "I would want to be a professional race car driver." My answer: "False. I would not want to be a professional race car driver." Another example: "I rarely lose my temper." My answer: "True." Stuff like that. You respond to hundreds of those types of statements and voilà! Therein are your personality traits. In theory.

I actually enjoyed taking the test and was interested to hear the results. The next day I met with a woman to talk about them. Everything was done on a percentile basis, and as we went over the results, she became more and more baffled. In all the primary markers except one (learning approach, for which I was in the eighty-fourth percentile), I scored low. And I mean *very* low. For interpersonal sensitivity, I was in the bottom eleventh percentile. For the adjustment category, the bottom ninth percentile. Sociability, bottom third. But the one that really puzzled her was my score for ambition, which was the lowest she had ever seen in her history of administering this kind of testing and data. I was in the bottom one percentile.

She asked me how I had managed to be so successful given that I seem to have no drive, few social skills, and an inherent apathy toward most of the ideas our modern business culture seems to find so important.

"I have no idea," I said. "I just love to wrestle. The success has come mostly by luck."

My "lack of ambition" must have been a part of my personality even from my inception, because I stayed in the womb for over ten months. When my wife, Bri,* heard the story, she said it explained me perfectly. She could just imagine me being completely satisfied sitting there with an umbilical cord for a feeding tube, being

---

*In text, Daniel Bryan refers to his wife, Brianna, as Bri, who is known to WWE fans as Brie Bella.

constantly fed and warm and never wanting to come out. When they finally induced my mother, one can imagine how painful it must have been. My mom, Betty, was a small woman, and when I, Bryan Lloyd Danielson, finally decided to come out on May 22, 1981, I was more than ten pounds. Looking back at the pictures today, I'm the fattest baby I've ever seen. More importantly, I seem to always be smiling. It doesn't take much to make me happy.

My mother has told me I was very quiet. I spent a lot of time on my own because I wasn't overly social, which is essentially the same as now. My father, Donald "Buddy" Danielson, remembered me being

easygoing but also having a really stubborn side. My dad's most consistent example of this involved cookies, which could be my favorite food group. He always talked about this time I was reaching for a cookie and he told me no. I reached again and my dad slapped my hand, then again said no. I started crying but continued reaching for the cookie. Each time my dad would lightly slap my hand, and each time I would cry a little harder, relentlessly reaching for the cookie. Telling the story, he howled with laughter but never did say whether he eventually gave me the cookie.

As a young child, I had a tendency to follow my older sister, Billie Sue, around everywhere. Our relationship growing up is probably why, even today, she remains very nurturing and protective of me. Billie Sue was—and is—so much more social than I am. I just followed her around, happy as a clam, and listened to whatever she said. I picked up on whatever she did. For example, when I first learned to talk, I didn't have a stutter, but my sister did. As I spoke more and more, I started to stutter as well. Billie Sue grew out of her speech issue way before I grew out of mine, which probably wasn't until I was nearly twelve years old.

2 "YES!" CONFERENCE
TUESDAY, APRIL 1, 2014—11:16 A.M.

Twelve hours and two hundred miles earlier, a kendo-stick-carrying Daniel Bryan appeared on WWE Monday Night Raw *to ferociously batter one of the game's most successful stars: Triple H, his WrestleMania opponent and thirteen-time world champion. Engulfed by Manhattan bustle, Bryan now prepares to share a stage with his foil—plus the likes of Hulk Hogan, John Cena, and Batista—at the final press conference before sports-entertainment's annual spectacle.*

WWE production staff members in headsets scurry through halls behind a stage at the Hard Rock Cafe while media start to fill seats for the official WrestleMania 30 press conference. In a quieter nook, Bryan decompresses with his Bella bride-to-be, Brie. Minutes before the live event kicks off, the could-be WWE World Heavyweight Champion feels the self-imposed pressure of speaking in front of the NYC media. According to Bryan, he pressed his suit in his hotel room until 4 A.M. because he is "pretty bad" at ironing, obsessing over creases and seams while tackling the anxiety of this public address.

"That stuff makes me more nervous than wrestling in front of seventy thousand people," Bryan reveals. "I am comfortable wrestling. I have fun

wrestling. You put me in some spandex in front of a group of people, I'm a hundred percent fine. You put me in a suit in a room of fifty press people and I get really nervous."

Anxious or not, you wouldn't know it when Daniel Bryan hits the podium. He picks up on the theme of "dreams," first discussed by Triple H, who's already spoken immediately prior to his bearded rival. Bryan's dream becomes incredible reality at WrestleMania 30, and he is ripe with gratitude toward the WWE Universe—those who have supported him up to this moment.

"I'm here because of the people," he says to the crowd in attendance. "They would not let their voices be denied."

The speech is impassioned, and there is much "Yes!"-ing, only to be eclipsed by an uncomfortable photo op (confrontation, more so) with Triple H, Batista, and Randy Orton—the three men Bryan will potentially kick, twist, and propel himself toward through the ropes at high speeds days later. Photographers get the shot as Bryan and his fellow performers share a pose that definitively represents this year's 'Mania. He's the focus. It's his path warmed by the spotlights.

Bryan walks away from the platform with the relief of a well-delivered statement, although he's still shaking off the remnant feelings about his previous press conference address around WWE's second-biggest annual extravaganza.

"I felt like SummerSlam was a fail," Bryan admits about his first-time press event speech months before. "This, I feel I did very well. It's always good to do something that puts you out of your comfort zone and you improve at it."

Bryan's next stop is New Orleans, and his Road to WrestleMania is about to switch from turf to sky. He, his lady fair, and a bevy of fellow Superstars exit Midtown en route to La Guardia Airport for a 3:30 P.M. departure to "NOLA."

Checked in and comfortably waiting, the bearded Superstar sits with his suit jacket across his lap and Brie immediately beside him. The flight looks to be star-studded; a glance around the waiting space spies six WWE Divas, three 400-plus-pound giants (Big Show, Mark Henry, and the

Great Khali), and even the man holding the prize Bryan's fought his en-
tire life to wear: WWE World Heavyweight Champion Randy Orton.
Suddenly the airline seating area resembles an arena locker room.

There's a unique mellow about the talent congregated outside the plane
gate, following such an important event. It's a brief calm before the
WrestleMania-week storm into which they're about to fly. The flight boards,
and Bryan, his fiancée, and the other extraordinary passengers embark on
their voyage to destiny. The next time they set foot on the ground, they'll
have arrived at the home of the Show of Shows.

A good six months before I started my professional wrestling career, I was a senior sitting in an English class where we were all reading our essays aloud. The teacher, Dr. Carter, liked arranging our desks in a U-shape around the room, so we didn't have to go to the front of the class. Stand up, read your essay, immediately sit down—that was all we had to do. I was terrified.

Some people thrive when they're being looked at and feed off the energy from being put in the spotlight. Not me. I hated it. Ever since I was a kid I've been shy. Personality is an incredible, fascinating thing. We are all born with certain tendencies and predilections in terms of the sorts of things we enjoy. Some of it's nature, some of it's nurture, but it's one of life's many amazing mysteries. We are all unique.

Watching my sister's children grow up, I marvel at how different they both are and how they got that way. She and I are equally different. For one, I don't think she ever had a problem speaking in front of people. Even now, she seems to do it with the utmost ease. At my wedding rehearsal, I put her on the spot. Not because I wanted to, but mostly because I am pretty much clueless on how any sort of practical thing works, including weddings and all the surrounding mayhem. I learned a little late that, apparently, a family member of the bride and one of the groom are supposed to welcome the new person into the family with a speech and a gift. I had no idea!

So three minutes before she'd go up to do it, I told my sister she needed to make a speech welcoming my wonderful bride-to-be into our family. This was not only in front of about thirty people—most of whom she barely knew—but also in front of a reality-TV camera crew filming the whole shindig for E!'s *Total Divas* . . . meaning it could be seen by well over a million people.

Billie Sue gave me kind of an exasperated look, asked my best man, Evan, for some advice, and then went on to speak. She did it with perfect poise and was funny, sweet, and, in her own way, elegant. Simply stated, she nailed it. Not only did she nail it, she was also aware of this gift-giving custom and gave my wife a clam-digging shovel to welcome her to our family. If roles were reversed, I probably would have thrown up, even after years of experience going out and doing interviews in front of strangers in, essentially, my underwear.

Before those years of experience, I was even worse. Sitting there in the U in senior English class, I was the fifth one in line to read my essay. I watched, one by one, as each person stood up, spoke—some better than others, but all of them decent—then sat down. Each time someone finished, the feeling of dread only got stronger.

It's not so hard, I kept telling myself. *Just get through it.* By the time Dr. Carter called my name, I was full of anxiety, moist with sweat, and, frankly, scared to death. I actually started off fine; I sped right through the first paragraph, sacrificing the maximum effect of my essay's message to wrap up quicker, which I thought was the way to go, given how I was feeling. Starting with paragraph two, I began to stutter, a problem I'd had since I was a small child. Becoming keenly aware of all the eyes looking at me, I read on, and the stuttering only got worse and worse. I paused, tried to start again, paused, tried to start again. By this point I was messing up ever other word—my sweat beading heavily from my forehead—and I was shaking. Finally I just stopped.

After a long pause, I looked to Dr. Carter and sheepishly explained that I didn't think I could continue. I couldn't do it. He allowed me to take my seat back in the comfort of the U, and, horrified, I sat down so the next student could take his turn. I never finished reading my essay, and I was the only one who didn't make it through. I was incredibly embarrassed.

I felt a similar unease years later when seven of my peers and I stood nervously on the WWE set as we were about to debut on the new television show *WWE NXT.* The eight of us were called "Rookies," though at that point I had been wrestling for ten years. None of us knew what to expect that night. We hadn't been told anything prior to standing there, ready to be seen on live WWE programming. About three minutes before showtime, a producer came in and told us one of the WWE Pros was going to come on set and speak. We were to react accordingly.

Another producer screamed out, "Going live in fifteen seconds!" Then, "Five, four . . ." The final three numbers were counted down by the motion of his hand. Suddenly the camera was panning over us and music was playing throughout the arena. The Miz, who was my assigned Pro, walked onto the set. He eyed each of us up and down, turned to the camera with his back facing me, and said, "Daniel Bryan, come here." I stepped forward.

The Miz started talking, but I could barely focus on what he was saying. I heard the words "Internet darling" and "a star in the minor leagues" and could only assume he was talking about me. He asked me if I thought I was ready, and ironically enough, my first word in WWE was "Yes."

Miz continued, "One thing you have to learn in WWE is you have to expect anything. So right now, I want you to go to the ring and I want you to introduce yourself. Tell everybody exactly who you are. I want you to show personality. I want you to show charisma. I want you to give these people a reason to watch you every Tuesday night." He rambled on for a little longer, then added, "Oh, and have a good catchphrase."

During the ten years prior to my NXT debut, I had garnered a reputation for being a very skilled wrestler. But I had also garnered a reputation for not having a whole lot of charisma or verbal skills.

My "character," if you could call it that, was essentially just me, and I could be as understated or as over-the-top as I wanted to be. For the most part, if I had nothing to say or didn't want to say anything, nobody could make me. Otherwise, since I lack a natural inclination for lighting up the microphone, if I was going to do an interview, I typically would ensure I had plenty of time to prepare.

Needless to say, having to do a live in-ring interview on no topic whatsoever with no time to prepare was not how I envisioned making my television debut. And I hated catchphrases.

It feels like an eternity walking to the ring in WWE when no one knows who you are. WWE fans tend to be very hard on people they don't see as "stars," and I could hear the groan when I came out to the Miz's entrance music. In the ring, I did my best to stay confident, or at least appear that way. By the time the ring announcer handed me the microphone, I still had no idea what I was going to say. I ended up thanking the fans for being so accepting even though the Miz was my Pro, and I told them I wished my Pro had been my true mentor, William Regal. From there, I basically babbled on about NXT for another thirty seconds. Losing my train of thought and seeing the crowd lose their patience, I started to worry. Luckily, Miz's music hit and out he came. Thank goodness. (Yes, I really said that.)

Miz immediately started ragging on me—well deservedly, I might add. He asked where my personality was; where was my charisma? We bantered back and forth until he finally asked me for a catchphrase. As soon as he asked, something I had just heard in my grappling class immediately came to mind. I told him if we were to ever step in the ring and fight, he would only have two options: He would either "tap or snap." It wasn't the best catchphrase in the world, and I actually couldn't use it because someone owned the rights to it, but it was enough for me to get through the interview and get a decent reaction. In response, Miz slapped me in the face and left me standing in the ring to end the segment.

Not exactly a home run, more like a solid single. I knew I needed to keep working on talking, but I considered this a success, especially given I had no idea what was coming. And that's one of the reasons NXT was the most unusual wrestling experience of my career: A huge part of it was unscripted, and none of the show's Rookies knew what was going on. I didn't know Miz was going to come out and save the interview, and I definitely didn't know he was going to strike me at the end. Miz is self-admittedly not the toughest guy in the world, and much later on, he confessed to me that he was mildly concerned I was going to fight him for the slap.

The rest of the episode played to my strengths, and I wrestled Chris Jericho, who was the World Heavyweight Champion at the time, in the main event of the show. Chris is a true pro, and even though the match was only five minutes and I lost, he made me look like a star. After the match, Miz started beating me up, and again I had no idea he was going to do it. Neither did he, apparently, as the instruction was sent to him from the producers through the referee in the ring. Despite the confusion and the chaos, it had been a decent debut. Yet it all went downhill from there.

3 "MAKIN' GROCERIES"
TUESDAY, APRIL 1, 2014—7:18 P.M.

The sun's only starting to drop when the wheels of the plane hit the New Orleans tarmac just a little after 6 P.M. If you've stood on a stage for a live streamed press conference for your organization's greatest event ever, it's already been a long day, made to feel longer with a three-and-a-half-hour flight (though easily a short skip for someone who's made a weekend trip out of Japan). There is no jet lag to record as camera crews capture Bryan and Brie's arrival and airport traipsing, before their ride to their hotel in NOLA's French Quarter.

Championships. Relationships. Nutrition. Daniel Bryan has his priorities. This is what delivers WWE's "Yes!" Man to the familiar storefront of the Whole Foods Market in Mid-City almost immediately after getting into town. He and Brie check into their hotel room, then split: Brie to an appearance, Bryan off to grocery shop—"makin' groceries," as New Orleans jargon goes. It's a common ritual for Bryan, whose weekend road routine usually includes arriving in a city on a Friday, then finding the nearest organic market and stocking up for several days of travel.

"Nutrient density is important to me," he explains. "Our schedule is brutal. Trying to replenish all that is just vital. You can't always trust stores

to cook super healthy. I'd rather have a protein shake and fresh fruit and veggies than a crappy chicken salad from a fast-food restaurant." He summarizes, "It's nice to have nutrient-dense food ready whenever you need it."

The produce lane is a different aisle than most WWE television viewers are used to seeing Daniel Bryan walk. He pushes a half-cart and carefully selects a serious amount of produce—vibrant carrots, greens, seven apples, seven bananas, multiple bottles of fresh juices—while fulfilling an unofficial shopping list for himself and his fiancée. He stops only to thoroughly check packages for ingredient listings and to sign an autograph for a fellow shopper/fan on top of a raspberry container sitting in his cart. Somehow, this is all routine.

"I've been doing almost all the shopping for us," Bryan says, explaining that his soon-to-be-spouse's erratic schedule has increased since the advent of the Total Divas reality series. "But I'm not as good of a shopper as Brie," he candidly admits. "I tend to overspend."

Bryan floats from section to section, seeking several days' worth of sustenance. A squared-circle Superstar who used to carry small packets of pumpkin seeds in his jacket pockets, the "Yes!" Man is known among his peers and fan base for his unique diet. In May 2013, Bryan developed an intolerance to soy that led to him abandon veganism. But as his shopping progresses into the dessert aisle, it becomes apparent how much he still enjoys a good vegan sweet treat. Bryan raves about avocado-based mousse with carob chips, but he's on the hunt for a specific peanut butter cookie for Brie. He ultimately settles for Uncle Eddie's chocolate walnut flavor, which you can expect the couple will share.

"I have a very bad sweet tooth, but I manage it. I manage it with these healthy treats," he coyly remarks.

This specific store location—which happens to boast a message of wholesome-food accessibility in this particular NOLA neighborhood— appeals not only to Bryan's dietary needs but also to the principles and values instilled since birth in the natural sprawl of Aberdeen. In brief, this is his kind of place, right down to the earthy scent in the air.

Bryan greets a cashier, pays, then heads back to the hotel to wait for his soon-returning fiancée. He's gone from suit to T-shirt, from a stage at the epicenter of New York City to the frozen food section of a grocery store in Louisiana. Now, as he stands holding brown paper shopping bags while he waits for an elevator in the lobby of the Roosevelt Hotel, Bryan involuntarily reminds you, by the sight of him, that he is everything a top WWE champion has never resembled. Yet in a matter of days he plans on raising up the most-coveted golden symbols in sports entertainment for the most emphatic "Yes!" succession yet.

The elevator dings, the doors close, and his first night in New Orleans quickly vanishes as WrestleMania Sunday takes one step closer.

It's often said you don't choose who you fall in love with, which I believe to be true. I also believe you don't choose *what* you fall in love with. Sometimes things just grab hold of your imagination and never let go—and that's been my experience with professional wrestling. My introduction to wrestling is one of my earliest memories, and I've loved it ever since.

I say "one of" and not "the" earliest memory because my earliest memory involves me burning my butt. After every bath at my Grandpa Austin's house, Billie Sue and I would wrap ourselves in towels and go stand by his wood-burning stove to dry off. In the cold Washington weather, the heat was always nice. One day around age four, I got a little too close and burned my little butt cheeks on the stove—so bad that each cheek blistered. More so than the actual burning, the most vivid memory is the pain I felt each time I'd sit on the toilet. I'm lucky I don't have scars, especially since I spend so much time on broadcast television in trunks. There have also been quite a few live crowds who have seen my derriere. How would parents explain those scars to their kids?

"If I show you, you have to promise not to tell anybody," whispered the new kid in class. It had been Abe's first day as a student at Aberdeen's Central Park Elementary School, but he had already

made friends. At the end of the school day, Abe was being chased around a table by my best friend, Warren, as he sang, "La cucaracha, la cucaracha! Please don't hit me in the butt." He and Warren came back to my house that same afternoon.

We found ourselves in my bedroom huddling around Abe's backpack. Warren and I were anxious and excited about what Abe was about to show us. Abe looked from side to side as if he suspected someone was watching us while he slowly unzipped his backpack. He double-checked to make sure we weren't going to tell anybody before he reached in and pulled out a stack of magazines. Wrestling magazines. Abe handed us each a magazine, and I pored over the pictures. Men with enormous muscles in ridiculous outfits fought equally ridiculous men. There were giants, midgets, Indians, cowboys, Russians, men with face paint and spikes—I had never seen anything like it! It was magic. Warren quickly lost interest, but I couldn't stop flipping through the pages. I convinced Abe to let me borrow a few of the magazines, and it was through their worn pages that I became hooked on wrestling.

It wasn't long before my parents found me reading the magazines that I was supposed to keep secret. Hiding things has never been my forte. Fortunately, I had nothing to worry about. Despite not being wrestling fans themselves, my parents weren't upset. They actually liked the fact that I was trying to read. Plus, they saw that it made me happy.

Before I knew it, my parents started bringing me home wrestling magazines when they saw a new one come out. Slowly but surely, I became a better reader, which was important because I missed a lot of school.

I have a lot of harebrained hypotheses, most of which are too idiotic to be printed. Ask Nigel McGuinness about my thoughts on the evolution of penis size. But this one idiot hypothesis mildly pertains to this story, so here goes nothing.

It is my belief that due to modern medicine, humans have stopped evolving in a way that produces healthier adults. I say this because many children who two hundred years ago would have died are now living to successfully reproduce. They thus pass on their genetic deficiencies to their children, who then pass them on to their children, and so on and so forth. I am one of those children: sick my entire childhood and even still often sick as an adult. Without modern medicine, I would have surely passed before I could procreate. Who knows, I still might. Regardless, I affectionately refer to myself as a defect.

Bri is also a defect. I will let her explain her own defectiveness in her own book, should she choose to write one. Before we started dating, I pointed this out to her, and also told her it would be genetically irresponsible for either of us to have children as it would weaken the evolution of humans going forward. What we should be doing as a species is breeding intelligent superathletes, like having John Cena make babies with Jackie Joyner-Kersee. It became our little joke, both of us being defects. And we will, at some point, try our best with the de-evolution of our species.

My persistent illness started with viral asthma, and, as we later found out, I was allergic to grass and trees and almost all animal hair—which didn't stop me from trying to sleep with my beagle Millie nearly every night. Oftentimes I would wake up with my eyes swollen nearly shut. After my allergies were discovered, I began getting weekly injections (easily up to 150 shots), which helped to a degree. Still, whenever I was outside or playing sports, grass would get the better of me. I ended up getting quite a few upper respiratory infections, and there would be times I would miss a week or two of school at a time. One December, I missed nearly the entire month leading up to Christmas break. Missing so much school, I suspect, made me even less social, but on the flip side, I became comfortable entertaining myself and developing my interests.

I still always managed good grades, mostly because school came relatively easy to me. Math seemed like a fun little puzzle for me to figure out, and I enjoyed reading. That pretty much covers elementary education.

Being out sick all the time, I never learned to swim properly because lessons were during school. I can't freestyle, backstroke, sidestroke. None of that. I never advanced further than beginner level. But if doggy paddling and treading water were in the Olympics, I might have a shot because I spent so much time practicing while everyone else learned how to actually swim.

Other than swimming, being sick didn't stop me from doing much. Despite my grass allergies, I was always playing sports, mostly because I love being outside. At different points, I played just about everything—soccer, football, baseball, and basketball. I ran track, did cross-country, wrestled, and even tried golf one summer with some clubs borrowed from a friend.

I played every sport and wasn't good at any of them. I never had the mentality necessary to be good at sports. They were just games to me and relatively unimportant; it was hard for me to care about winning and losing. As long as there wasn't too much pressure, I had fun. That's why I loved practice. Some people hated drilling, and they saw practice as work. I saw it as being able to play against my friends, with no pressure. I liked the drills in almost every sport because it was fun for me to see functional improvement.

A good example of my athletic mindset was how much I enjoyed track. Even though I only did track for a couple of seasons, it was my favorite because there were so many events to participate in. I did shot put, threw the javelin, and ran a variety of distance races from the 100-meter to the 3,200, plus I tested my skill with the discus and all the jumping events. Again, I tried everything and was rotten at everything—especially the pole vault, which I loved. Really, what's not to love? You run with a stick and use it to jump as high as you can and then land on a big fluffy pad. The thing is, I'm not a huge fan of heights, so I would practice and practice and practice, because it was fun, but never cleared anything past eight feet. People can high-jump eight feet.

My only real accomplishment in athletics was being named MVP of the C squad my sophomore year in basketball. At least, I like to tell people I was the MVP. The award I got was actually a Coach's Award for hard work, and all of the good sophomores played on varsity or JV. I suppose it's not much of an accomplishment after all.

My love of sports turned into a love of sports cards, even though I tended to look at them more as an investment than as a hobby. My generation of kids was the first to save their sports cards because they'd be worth money someday. Back then, I thought my sister was stupid for saving her money instead of buying cards like I did. I believed the cards were going to appreciate in value, unlike my sister's savings, which she just kept in her bedroom, accruing absolutely no interest.

Bryan with his "World Champion" dog, Asparagus, 2007

It was predominantly baseball cards at first, then expanded to basketball cards and football cards. I even had some wrestling cards. Interestingly (or unfortunately, depending on how you look at it), I didn't ever like the Michael Jordan types. I ended up collecting a lot of players who were good but not necessarily stars. In baseball, instead of liking Ken Griffey Jr.—who was on the Seattle Mariners and whose cards were always worth a lot—I liked Roberto Alomar and Paul Molitor. I figured, "Oh, Paul Molitor's so good. When people realize how good he is, his card is going to be worth money." Sometimes I'd trade a card of Frank Thomas—who was huge at the time—for a couple of Roberto Alomars. Even though I wasn't great at understanding the real value of sports cards, my first attempt at being an entrepreneur involved trying to sell the cards with my friend Scott.

During the summer—weather permitting—we would set up a table outside of my house, organize our cards all businessmanlike,

and tape up a sign out front that read BASEBALL CARDS FOR SALE. There was never a ton of traffic on our street, and usually our only "customers" were kids who didn't have any money so would end up playing football or Wiffle ball in the front yard.

After one summer, Scott and I combined all the money we saved, which was a total of $40. In our heads, this must've seemed like a million dollars, because we were convinced we'd be able to start this trading card empire with that cash. We only ended up being able to pay for a single box of Leaf baseball cards, which was a disappointment.

Still, I continued collecting cards until I was fourteen, and I kept them in the attic in case they'd be worth something someday. They're not. Unfortunately, sports cards of that time—much like the comic books I also still have—were so mass-produced that there's no scarcity, and they're worth *less* than when I collected them in the '80s and '90s. It turns out my sister made the better decision after all. That's where a functional understanding of economics would have really served me well.

Just like the wrestling magazines helped out my reading, sports cards served a purpose as well. There are all sorts of statistics on the backs of the cards, and I was hell-bent on figuring out what they all meant. Figuring out things like batting averages and field goal percentages gave me a better understanding of division, percentages, and decimal points, and it made math seem fun rather than a bore. Plus, looking up the value of cards in the pricing magazines helped when it came time to find things in the dictionary or scan reference materials in the library. Education can be fun if framed in the right way.

Selling sports cards wasn't the only way I tried to make money as a kid. After my parents' divorce, we didn't have much money. My mom didn't have any sort of college degree and was having a hard time finding a job, so when Billie Sue and I were old enough—around ten or eleven—we each got paper routes. Every day, rain or shine, a big stack of newspapers would get dropped off at our house and we'd hop on our bikes to go deliver them. Like most other things, I turned it into a game and it didn't really even feel like work, though we also had to go door to door and collect people's payments at the end of the month, which I was not good at.

In theory, for each of our paper routes we were supposed to net around $100 a month. We'd give about half of what we collected back to the *Daily World* and be able to keep the other half. Of that, my mom would let us keep a small portion, and the rest would go into the family budget, our savings, and tithing to the church. Unfortunately, our salary didn't always work out that way.

I have always had an irrational fear of asking people for money, possibly because we had so little of it. Even something as simple as going to collect $7.25 a month from people who had signed up for the service somehow terrified me. Around the fifteenth of each month, we were supposed to start collecting, and we had about a week to get it all in. Although I was vigilant in getting people their papers on a daily basis, I was less so when it came time to collect. At first it didn't seem like a big deal, but then I would encounter customers who seemed bothered or angry when I came to the door asking them for their payment, especially if they owed more than a single month.

Sometimes when you went collecting, people wouldn't be home, so if you tried to collect a couple of times in a month and missed them each time, you would just get both months' payment the following month. There was one house that I had missed for a couple of payments in a row, which wasn't so unusual because there is a lot of shift work in town. By the time I finally reached them, they owed for four months, around $30. The guy exploded on me when he found out how much he owed, and somehow I felt I was in the wrong. I became even more hesitant to collect after that moment.

Soon after, if there were people who owed more than two months, I just stopped collecting from them altogether. There were also some houses I was already skipping because their homes would creep me out. It got so bad that one month when it came time to send *Daily World* their money, we actually owed them more than I had collected.

My mom was beside herself and didn't understand what had happened. We were already struggling, and then what was intended to be a source of income turned into a debt. After that, I started doing a little bit better, but we still never made as much as we should have because I simply hated collecting.

As soon as my sister turned sixteen, she got a job at McDonald's, and when I turned fifteen, she was able to help get me a job there, too. At that age, all I was supposed to do was work a couple of hours a week doing the mopping, sweeping, and removal of garbage. One day, they were shorthanded in the kitchen because someone didn't show up. They showed me how to cook the burgers on these mini trays, and it wasn't hard; I did it and I became very efficient at it.

I must've done a good job, because shortly thereafter they put me in the kitchen for every shift, even though I wasn't supposed to be, and I was working more than twenty hours a week (the limit for my age in Washington state at the time). I think they just forgot how old I was. It became my duty to get the meat tray filled, and I never did the mopping and that stuff again.

Long prior to my years in the workforce, my passion for wrestling deepened when I discovered I could actually watch it on television. We didn't watch much TV and didn't have cable, so the thought had previously never occurred to me. Suddenly the characters that I read about in magazines had sprung to life. Seeing the Ultimate Warrior lift a grown man above his head and drop him to the mat for a press slam was even more impressive than it looked in the pictures. A photo of someone standing on the top rope was no match for watching the grace, movement, and destruction of a "Macho Man" Randy Savage elbow drop.

Since I had no concept of television programming, I'd flip through the channels every time I'd turn on the TV, in hopes of catching some form of wrestling. It took me some time (I can be a slow learner), but I finally realized that it came on every Saturday morning.

I was the sole wrestling fan in the family, but the only time I remember anybody in the house getting annoyed with my fandom was during the NFL play-offs. It seemed to me that football season was my dad's favorite time of the year. He loved watching football and the Seattle Seahawks, our hometown team, whom he'd followed since their first season in 1976. Most years they were pretty bad, but in 1988 the Seahawks won their division for the very first time and were play-off bound. The game was on a Saturday against the Cincinnati Bengals, and all week my dad had talked about watching it, but I insisted on watching wrestling.

I must have been arguing relentlessly to watch my Saturday morning show, because my dad, usually as patient as could be, was finally exasperated. "The play-offs only happen for a couple weeks a year and the Seahawks are playing," he said. "Wrestling is on *every single week!*" I eventually gave in but was disappointed because the British Bulldogs were wrestling that day. (I loved Davey Boy Smith and Dynamite Kid—not so much because Dynamite was one of the most revolutionary performers of all time as because I thought their dog, Matilda, was so cute.)

At first my friend Abe was the only other kid I knew who was really into wrestling. When I would occasionally go over to his house, we'd play with the giant rubber LJN Toys action figures. It seemed like he had all of them—not just the popular wrestlers like Hulk Hogan and Jake "the Snake" Roberts, but even some of the more obscure characters like Special Delivery Jones and Outback Jack. Plus, he had two rings, so we could each make them fight. Before long, though, Abe lost interest in wrestling, and it just became my own little thing for a while.

It wasn't until I was in middle school that I found other kids who liked wrestling, too. The biggest development was when I found out that my friends Tony Sajec, Schuyler Parker, and John Manio had created their own wrestling league, which they called Backyard Championship Wrestling (BCW), despite most of the action taking place indoors. Sometimes they'd wrestle each other, but most of the matches involved Big Bad Brown, a giant teddy bear who was also their champion. At some point, they invited me and my friend Evan

Aho over, and it became a regular thing. Eventually, Big Bad Brown retired and our wrestling evolved into something else entirely. At first it was at Tony's house (where Big Bad Brown resided), and we'd just kind of wrestle on the floor. Soon we moved the fun to my house, and by the end of high school, my best friends were the guys who would watch wrestling pay-per-views at my place regularly. It was Mike Dove and his brother Jake, Evan and his younger brother Kristof, Tony, Schuyler, and John. The first WWE show I ordered was the Royal Rumble in 1996. Then we got WrestleMania XII, which had the epic main event Iron Man Match between Bret "Hit Man" Hart and Shawn Michaels.

Before the shows started, we'd clear everything out of our family room and lay out a mattress on the floor, thus transforming the room into the BCW Arena. The corners of the room were the turnbuckles, the walls were the ropes we'd bounce off of, and the couch was the top rope in case we wanted to do a Macho Man elbow drop or something.

If you've been a wrestling fan for an extended period of time, you've probably either seen or heard of Mick Foley's backyard wrestling adventures, particularly the moment in which he jumped off the top of his house. Our wrestling was different. Sometimes we would actually try to seriously learn the moves we'd seen on TV, but more often we would just be goofing off. My friend Schulyer was Hip Skip, whose character never stopped running for twenty-four hours straight. He would come running from down the street, open the sliding glass door, run in, do a match, then run back out. There was also El Bate, a wrestler in a Batman mask who'd often appear in videos we'd make for our Spanish class (despite *el bate* actually meaning "baseball bat," not anything to do with Batman).

I liked to think that because we weren't doing the crazier stuff, what we were doing was safe. The truth is, it wasn't, which is why WWE now does all those videos telling people to not try it at home. And since it was my house and I seriously wanted to be a pro wrestler, I was constantly practicing things I thought I might need to know, like backflips off the couch. We did it all on a mattress, so we never thought of landing on someone as dangerous. We only looked at the jumping, twisting, and backflipping as the dangerous part. Unfortunately, one time, I jumped off my couch for a twisting senton and landed back-first directly on Kristof's face, breaking his jaw. He had to have his jaw wired shut and was only able to eat through a straw for weeks.

I didn't want anything to stop our wrestling, so I never told my mom what happened. We had already been given a warning after cracking the drywall in the corner that we used as a turnbuckle, and I thought something as serious as this injury would end our wrestling for good. My mom didn't find out until much later when she was talking to Kristof's mother, Pam, who had been very cool about the incident. When Pam made mention of Kristof's broken jaw, my mom was like, "Wait—what?!"

Luckily, despite my injuring him, Kristof remains my friend to this day. He and Evan and Mike were all groomsmen in my wedding, almost two decades later. Kristof still tells me that at some point he's going to break my jaw in return. Whenever I see him, he always asks, "Is it now?"

Other than wrestling with my friends and working, I was relatively antisocial and completely content to stay at home. As you can imagine, that made me a real hit with the ladies. I only really dated one girl in school, during a period when I lived with my dad in Castle Rock, Washington, about an hour and a half away from Aberdeen. Her name was Becky; she was a senior and I was a junior. I think she just liked me because I was new and Castle Rock was a small town. We went to movies or out to eat, and even went to her senior prom together. After one of these events, we would end up in her parents' basement making out on the couch. One night, during a particularly long makeout session, Becky was on top of me, and in the heat of the moment, she whispered into my ear, "Be gentle." I laughed so hard that I accidentally threw her off the couch. Despite my subsequent calls, we never went out again, and soon she was dating a college guy with a unibrow. So it goes.

My hometown of Aberdeen, Washington, is a blue-collar town filled with good, hardworking people. It's built on the timber industry, and there are signs all over that say WORKING FORESTS = WORKING FAMILIES. Unfortunately, when logging is down, a lot of people get laid off. At one point, Aberdeen had the highest tavern-per-person ratio in the state, or at least that was the rumor. It also rains, on average, over eighty inches a year. (The year I graduated, for example, it rained a hundred days in a row.) Nirvana's Kurt Cobain is probably our most famous resident. I'm not sure if it's related, but Aberdeen has a relatively high number of suicides every year.

The rain always comforted me as a kid. Even in the winter, I would leave my window open because I liked the sound of the raindrops as I went to sleep, and I liked the room being really cold, with me really warm underneath my blankets. Looking back, I realize how much I love the rain, and I recognize that without all that water, you can't have all that green.

Our house was next to a big sprawl of woods in a suburb of Aberdeen called Central Park. It was basically just our place, the people next door, and a large parcel of wooded area we called Oscar's Creek, named after one of the neighbor's Labradors who loved to play in that spot. I remember rope swings over ravines—even with my fear of heights—and essentially growing up around all the trees. Being around living things like trees, plants, and ferns is what I prefer, and being raised in this environment is definitely what made me love nature.

Sometimes my dad took us fishing, and I hated it. He told me that fish don't feel any pain, but I didn't believe it. Catching a fish is a very violent affair. I always put myself in the position of the fish; I envision me spotting a cookie, eating the cookie, then suddenly getting hooked by the mouth, dragged across the street, dumped in some water, and forced to stay under the water until I die—exactly what happens to a fish, but the opposite. Years after our fishing trips, I still have this (awesome) picture of me, my sister, and my dad, holding two fish. He's smiling. My sister's smiling. And there I am, looking at the fish, horrified.

Bryan, his sister, Billie Sue, and father, Buddy, make peanut butter balls

Writing about my father is the most difficult part of this book. I love my father. All of him. My mom says to this day that in the absence of alcohol, my dad was the best man she's ever known. She says that still, over twenty years after their divorce. But then there's the other side. Addiction is a terrible thing, and one with which my family has a long history. My father was the youngest of six children, all of whom either had alcohol or drug problems, or were complete teetotalers. My dad battled with alcohol addiction his entire life.

I related to my dad better than I did to anybody else. Billie Sue says it's because we're exactly the same, minus the alcohol. I always take that as a compliment because he was smart, kind, and funny. He was genuinely sympathetic toward people. And most importantly, he always made sure we knew we were loved.

My parents were high school sweethearts who married relatively young (my mom was twenty, my dad nineteen). My mom waitressed

to help put my dad through school as he got his engineering tech degree, but once he graduated, he went to work in the logging industry as a log scaler, measuring and grading the cut trees. My dad loved the outdoors and loved logging, which, unfortunately, isn't the most stable job in the world. Shortly after I was born, we moved to Vernal, Utah, where my dad had gotten a different position that was supposedly going to be a little more steady.

According to my aunt and uncle, my dad always had an issue with alcohol, but my mom first noticed it when we lived in Utah. We were only there for six months before we moved to Albany, Oregon, so my dad could pursue scaling again, and then back to Aberdeen. During all that time, my dad was caught in an addiction cycle. He'd be in and out of alcohol programs, which brought times of sobriety—three weeks, six weeks sometimes—then it would start again. Sometimes he left for days at a time, and my mom would be worried sick. I really didn't notice any of it, though, because my mom protected my sister and me from seeing him when he was drunk. I remember we'd always be put in the back bedroom of the house to watch *Pete's Dragon* or *Mary Poppins,* and occasionally we would hear yelling over the sounds of the TV.

My dad's drinking got substantially worse when his father died of emphysema and then, a year later, his mom died of cancer. After that, my parents were pretty much divorced, although I don't remember the exact timing of it. My mom and my sister don't either. It's strange how there can be such collective forgetfulness.

All of that said, my dad was still a very loving father. The only reason I bring up his drinking is because it helps explain why I don't drink and never have. When kids started drinking, I immediately saw it as a negative and not cool at all.

Though they were separated, we would still go over and see him all the time. My dad played catch with me, came to my sporting events when he wasn't working, and took us camping. We went to my dad's house on Christmas Eve, and he played Santa until we got old enough to know it was him. On Christmas morning, we'd wake up, eat cinnamon rolls my mom made on our wood stove, then open presents (including perhaps my favorite Christmas present, a set of thirty RF Media VHS tapes of all the Extreme Championship Wrestling house shows).

One of the things I especially loved doing with him was going clam-digging. In the Pacific Northwest, we have razor clams, a meaty shellfish that can grow up to six inches long. To find them, you look for little indentions in the sand and pound your shovel next to them. If a hole starts bubbling, it's a clam hole. Then all you have to do is start digging, and if you're fast enough and get your arm into the hole, you can grab the clam before he digs away—and they are *fast* diggers. My dad was great at it since he'd been doing it ever since he was young. He'd dig some, then people-watch some; dig some more, then people-watch some more. It's kind of the way I've always approached life.

As a kid, I was never very good at clam-digging, but I loved playing in the sand. The older I got, the better I got, yet my dad was always much better than I ever was. I still tend to break the clam's shell when I'm digging. After getting our limits of fifteen clams per person, we'd go back home, and within a day or two we'd be having fried razor clams for dinner, which has always been one of my favorites.

Something I always appreciated about each of my parents is that neither ever talked bad about the other. I'm sure after the divorce they each wanted to, but they never did. Eventually my dad married a wonderful woman named Darby, who stood by him through thick and thin. She has a terrific sense of humor and treated Billie Sue and me great whenever we'd come over. We'd play cards or watch Seahawks games, and even if we were doing nothing, we still had a good time.

My parents' divorce was very hard on my mother because she'd been a stay-at-home mom. She didn't have much more than a high school education and had done a lot of waiting tables until my sister and I were born. My mom didn't know what to do, as there were

very few jobs in Aberdeen that would pay a woman with no education and limited job skills, who hadn't worked in years, enough money to support a family. But my mom wouldn't give up. She started by volunteering at the Satsop nuclear power plant, giving tours and such. She worked so hard that they hired her, but the power plant was never fully completed, and after a couple of years, my mom was laid off. My sister and I never heard a complaint from her about any of it. Soon she started going to the community college, even though she had to take some classes that didn't even count for credits toward her degree, just so she could catch up. My mom worked hard while back in school, and on top of that, she worked two jobs, each at a different department store. And she never—to use a wrestling term—"sold" being tired to us. Looking back, I will never know how she did it, because she was always there to pick us up from our various practices, she always came to our games, and she made us every meal. (We never ate out.) I can't imagine how she had enough hours in the day.

My mom worked her butt off and graduated with her bachelor's degree in 1999, a few days before I graduated from high school. She went on to get her master's degree in counseling psychology, and she's worked in that field, helping people, ever since. My mom also remarried—although well after I started to wrestle. Her husband is a terrific, smart man named Jim, and they live together to this day.

4 TRAINED TO WIN
WEDNESDAY, APRIL 2, 2014—11:32 A.M.

Daniel Bryan emerges from his hotel room equipped with his water bottle and classic black-and-white composition notebook—the only tools he needs for a late-morning workout. On foot, Bryan heads a few blocks away to the New Orleans Athletic Club, receiving a drive-by salute from a fan who hollers from her car, "We love you, Daniel!"

Not your standard Planet Fitness, "N.O.A.C." (as embossed on its front door) has roots dating back to 1872 and interior walls accented by sepia images of athletic gentlemen from yesteryear. It's a real workmanlike exercise facility, quirky yet appropriate. Transitioning from uniquely patterned tile, hardwood floors creak heavily as Bryan steps in for some conditioning.

The first training phase for the former WWE Champion? Sign up. Daniel sits in a wooden chair in a registration room lined with fading photos of old-school strongmen and athletes. For enrollment purposes, he's asked for full name, phone number, and other standard info, then gets his picture snapped by an employee with a small webcam. He takes one towel and heads off into the massive, multilevel gym with spiral staircases, ornate banisters, and a swimming pool that looks like one found in a backyard beside a garden . . . but it's inside.

His motions are slow during muscle stretches, his focus on strengthening all the smaller muscles in the shoulder. Between Hindu push-ups, Bryan pauses to provide more insight into his regimen.

"I'm focusing mostly on conditioning and technique," he says. "I'm going ultralight and ultra-conservative with my training because the last thing you need is to set a personal best and tear out your shoulder. I do a lot of movement prep before I start and a lot of stretching when I'm done."

At WrestleMania, WWE's "Yes!" Man comes eye-to-villainous-eye with the Game—a nickname Triple H earned over time for both ring dominance and physical prowess. He is an opponent unlike any other Daniel Bryan's ever faced, but the same can be said of Triple H about Bryan.

The Cerebral Assassin (another of Triple H's intimidating monikers) is as calculating as he is powerful, and he's adapted a new conditioning regimen to combat the in-ring style of his opponent. It's a truth Bryan welcomes and, in fact, lauds.

"The idea of the lumbering big man doesn't work anymore. There were times when I first started training to be a wrestler that I thought I needed to get bigger because that's what wrestling demands, so I was doing strength- and size-based workouts," Bryan explains. "But even if you look at [400-pound WWE giant] Big Show, he's dropping weight and adding mobility because that's what it takes to exist in today's wrestling era."

He proclaims, "Wrestling is evolving. What worked ten years ago doesn't work now. The fans demand more because they've seen more—not only from guys like me. They've seen it from Cesaro . . . Seth Rollins . . . Big E.

"All this is changing," Bryan says, promising a revolution in WWE

When you're a kid, people constantly ask you what you want to be when you grow up. I don't recall if it was immediately at first sight that I knew I wanted to be a professional wrestler, but looking back, I don't remember ever wanting to be anything else. Of course, when you're young, nobody laughs when you say you want to be a professional wrestler, because a lot of kids want to be something that seems relatively implausible to adults. But as you get older, you're expected to start thinking more realistically about a career—especially if, like me, you in no way, shape, or form stand out in a crowd. No matter, whenever anyone asked, I always said I wanted to be a pro wrestler. Sometimes people would laugh; sometimes they would say that it sounded fun but I should probably go to college first. The response that gave me the hardest time was this: "How do you get into wrestling?" I had no idea.

In *Pro Wrestling Illustrated,* they had these advertisements that read, "Learn to be a professional wrestler!" You'd pay $20 to get the book and become a pro wrestler. That simple? I was sold. I bought multiple books like that. I use the term "book" loosely because they were more like a phone book of resources (although reduced to about twenty pages) than actual guidebooks.

They told me that I had to get some wrestling gear and suggested reputable gear places. They said I needed to get some wrestling boots and noted places where they could be ordered. That's essentially all they did. The most important instruction was that I needed to go to wrestling school and I needed to go to a good one. One of the books highlighted the Malenko School of Wrestling, and I knew exactly where I needed to go. I was a sophomore in high school, and Dean Malenko was my favorite wrestler.

It's interesting how tastes can change in just about anything. When I was first introduced to wrestling, I loved the colorful characters and adored pretty much anybody who came to the ring as an animal. Jake the Snake, Koko B. Ware, and the British Bulldogs were always at the top of my list, but my absolute favorite was the Ultimate Warrior. Though he wasn't a great technical wrestler (not that I knew any better at the time), Warrior sprinted to the ring and, with incredible energy, shook the top rope like a maniac. He wore neon tights with matching tassels and had the physique of a superhero. He was everything I loved about wrestling when I was nine years old.

As I got a little bit older, I started liking wrestlers not just because of their persona, their appearance, or their entrance but mostly because

of their performance inside the ring. I was drawn to guys like Bret "Hit Man" Hart and Arn Anderson—excellent ring technicians, but still big men.

Although I always wanted to be a wrestler, I had doubts because the guys I saw on TV were so big. Even a guy like the 1-2-3 Kid, who was an underdog because of his size, was over six feet tall. I was only five foot eight. Then, in 1995, World Championship Wrestling created the Cruiserweight Title and brought in some wrestlers who started to give me hope that my size wouldn't be an issue. All of a sudden on my TV every week were guys like Eddie Guerrero, Chris Benoit, and Dean Malenko, who were my height or shorter and had wrestled in Mexico, Europe, and Japan, learning different styles everywhere they went. Guerrero and Benoit wrestled each other in a match on *WCW Saturday Night* that was so good it made me start recording wrestling so I could watch the matches again and again.

Dean Malenko was the one who appealed to me the most. A no-nonsense wrestler, he was introduced as "the Man of 1,000 Holds," and when he first started in World Championship Wrestling (WCW), they shot vignettes of him stretching guys with various submissions. My favorite was his Texas Cloverleaf, where he figure-foured a man's legs with his arms and then turned him over onto his stomach, looking like he was bending his opponent in half. I started trying it on all of my friends, and true to form, it hurt.

In 1996, at WCW's Great American Bash (the first WCW pay-per-view I ever ordered), Dean wrestled a debuting Rey Mysterio Jr. for the Cruiserweight Championship in the match that convinced me there was no excuse for me not to follow my dream. Both men were shorter than me, but between Dean's aggressive mat wrestling and Rey being the most spectacular high flyer I had ever seen, not a single person watching would have noticed. They transcended the preconceived notion that most people had (myself included) that wrestlers had to be big.

Shortly after I turned sixteen, I called to inquire about the Malenko School of Wrestling, using the number I saw in one of my books. A lady named Phyllis Lee picked up and answered all of my questions, including cost. It was $2,500 to enroll, but you needed to give them a $500 deposit to secure your spot. For whatever reason, I had presumed that there were people lined up all over the world to go to Dean Malenko's school and that I would need to send in my deposit as quickly as possible to ensure there'd be a place for me.

Working at McDonald's and filling their meat trays, I saved up enough money for wrestling school that summer. Once I had the deposit, I immediately called the school and I said I wanted to hold my spot, and I sent Phyllis Lee my $500, solidifying what I thought was my postgraduation plan, nearly two years before I even graduated.

By this point, my mom had accepted that I was going to try to be a wrestler, but she wanted me to go to college while I did it. Surprisingly, Dr. Carter, my junior- and senior-year English teacher, was very influential in my decision to wholeheartedly pursue wrestling and not go to college immediately. One day he was talking about his stint in the Peace Corps and how that experience gave him a whole new perspective on the world. It made him realize he wanted to teach. He questioned how students were supposed to go straight from high school to college and know exactly what they wanted to be without much real-world experience. While most of my teachers thought I should have a backup plan before I started wrestling, Dr. Carter encouraged me to try wrestling first, and if it didn't work out, the colleges would always be there. Even though I was a relatively good student and graduated with honors, the closer I got to graduation, the more I hated school. I enjoyed learning math and science, but the classes were slow. I loved Dr. Carter's English class, though most of school felt pointless and seemed like an inefficient use of nearly eight hours a day.

I spent as much time as I possibly could mentally and physically preparing for wrestling the best I knew how. I wanted to get in the best shape possible, so I developed my own training regimen, which meant working out on my own time and not during phys ed. I read books on strength training. I worked on bridging to strengthen my

neck and worked on backflips because I thought I'd have to be a high flyer. I bought Japanese and Mexican wrestling tapes through a catalog I found on the Internet. I watched as much wrestling as I could and wrote down every move I saw in a binder filled with things I wanted to learn. The issue was that I needed to work so I could pay for wrestling school. At the time, I was working two minimum-wage jobs, one at McDonald's and one for KB Toys. With all of that, I didn't think I had time for school, so I lied to get out of it—the biggest lie I ever told.

I'm pretty much the worst liar I know, which is why today I'm surprised that my plan worked so well. I told my teachers I had gotten this job at one of the logging places in town, which would pay way more than my other jobs, but they needed me to work during the day. I asked if I could do all my schoolwork at home and just come in to take my tests. Everyone was cool with it. All I'd need is a letter from my mom saying it was OK and a letter from the boss saying the job was legit.

The job was not legit. It was just an excuse not to go to school. So I forged both letters—one from my mother and the other from my fictional boss—then I just stopped going. It was way easier than it had any right to be. Sometimes I still have nightmares that I never actually graduated from high school. In the dream, I walk up to get my diploma and someone pulls me aside and tells me they caught me and I will have to repeat my senior year. I still feel guilty about this deception.

Everything I was doing in my life was to get ready for wrestling, but I couldn't prepare for what happened next. Three months before I graduated and was planning to head down to Florida, I got a call from Phyllis Lee to explain that, unfortunately, the Malenko School of Wrestling had closed down. Phyllis apologized, and when I asked for my $500 deposit back, she said, "I'm sorry . . . we don't have it anymore." I couldn't believe it. When you're only making $4.90 an hour, $500 is *a lot* of fucking money. Also, not only did I lose the money, I lost the chance to be trained by my favorite wrestler.

In three months I was graduating, and I had no idea what I was going to do. I wallowed around for a couple of weeks after I got the news. I called other wrestling schools, but none of them made me feel confident I was going to get good training. I didn't know where to go or who to trust. Finally, what seemed like bad luck ended up being the best thing that could have happened to me. Shortly after I was told Dean's school was closing, Shawn Michaels announced he was opening up a wrestling school of his own.

While I was watching *Monday Night Raw,* an ad flashed a 900 number, which I called—for a significant fee—to request more information about the Shawn Michaels Wrestling Academy. I figured a Shawn Michaels wrestling program had to be great, but as soon as I called, I started to worry it was a scam. The phone number cost money, but then all it told you was to mail them another $20 in order to receive the information. Despite being hesitant, I gave it a shot. When the pamphlet for the school came in the mail, I was demoralized again. The school was going to cost $3,900, which was $1,400 more than I had planned and even worse because I had lost the $500. The pamphlet contained another number to call to say if you were interested. Yet again the call cost money, and I almost didn't do it. I didn't know what else to do, though, so I called. When I finally talked to somebody, it ended up being Shawn Michaels's mom, Carol, who was handling a lot of the logistics of the school.

Carol was absolutely wonderful and a godsend. Since I had limited social skills and didn't even know what questions to ask, my mom talked to Carol more than I did. My mom was, naturally, concerned. As a family, we weren't exactly well traveled, and Shawn's school was in San Antonio, Texas. To us, that was so far away, it might as well have been Mars. My mom worried about my safety in such a big city, especially since I wouldn't know anyone there and wasn't overly good at making friends. We didn't have great Internet at the house in 1999 (it was dial-up) so it was really hard to get information. We tried to find an apartment, but we didn't know anything about the neighborhoods in San Antonio, and it was an expensive city.

My mother had a ton of questions, and Carol answered them all. I'm sure it helped that she had watched her own son embark on the same journey years ago, so she knew the stress a mother would experience. Carol explained to us that they had made an agreement with an apartment complex in San Antonio for the people coming in from out of the area. It wouldn't be supernice, but it would be in a safe neighborhood. If I wanted a roommate, they'd put me together with someone else coming to the school and we could sign a lease together. Though my mom still had concerns, Carol was able to reassure her enough so that she wasn't a nervous wreck when I ultimately left.

Fortunately, the Academy accepted month-to-month payments of $1,300 if you didn't have the full $3,900 tuition up front. I

Bryan and friends Mike Dove (left) and Evan Aho graduate high school, 1999

cut all unnecessary spending and saved every penny I could. Even though she had hardly any money, my mom helped me out, too, without which I wouldn't have made it.

The night I graduated from high school, I went to our class graduation party and said good-bye to my friends, who were all superstoked that I was going to wrestle. One of my friends even made me a little championship belt. I left the party around midnight and I went straight home to pack up all my stuff in the car, then started driving to San Antonio. I didn't sleep because I was too excited.

The drive from Aberdeen, Washington, to San Antonio, Texas, is just a little under 2,500 miles, and there're really only two major roads. You take I-5 south for over 1,000 miles until you get to Los Angeles, and then you take I-10 east for over 1,000 miles until you get to San Antonio. Pretty easy, actually. This was my first of many long cross-country trips, and not only did I enjoy it, I discovered that I'm a good long-distance driver. The only time I stopped was for gas or to sleep a couple of hours. I probably could have been a relatively good truck driver, though my dad would've been furious. He had this funny disdain for truck drivers, having dealt with them for years in the logging industry. The only rule my dad ever really had for my sister about dating was this: Never marry a truck driver.

For the trip, I only packed what fit in my little teal 1992 Geo Storm. I brought some blankets, pillows, and a sleeping bag. I had a bag of clothes, a small TV with a VCR built in, and a box of all my wrestling tapes, which took up the most space, by far. That was it.

I broke down somewhere in Arizona, which slowed me down and cost me several hundred dollars (vital dollars, I might add), but other than that, the trip was enjoyable. My first night in San Antonio? Not so much.

MapQuest had just kind of become a thing, so I had the printouts and an actual map to help me figure out how to get to the apartments. I arrived in San Antonio around 11 P.M. on June 25, 1999. When I got there, everyone on the freeway was honking their horns and screaming. I mistakenly thought they were honking their horns at me, and I got very nervous. I pulled off at an exit, but the same thing happened. Finally I tried going to the apartment complex, but by the time I found it, it was unreasonably late and the office was closed. There was a grocery store down the street, so I parked there to try to get some sleep because I didn't know what else to do. People were still driving around with their hands on their horns and making noise, so not only was it impossible to sleep, but I still had no idea what was going on.

This was the end of June in Texas and it was hot as hell, and even hotter in my car. I didn't want to keep it running because that would burn gas, but it was so hot—especially for a kid who grew up in Aberdeen—that I kept having to turn it on for quick doses of air-conditioning. Occasionally I'd roll the windows down, but then I got scared because of all the insane honking and yelling.

Eventually a man from the grocery store came up to me and asked me what I was doing. "Oh, I was kind of just sleeping here," I replied.

"I don't have anywhere else to go." He didn't care. He told me there was no loitering and that I'd have to move on. Before he left, I asked him if all the honking and yelling was normal around the area. He looked at me like I was an idiot and said, "No, they're doing it because the Spurs just won the NBA Championship." That explained it. I felt dumb as a brick as I relocated to a big strip-mall parking lot, where nobody bothered me for the rest of the night. I didn't get any sleep, of course.

Even though I arrived before my official move-in date, I was able to get into my apartment early the next day thanks to the nice ladies who worked there. You could tell some were mothers by the way they sympathized with my naïveté.

The apartment was a small one-bedroom. I shared it with another trainee named AJ from Florida, who slept in the bedroom (mostly because he owned a bed) while I slept in my sleeping bag on the living room floor. He was around thirty, which felt so much older than me at the time, and he had long, black hair, wore leather jackets, and had a cool car. He *looked* like a wrestler and, in fact, he did have wrestling experience. AJ came to train with Shawn hoping not only to improve but, like several other guys who came to the school, to get an "in" with WWE.

AJ also had life experience, which really helped out because I didn't know how to do anything when it came to living on my own. For example, I didn't realize there is a difference between regular dish soap and soap you put in a dishwasher. My family never had one. I put regular soap in the dishwasher, turned it on, and left the apartment. When I came back, there were suds all over the floor. AJ knew right away that I had put the wrong kind of soap in and explained the difference. Then he called up the nice ladies at the office.

"Your dishwasher's broken and it flooded our kitchen!" he told them. When the repairman came to inspect, he asked if we used the wrong dish soap, and AJ responded, "Of course not. Do you think I'm an idiot?!"

I suspect he went through the whole charade because he didn't want to clean up the suds and figured I couldn't do it properly. I was that oblivious to just about everything.

By winter, AJ had left San Antonio, and it started getting cold. The apartment was freezing and no matter how high I turned up the thermostat, the heat would never come on. I spent over a month bundled up in my warmest clothes before I finally called the office. The repairman came by, looked at the thermostat for less than three seconds, and pushed a switch that read COOL to the position that read HEAT. I felt like an idiot for missing something so obvious.

The Shawn Michaels Wrestling Academy was in a grubby part of San Antonio on top of a Mexican restaurant called Doña Juanita's. It wasn't quite what I expected. I thought it would be more like the WWE Performance Center is today, but inside, there was just a ring with a few weightlifting machines, and it was really, really hot. The guys who lived next door would sit outside on top of their cars and drink beer all day. I was constantly terrified that my car would get broken into or stolen. I later found out that someone was giving them cases of beer to watch our cars. I don't think anyone's car was ever broken into.

On the first day of training, we all got to the Academy early. I get nervous doing just about anything for the first time, whether it's going to a new yoga studio or taking a class at the botanical garden. Needless to say, walking up those stairs and finally reaching the moment of my first wrestling class had the butterflies in my stomach going crazy. AJ had told me a rule in wrestling was to introduce yourself and shake hands with everyone in the locker room, so I greeted all my fellow trainees. Some of the guys were already laughing and joking, and the comfort they projected put me a little more at ease. But then the room went quiet as Shawn Michaels walked in.

Shawn Michaels, in my opinion, is the best American wrestler of his generation. Being the best in wrestling is subjective, of course, so not everyone will agree, but he was a true Superstar in my eyes and the first wrestler I ever met. When I was seven, I watched him as part of The Rockers when he first came to the WWE. My friend

Schuyler impersonated him all the time when we were in middle school. This was the guy who won the Royal Rumble the first time I ever ordered pay-per-view in 1996, and he was in the main event of the first WrestleMania I ordered, in which he competed in a sixty-minute Iron Man Match with Bret Hart to win the WWE Championship for the first time. If Shawn Michaels had a big match on pay-per-view, I ordered it because I knew I'd be getting my money's worth. He had retired a year earlier because his back had gotten really bad, and the general feeling was that he would never wrestle again. When he walked in the door that first day, I was in awe.

Once 9 A.M. hit, Shawn gathered us around and introduced himself and the other trainers, and soon after that we started training. My first day of training was a real eye-opener. I had tried to come to the school in the best shape possible, and I was confident in my conditioning, but we were on the second floor of a building with no air-conditioning. We started with conditioning, doing some running, some body-weight exercises like squats and push-ups, and some circuit training. I looked around and could see the heat taking its toll on the other trainees. A few of them started throwing up during this portion of the training, which lasted more than an hour. Next, we did some gymnastic-type rolls inside the ring. Between the heat, the exhaustion, and the dizziness created by the tumbling, guys were throwing up left and right. Some made it to the bathroom, some only made it to the window to puke onto the sidewalk below, and some didn't make it to either. They just vomited on the floor. I did my best to resist the urge, and out of all the guys, Lance Cade and I were the only ones who didn't throw up. We finished off the day running sprints, and at the end, Shawn gave us a pep talk. I was so exhausted I don't even remember what he said. For me, beginnings are always the hardest, and I felt great knowing that I'd completed my first day of wrestling training.

Though Shawn had started a part-time class earlier in the year, we were his first full-time class, and as a class, we were very successful. In many wrestling schools, a majority of the guys who start training never even have a match. Out of the twenty guys who started in that first class, more than half ended up being able to wrestle at least a couple matches, and three of us—Lance Cade, Brian Kendrick, and myself—ended up holding championships in WWE.

Lance caught Shawn's eye from the very beginning. He was a big guy from Nebraska—tall (six foot five), muscular, and athletic. He was good-looking, too, with his long blond hair, and only eighteen at the time. That first day of training, among all the calisthenics and rolls, we also did something involving jumping. Lance could jump to the moon, and when Shawn saw him jump so high, he immediately said—in front of everyone—"I smell money." It was clear that Lance was one of Shawn's early favorites.

It took me and Brian Kendrick a little longer to catch Shawn's attention. We were both smaller—me at five foot eight and Brian at five foot six—but we would work our hardest at every drill, no matter how mundane. In fact, because of our shared work ethic, it didn't take long for Brian and me to become friends.

Brian is great, both as a wrestler and as a person, and I was lucky we attended class at the same time. He had grown up in Lacey, Washington, only about an hour from Aberdeen, and he loved wrestling every bit as much as I did. He had his own collection of wrestling tapes, and sometimes he'd come over and we'd watch the tapes together, talking about things we'd like to learn. Brian was probably twenty when we got down there, but he had a much better understanding of how the world worked than I did. He was also free-spirited and didn't care what people thought about him. A couple of years earlier, Brian had gone to a wrestling school in Austin, Texas, and even though he had a couple of matches, he felt like that school was a scam, so he quit and saved his money. When Shawn's school opened up, Brian jumped at the chance. In an effort to save on rent, he stayed at his aunt's house in Austin and drove the ninety minutes to class every day, then back home to work his pizza job at night. He worked harder than anybody else in our class.

Even though it was Shawn's school and he was there for almost every class, Rudy Boy Gonzalez was our primary trainer. Rudy was a character. Though only five foot eight, he had an enormous stomach that was hard as a rock, plus the biggest head I had ever seen. But he was really agile and hilarious, to boot. He'd been wrestling for years, and he was an excellent trainer and one of the main reasons for my early success.

Mandatory class days were Tuesday, Wednesday, and Thursday from 9 A.M. until noon, but Brian and I were training way more than that. Rudy stayed late working with us, and he'd open the gym any day we wanted to come in and train. At first he would just help us with the basics we learned in class, though soon he was teaching us anything we wanted to learn, like Space Flying Tiger Drops or moonsaults to the floor. If Brian or I saw something on a tape and wanted to learn it, Rudy would try to teach it to us. There are some things we just weren't physically capable of doing, but you don't find that out until you try. Every time we fouled something up, Rudy gave us some advice or shared his perspective on how we could have done it better. Just being there for us and so liberally sharing his knowledge, Rudy inspired us to work harder. His passion for teaching really stood out.

Shawn's passion for wrestling was apparent as well, and seeing it humanized him for me. Gradually, he turned from being a Superstar I was in awe of to a coach I respected (admittedly, with a little bit of awe). Shawn was so passionate that occasionally he would get in the ring and actually take the moves, even though he wasn't supposed to because of his back. One time we were learning back body drops, one of the higher bumps in wrestling, and none of us were taking them very well. We might have landed fine, but we weren't getting the height to make the move look spectacular.

Shawn was a masterful bump taker. He excelled at making his opponents look great by taking an ordinary move like a back body drop and getting so high that it looked as if his opponent had just thrown him fifteen feet in the air. Given we were getting nowhere near that high, Shawn would stop us, tell us how to get more height on our bump, then have us try again. He kept explaining and explaining, but try as we might, none of us seemed to be getting any higher. Finally he got so fired up that he got in there and took a back body drop himself to show us, catching so much air that his foot hit one of the beams on the ceiling.

All of a sudden from one of the doors I heard a woman scream out, "Michael Shawn Hickenbottom! What are you doing?!" It was Carol, Shawn's mom, and she gave him an earful in front of all of us for going against doctors' orders. Instantly he stopped being the Superstar wrestler Shawn Michaels and turned into a son being scolded by his mother.

Another thing that took Shawn off the pedestal I had put him on was his painkiller issue, which he talks about in his book. Most of the time he was great, but occasionally he would show up with his sunglasses on, watch class for a little while, then fall asleep in his chair. Since I was naïve enough not to know what painkillers were, I thought maybe he was drunk. Either way, I realized that no matter how successful he was, Shawn Michaels was just another dude with his own struggles, who also happened to be great at wrestling. And actually what put him back on the pedestal was not his wrestling—which, when he made a comeback several years later, may have been better than ever before—but his ability to kick the painkillers. Addiction is a son of bitch, and he beat it.

For a long time I focused on wrestling to the exclusion of everything else. Even though I didn't have very much money, I worked as little as possible. I would get whatever crappy minimum-wage job I could find that would work with my schedule, and as soon as I saved up enough money to pay my bills for a month or two, I would quit. One time, I thought I'd hit the jackpot with a job as a stock boy for Victoria's Secret. My first day was supposed to be on a Friday, but last minute, I was asked to do ring crew for a show. I called in and asked if I could start on a different day, and the manager told me she'd call me back with my new start date. She never called me back. Instead of working with bras and panties, I ended up getting a pretty good job at a Christian bookstore where we shipped Bibles

to churches. I had it for a month, then quit. Luckily, my half of the rent was only $200 and I knew how to live on very little money. That meant I would have to eat peanut butter and jelly tortillas (which were cheaper than bread) all the time. If you don't require very much money to live, it gives you a certain amount of freedom, and that freedom allowed me to commit a hundred percent of myself to wrestling.

Wrestling training is difficult, mostly because the contact is so unique. There's a lot of contact in sports like football, but not the same kind. If I'm a wide receiver trying to jump for a pass in the middle of the field, there's a good chance I'm going to get leveled, but the receiver tries to *not* get leveled, and the quarterback attempts to throw the ball in the best possible position for the receiver to make the catch *and* do so without his head getting taken off. Wrestling is different. When my opponent gives me a shoulder tackle, I try to "attack the mat," taking a bump as hard and as fast as possible, plus try to do it safely. Trying to unlearn years of attempting to not fall down is hard, and hard on the body.

As training went on, guys started dropping out. Some people walked away because of injuries, some because they had personal issues, and some because wrestling turned out to be tougher than they thought. My roommate AJ ended up leaving halfway through the class because he had some issues to address back in Florida. Fortunately, he paid his half of the rent for the rest of the term of our lease, for which I was grateful. It opened up space in the apartment for Kendrick to come stay so he wouldn't have to drive to Austin every night. Not only did I enjoy his company, but it gave him more time and energy to train, which made us both better.

Slowly but surely, we learned enough to have matches, starting with basic matches in training after about seven weeks. At first Shawn and Rudy would just tell us exactly what to do. While we were in the ring, Rudy would say something like, "Bryan, grab a headlock." I would grab the headlock. Then he would say, "Now take him down." I would take the guy down. He would tell my opponent to head-scissors me, which he would, and we would continue until Rudy would end the match by calling for a move like a small package and telling the pinned person not to kick out.

Soon we were coming up with our own matches at the Academy. Boy, were they rotten. If you have never seen someone's first attempt at having a match, it's comical, and mine were no different. But as we kept training, the matches got better.

I was sitting at home on a Sunday afternoon when Rudy called me and told me I was having my first professional wrestling match in two days. I was so excited I could barely talk. When I finally could, I mumbled a thank-you and then asked, "What should I wear for gear?"

Rudy said not to worry; he knew a guy and was coming over to pick me up in about an hour.

A few weeks prior to this call, Shawn was talking with us after class. He said if we hadn't already, we should start thinking about our wrestling names. I didn't have any good ideas other than using my real name, so I asked Shawn what he thought. He tucked his chin, thought it over for a second, then responded with, "How about 'the American Dragon'?"

I didn't really like it, but was too afraid to tell him. "Why?" I asked.

"Because you wrestle like a Japanese guy," he responded. I took that as a compliment. Thus, the American Dragon was born.

The gear guy lived four hours away in Matamoros, just across the Mexican border, so I was ready with two peanut butter and jelly tortillas for the trip when Rudy picked me up. He didn't know exactly where the guy's house was, though, so we had to pick up another wrestler who lived on the U.S. side of the border to show us where to go. As we were crossing the border, I found out they didn't even have the gear guy's telephone number, so we were just going to stop by and see if he was home. It felt really poorly planned.

As we got closer to the gear guy's house, I distinctly recall seeing all these dogs tied up on the roofs of houses. I asked why the dogs were on people's roofs, and Rudy's friend said, "Oh, so people don't eat them." I was terrified.

When we finally arrived at the gear maker's house, luckily, he was home. Rudy described what he wanted my gear to look like: long red and blue tights with dragons on the sides, along with a similarly colored mask that looked like a dragon to cover up the blank stare I had when I wrestled. We would supplement whatever he created with amateur wrestling shoes and white kick pads we'd gotten from a martial arts store. The gear guy said he could get it done that night, but it would take him about four hours. He didn't even measure me, which made me question whether the whole escapade was a good idea.

To kill time, we ate at a nearby Mexican restaurant. Despite all the free tortilla chips, that only took about forty-five minutes. In trying to figure out what we were going to do, the guys decided they would take me somewhere I'd never been: a strip club. My vote to not go wasn't counted.

One would think that seeing your first live naked woman would be exciting for an eighteen-year-old, but it wasn't. I was horrified. In this particular case, seeing my first live naked woman coincided with seeing my first live naked C-section scar. Rudy and his friend watched and laughed as I shrank away from a woman who came up, licked my ear, and said something to me in Spanish. I had no idea what she said, but all I wanted was to get out of that club. It looked like the dirtiest place I had ever been inside of, and I was scared to death the entire two hours we were there.

We finally went back to the gear guy's house around 3 A.M. The gear was done, and, remarkably, everything fit great. The mask was a little tight in the nose, but for not having measured me he did an amazing job. Despite being horrified an hour earlier, when I looked in the mirror, I was thrilled. That's when my first match finally felt like a real thing.

5 THE REAL KICKER
WEDNESDAY, APRIL 2, 2014–12:55 P.M.

After more than an hour of training, Bryan takes a pause in one of the many rooms of the New Orleans Athletic Club, this one overlooking the indoor swimming pool on the lower level. With several substantial sips and gulps, he finishes off a French vanilla protein shake with a raspberry-flavored electrolyte mix-in. The pounding of speed bags in the background is a prelude to Bryan's next round of exercise. He targets a stuffed punching bag but spares it fisticuffs in favor of swift, daunting kicks. Bryan throws his leg forward and connects with precision, leaving sweat gleams and indents. Again. And again. The blows are unsettlingly potent, but it's the change in his eyes that is most unnerving. Not to mention the likely thoughts and visions behind them.

After a solid workout, Daniel Bryan walks through the French Quarter back toward his hotel. A brief encounter with some excited WWE fans outside the entrance keeps his energy high as he heads back up to his room. The drapes are drawn, spilling light onto half-unpacked suitcases, the Whole Foods bounty, and various itineraries. Bryan's first order of business is a quick call and catch-up with Brie, whose voice is only a light buzz between his questions in the otherwise quiet room.

Bryan pushes the vitamins and WrestleMania swag around on his desktop to find the room service menu and discuss grub options with his wife-to-be. The choice falls between chicken fingers and a far more likely organic, farm-raised chicken breast with varieties of greens, from bib lettuce to arugula. The two plan for the afternoon and evening ahead, plus the opportunity to spend ever-dwindling time together.

Shawn started his promotion, the Texas Wrestling Alliance (TWA), shortly before I moved to San Antonio. It was designed to give his trainees a place to put their instruction into practice, a place for us to be able to keep learning once we graduated and actually had to go out into the wrestling world. Along with the students, it was filled with experienced independent wrestlers from all over Texas.

Originally I was supposed to wrestle Lance in my first match, but due to an injury, they pulled Lance out the day before and put Brian in his place, which made me feel a little more comfortable since he and I had trained so much together. Brian had decided long before that he was going to wrestle under the name Spanky, which was in part a reference to masturbation, and with the gimmick he didn't need to drive down to Mexico to get gear. He went to Goodwill, got some sort of flowery pajama bottoms, put on his amateur wrestling shoes, and—voilà!—he had gear that was a great fit for the character.

While Brian had a good grasp of the character he wanted to portray, I didn't. In fact, I wasn't even thinking about it. I didn't think about music or what I wanted to do during my entrance. I hadn't really thought about anything other than the technical aspect of what I'd like to do wrestling-wise. Shawn took care of the music thing. He suggested Bruce Springsteen's "Born in the U.S.A.," which is not the worst entrance music of all time, but it's pretty close. I was too nervous to second-guess the decision.

On October 4, 1999, Brian and I wrestled our first match in San Antonio at a country-western bar called Far West Rodeo. Brian came out dancing in his Goodwill pj's to Christina Aguilera's "Genie in a Bottle," and I came out in my dragon mask and spandex tights with my lame music. In general, first matches are rotten, and ours was no different, though there's no denying we worked hard. We were trying to do a lot of stuff that you probably shouldn't be trying in your first match, like German suplexes and moonsaults. Though I had been nervous, after I got in the ring and started wrestling, I went into a weird state where I was just having fun. I'm not sure the two hundred fans in attendance knew what to make of us, but they were very generous, cheering loudly after we wrestled to a ten-minute draw, maybe because we were wrestling a more action-packed style than they were used to seeing.

We walked to the back afterward, and a bunch of the wrestlers congratulated us on our first match. Shawn, in particular, was thrilled with our performance. When I went to sleep that night I couldn't believe I had done it: I had wrestled my first match, it went well, and I didn't fall on my face.

TWA was running a couple of shows a week by the time of my first match, and soon I was wrestling several times a week, mostly against either Brian or Rudy. Not only that, but TWA had gotten a local television deal, so our matches aired on Saturday night around midnight. The shows were only thirty minutes, but it gave us the experience of doing short TV interviews, which I was horrible at for a long time. But, hey, practice makes perfect.

In November of that year, Shawn arranged for Lance and me to wrestle in Frontier Martial-Arts Wrestling (FMW), a Japanese company, in exchange for his going over to referee a big match of theirs. Getting an opportunity to go to Japan so early in my career had me over-the-moon happy.

We did a press conference with Shawn once we got to Japan, and then we went to FMW's big show to watch while Shawn refereed. I had seen a ton of Japanese wrestling, most of which was very technical and athletic, and I loved the style. FMW was a little different, though. It had some awesome technical wrestling and aerial moves, but it also had a lot of brawling and hardcore wrestling. This was not exactly typical in Japan, but with so many different wrestling

companies, this happened to be FMW's niche. Their biggest star was a high-flying character named Hayabusa, who was wrestling Mr. Gannosuke in the match Shawn officiated. As we watched the promotional package, I couldn't believe it. To build up the match, Mr. Gannosuke had exploded a bottle rocket in Hayabusa's butt! That's right, he shoved the bottle rocket in Hayabusa's butt and lit it, and it exploded. Shawn's eyes were priceless when he first saw it. His brain seemed to explode. They assured Lance and me that there would be no fireworks put in our butts.

After that show, Shawn flew back to San Antonio, while we stayed. We did a week's worth of training at the FMW dojo with Masato Tanaka, a great wrestler we'd seen before in Extreme Championship Wrestling. Tanaka is a thick, muscular, and notoriously tough Japanese guy. Yet in my mind, I mostly remember this image of him as he left the dojo, hopping onto his little moped bike and saying, "Bye-bye!" in an unexpectedly high-pitched voice.

After our training, we commenced a ten-day tour, for which we were paid $1,000. Given how poor I was, it seemed like an incredible amount of money. I thought I'd never have to work again.

There were a lot of things that confused me on my first trip to Japan. Our first night in a hotel room on the tour, Lance pounded on my door and asked me if I'd been in the bathroom yet. I told him I hadn't, so he barged in and led me straight to the tiny bathroom. The toilet had lights and buttons on it, one of which he pressed, then told me to stand back. This little rod came from under the toilet seat and sprayed water right where a person's butt would be. It squirted so hard that the water went all the way out the bathroom door. I learned it was a mechanical bidet. Before the trip I didn't even know bidets existed.

A lot of the small Japanese towns we went to didn't have Western-style toilets. They had what we called Japanese toilets, which were essentially porcelain holes in the ground. Nobody told us how to use them, not that we shouldn't have been able to figure it out. I had to take my pants off completely and sometimes even my shirt if I had to poop, just to make sure I wouldn't get anything on myself.

Years later when I worked for New Japan Pro Wrestling, veteran wrestler Scott Norton told me a horrifying story of how he was already dressed for a big match but then had to go to the bathroom. They only had the Japanese-style toilets, so he pulled his singlet down and gave it a go, but somehow he got poop on himself. His match was up next and he didn't have time to change gear, so he went in and showered with his gear on. Given that Scott experienced this even after all the times he'd been to Japan, I don't feel so bad now.

One night, some of the guys took Lance and me out to this bar-type place where all the servers were women who walked around in bikinis. All of a sudden this DJ yelled, "It's *party* time!" in English, with his Japanese accent. The girls took their tops off and ran to sit on customers' laps, where they bounced up and down to the music. The song would end and they'd just get up, put their tops back on, say, "Bye-byyyye!!" then go back to serving drinks again. Lance and I were both still eighteen, and it was the craziest thing I'd ever seen. The Japanese wrestlers laughed at how uncomfortable we were.

I also had a hard time with the food. Back then, I didn't like experimenting much with what I ate. I liked the basics, like peanut butter and jelly sandwiches, fruit, salads, and sometimes, when I was feeling adventurous, ramen noodles. In Japan, the guys would occasionally take us for sushi, and I struggled to stomach the raw fish. Today, I love Japanese food—and all sorts of food, really—and my mom, who would see me turn away all but the most basic, is amazed.

Despite all my cultural confusion during my first trip to Japan, I had a great time. We wrestled seven matches in ten days, and Lance and I teamed up every show to wrestle two of the FMW guys. I learned something new every night from the Japanese wrestlers.

The final two shows of the tour took place in Korakuen Hall, a small but legendary building in Tokyo where anybody who's anybody has wrestled. Wrestling in there was an amazing experience, and the

crowds were awesome. They weren't necessarily excited to see either me or Lance, two young, green wrestlers that they barely knew, but they applauded when we did something good and were very forgiving when we weren't so good. The last match was my favorite of the tour. We faced off with two of the younger wrestlers, and for the first time, I did a springboard front somersault dive into the crowd—a move that would turn into a staple for me years later.

At the end of the tour, they thanked us, gave us our money in cash, and told us they would love to have us back. Really they only wanted Lance back, because even though neither of us was very good, Lance was big and had a cowboy gimmick that appealed to the Japanese audience. When he went back to FMW for a second tour without me, I realized the deal. At my size, if I wanted to be successful I would need to get a whole lot better.

The trip to Japan was a great learning experience, both from a wrestling perspective and in opening my eyes to different cultures. The only negative aspect was midway through the tour when I got knocked out for the first time. During a tag team match, I tried a moonsault from the second rope to the floor, but my toes slipped and I hit the concrete floor headfirst. When I came to, I was in the ring and had no idea what was going on. I knew I needed to tag Lance, so I grabbed my opponent in a full nelson and suplexed him right on his head. Why I did that, and not just a basic move like a snap mare or a headlock to stop him, I have no idea. To make it worse, he was being really gentle with me, knowing I was hurt, yet I just dumped him with a dragon suplex. And then I tagged out. I don't think I got in the rest of the match, which is a good thing. Though it was the first time I got knocked out, it wouldn't be the last. As far as injuries go, concussions have been the number one thing to plague me throughout my career.

In February 2000, a couple of months after the Japan tour, Shawn got us an untelevised (or "dark") tryout match with WWE at Smack-Down in Austin.

It was me and Shooter Schultz, another of Shawn's students, against Lance Cade and Brian Kendrick. Originally we were told by a WWE producer that we'd have twelve minutes to wrestle, so naturally, we planned out a twelve-minute match. Then, shortly before the show was about to start, we were told we only had six minutes. None of us knew what to do because that had never happened to us before, whereas now I realize that's a common occurrence in WWE. We told Shawn, and that's where it was good to have Shawn Michaels as an advocate. He was expecting WWE agents to take a thorough look at us, and so he went off, yelling about "his guys" and demanding more time for us. We got ten minutes.

The four of us went out there and threw everything we could at the match—to a mild reaction from the Austin crowd. We did a lot of things I now know we shouldn't have done. Lance performed a chokeslam, a move several people on the roster used, which would typically make that move off-limits for anyone else to use. We also did several dives out of the ring, one of which gave me my first documented concussion. We weren't used to the ramp being there, and Lance took a misstep when he tried to catch me off my springboard somersault dive. I landed on my head on the ramp, which knocked me loopy. Afterward, the WWE doctor told me I had a concussion, all right, but not much was known about concussions at the time, so he just advised the guys to make sure I didn't go to sleep after it.

When we got back through the curtain, Shawn was there waiting, and he was all pumped up for us. "Yes! That was *awesome,*" he said. He started telling anyone who would listen that they should sign us. Shawn is a great guy to have in your corner. Immediately following our tryout, he started putting pressure on WWE to sign us. Our tryout was on a Tuesday, and by Thursday Shawn still hadn't heard anything, so he called and threatened to take us to WWE's rival wrestling promotion, WCW, since he was friends with Kevin Nash, who had a lot of influence there. That Friday,

WWE offered all four of us—me, Brian, Lance, and Shooter—developmental contracts. Like I said, Shawn is a great guy to have in your corner.

Our developmental contracts were for $500 per week, which made me feel like the richest guy in the world. I had recently gotten a job at Great American Cookies inside the mall nearby, and though I usually gave at least two weeks' notice whenever I quit a job, this time, I just stopped showing up. I didn't even go in to get my check for the time I worked there, which is unlike me.

The timing of the deal worked in my favor as well. The following week, I was doing my first ladder match, where Brian and I wrestled against a team called the Board of Education for the TWA Tag Team Title. It was the first time we were in the main event of a TWA show, so we wanted to pull out all the stops. At one point I set up a twelve-foot ladder in the ring and jumped off the second rung from the top, somersaulting over the top rope onto my opponent, Ruben Cruz, on the floor. The ladder moved as I jumped off, which didn't allow me to get enough distance to hit him. Ruben nearly sprinted forward to try to catch me, but it wasn't enough, and I landed hard on the floor, separating my right shoulder. We continued wrestling for another ten minutes, which included me foolishly executing an elbow drop off the top of the ladder, which I'm sure didn't help matters. Brian and I lost the match but brawled with the Board of Education afterward, getting the upper hand and setting the two of them up on a table on the floor. Brian and I dove off the top turnbuckle onto our opponents and crashed through the table. This was my first time through a table, and it was bad enough given the state of my shoulder, but as I went through, my head hit the leg of the metal guardrail, knocking me out for more than a full minute. I wasn't able to wrestle for the next six weeks, so I felt *very* lucky to have that guaranteed $500 a week. If it had happened a week sooner, my entire career would have been much different.

That match changed my perspective on how I should wrestle. Due to my size, I thought I needed to wrestle a more daredevil style, but it wasn't practical because no matter how exciting the style might have been, if I kept getting hurt, I would have a pretty short career. I resolved to switch to a more mat-based wrestling style since all of my injuries had occurred during big dives to the floor. I figured if I was going to have any longevity, I needed to be more grounded and technical, like Dean Malenko. That's why it was a godsend when WWE called and sent us to their developmental system in Memphis, Tennessee, where I first met William Regal.

The follow-up to the ladder match with the Board of Education was a steel cage match that ultimately further reinforced my need to take fewer risks and make smarter decisions inside the ring. To make the cage match feel like the final, definitive blow-off brawl between our teams, we decided that all four of us in the tag match would blade—in other words, purposely cut ourselves to draw blood. It was my first time, and I admit it was a terrifying prospect.

Shawn showed us how to make a blade: You get a straightedge razor and cut it to get one really sharp tip. You then affix that to your wrist tape so you can access it during the match. There are two methods for actually drawing blood: You can either stick it into your forehead and twist, or you can stick it into your forehead and slice. The smart way is to stick and twist; that's the way that leaves the least amount of scars. (I've never been confident that that method would get me enough blood, so I've always been a slicer. I have a couple of scars on my forehead today, so now I realize I probably should've learned the twist method instead.) The most nerve-wracking part to me, though, was that I didn't know what to do with this incredibly sharp blade in my fingers once I was done. Shawn told me he'd usually stick it down his pants or—to my utter shock—sometimes he'd stick it in his mouth. Neither of those sounded like good a place for this razor-sharp object.

Preparing for the match, I had ripped my mask on the cage wall to provide easy access to my skin beneath it. When the time came, I readied myself, then stuck the blade into my forehead and scraped it across. It didn't hurt all that much, but what I did immediately

notice was a very distinct sound, the sound of ripping. Instead of cramming it down my tights—which sounded crazy—I quickly handed the blade to the referee and instructed him to stick it in his pocket. Unfortunately, I only got one single drop of blood and nothing more than a scratch on my forehead, so I learned another valuable lesson that night for the future: have multiple razors on me.

Though all four of us tried to blade in that match, the only person who actually got good blood was Brian Kendrick. Our failure and poor plan, frankly, just reflected the stupidity of being a rookie and trying to do things that weren't necessary. Like with anything else, you learn from experiences like this.

6 ROCK–N–SAKE CONNECTION
WEDNESDAY, APRIL 2, 2014—8:42 P.M.

Contemporary apartment buildings line Fulton Street, a narrow city block with a cluster of trendy restaurants and bars, including Rock-n-Sake Sushi. Outside, a minivan cab pulls up and delivers Daniel Bryan and Brie Bella to their evening dinner destination. Brie, a WWE Diva turned reality TV star, glides out and instantly turns the heads of passersby. She's followed by Bryan—affectionately referred to by Brie as "Sweet Face"—who hops out of the vehicle in his gray lace-up TOMS and plaid button-down, his signature outside-the-ring gear.

The couple enters the restaurant, spies the menu, and advances toward a table in the far back corner. Later, immersed in fairly loud pop music and dim lighting supported by neon jellyfish lamps overhead, Bryan explains it's "not our kind of scene," but the food—fresh fish and crisp salads— is good, with the Yelp reviews to support the claim.

Plate after plate of small dishes start descending upon "Braniel's" table as the two get close for conversation and recaps of their respective days apart. They snap loose their chopsticks and dig in to a variety of shared special-ties. Tuna tacos, cucumber salad, sushi rolls, gyoza, green tea, and a PB&J roll for dessert (remember: sweet tooth) are all slowly enjoyed by the duo in

between conversation and giggling, like any other couple at dinner. They
pause only for a WWE fan who discovers them and asks for a quick pic.
(Beautiful Brie plays photographer, ironically.) To some, this interruption
might be a faux pas, but "the People's Couple" is happy to oblige.

After finishing his food, "Daniel-san" scrolls through his iPhone while
Brie leans in to take a look, a glow from the device illuminating what's
easily the most gorgeous face in the restaurant. The days ahead will be fast
and furious, as they know. They're content tonight because they're together.

I am not a natural meat eater. When I was a child, my dad would go
hunting and bring home big deer and elk, so we'd have a freezer full
of deer and elk steak. My mom would always cook it for dinner, but
I never really liked it. I think it was the texture, but it could have
also been that I'd see my dad hanging the carcass at his friend's place.
It was jarring to see the dead eyes of such beautiful creatures. I would
shuffle the meat around my plate in an attempt to make it look like
I ate more than I did, then go after the green beans and mashed
potatoes.

Whenever it was up to me to make food for myself, I always went
for things like peanut butter and jam sandwiches. I was a little spoiled
in that regard because my mom always made homemade jam out of
the raspberries in our garden, not to mention her homemade bread.

As I started trying to learn about building muscle, I read the fitness
magazines, all of which told me I needed a high-protein diet filled
with meat; chicken and tuna seemed to be their gospel, and it was
preached in every magazine. I hadn't learned to question the media
yet, so I just did my best to gulp it down.

In 2004, when I met Austin Aries, I was surprised to learn he was
a vegetarian. He was in great shape without eating any meat, and I
really looked up to him for that. Separately, I switched from reading
predominantly fiction books to predominantly nonfiction for the
next several years, and all of a sudden, I had a growing awareness of
the horrible condition animals were kept in within factory farms, as
well as the substantial increase in carbon emitted in the produc-

tion of meat, as opposed to plants. I found that when you get deep into science and world problems, a lot of issues start running together. In 2007, inspired by Aries and the books I was reading, I tried going vegetarian. Unfortunately, I didn't do it correctly and ate things that were easy instead of eating things that were healthy. I'd eat tons of bread just to feel full. It took a toll on my body, both in the way I looked in my spandex and in the way I felt. I was exhausted all the time and had no energy, and after about four months, I thought vegetarianism just must not work for my body. Had I actually spoken with Aries about how to do it properly, or if I'd read a book on the subject, I'm sure I would have seen the error of my ways.

A few years later, in 2009, with all the hard grappling and kickboxing training I was doing, I ended up getting three staph infections. One isn't so uncommon when you're on mats all the time. They scrubbed the gym every day, but there's bound to be bacteria on the mat with all the people coming in and out. But then I got a second infection and a third that December, which scared me because I had finally been signed by WWE and was just waiting for the call from them to come start. I worried that if they needed me for TV and I told them I couldn't do anything because of my staph, they'd fire me without even being given an opportunity.

I thought it was strange that other guys at the gym who trained just as hard as I did, if not harder, didn't seem to be getting any infections at all. It's not as if there was a staph epidemic. So after the third one, I had a lengthy discussion with my doctor in Las Vegas. We discussed not only my staph infections—which he attributed to my weak immune system—but my elevated liver enzymes and high cholesterol as well. He suggested going vegan, with the theory being that meats, cheeses, milks, and some other foods take a lot of energy for the body to digest. By eliminating those things, I'd free up more of my body's natural energy to fight off bacteria. If I did it, he expected me to see a huge improvement in my overall well-being, as long as I did it properly. This time I did.

My doctor gave me a list of books to read before switching to the vegan lifestyle. I read *The China Study*, *Thrive*, and *Becoming Vegan*—and they gave me a better understanding of how to eat to increase my health and keep my strength.

At first I had a really hard time with this new diet, but the longer I did it, the better I felt. It required a whole new way of eating, especially on the road. I would bring most of my own food, because oftentimes there would be nothing healthy and vegan to eat that had the protein I required. It was frustrating, especially after shows, when Sheamus and Ted DiBiase would eat fast food and all I had was a dried-out hemp bagel with almond butter on it. Sometimes all I wanted was just something warm, but there was very little available. Daytime food became frustrating for the guys, too, because finding a place that fit my needs was often difficult. There was a period when William Regal was riding with us as well, which made it harder because he needed to eat gluten-free. Between him avoiding gluten and me being vegan, the two of us were driving Teddy and Sheamus insane.

My diet also had implications for how people saw me. My first NXT match against Chris Jericho went really well and when Chris got to the back, he expressed to Vince McMahon what a great job I'd done. As Chris tells it, Vince responded almost in disgust, grunting and then saying, "Him? He doesn't even eat meat!"

My family's reaction to me turning vegan was just as funny, especially with my dad being such a big hunter and meat eater. Still, they were supportive and did their best to make me food when I was back visiting. For my birthday, my mom even went through all the trouble to substitute vegan ingredients into her pumpkin cake, my favorite of all desserts. She didn't know much about veganism, but she tried to learn just for me.

Despite the difficulties and frustration of finding food on the road, I felt the best I had in years. I had energy, slept better, and overall, felt pretty good. It helped that when I was living in Las Vegas there was a vegan place called Red Velvet Cafe that made amazing cupcakes. I worried that I wouldn't have anything fun to eat on my cheat days, but I ended up having nothing to worry about, because those cupcakes were better than regular cupcakes!

My diet was based on fresh fruit and vegetables, and I used things like beans, quinoa, and tofu for my protein. Soy was the predominant source of available protein on the road; I was constantly in search of places that had unprocessed veggie burgers, and most of them had a large quantity of soy in them. Unfortunately, a lot of soy is genetically modified, and shortly after WrestleMania in 2012, I started getting really sick again. I couldn't figure it out for a long time, but then we did a blood test and found out I had a severe intolerance to soy.

When I was home and cooking my own food, avoiding soy was easy. Being on the road, however, was a different story. I tried going soy-free on the road for a while but became more and more frustrated at all the vegan foods I could no longer eat, leaving me with no good alternatives for protein. I was drinking four or five vegan protein shakes a day, and the whole thing was driving me crazy. With a heavy heart, I made the decision to start adding some animal products back into my diet. It almost made me feel defeated, as if I had taken a stand but then failed.

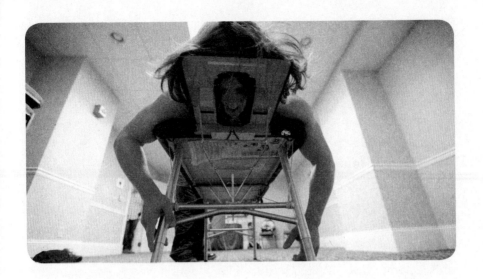

7 WORK OF ART
THURSDAY, APRIL 3, 2014—10:58 A.M.

"Braniel" exits their hotel room and splits at the elevator; Brie greets some WWE fans en route to the salon, and Daniel arrives at his appointment for Active Release Techniques (ART) therapy in a quiet hotel suite turned therapeutic studio.

ÖKO water filtration bottle still in tow, Bryan consults with the practitioner, describing tenderness and various effects of the highly physical lifestyle of a professional athlete. He lies flat on the table—belly up first, then on his back—and the specialist uses hard pressure to break up scar tissue in overused muscles.

Bryan's neck and limbs are swayed back and forth; he's then locked up in what resembles a half nelson. And repeat. By session's end, any initial discomfort yields loosening of the muscles. He's primed for the next phase of today's wellness: a workout.

Lance, Brian, Shooter Schultz, and I moved to Memphis in mid-June 2000, almost one year to the exact day that I left Aberdeen for San Antonio. Moving to Memphis was a little nerve-wracking for all of us, mostly because we had never been outside Shawn's

protective womb, as far as wrestling was concerned. Shawn was always very protective of us, and he treated us like his kids. There were a lot of things we didn't know how to do that Shawn made sure we had help with, like getting our apartments or having his wife, Rebecca, take Lance and me to the passport office before we went to Japan. In Memphis we were forced out from under Shawn's wing and had to learn to do everything on our own. It was probably about time. Brian, Shooter, and I got a three-bedroom town house together, and shortly after moving in, we went to Raw in Nashville and Smack-Down in Memphis to show our faces.

We drove with Terry Golden, the promoter and owner of Memphis Championship Wrestling (MCW), which was the name of the developmental promotion. Terry was really nice to us, but it was a far cry from going to the shows with Shawn. The Raw in Nashville was the first time I met William Regal.

Regal was an intimidating figure, particularly to someone like me who'd been wrestling less than a year. He's tall with a strong jawline, and he had a reputation for being a shooter, meaning he legitimately knew how to hurt you. He had started wrestling at age fifteen, doing shows at carnivals where he'd sometimes have to take on members of the audience. Regal came up the hard way and wrestled all over the world before coming to the United States to compete in WCW in 1993. What makes him even more intimidating is how he speaks very softly, sometimes so softly that you strain to hear him, and that he has the confidence of a man who knows what he's capable of.

Regal was in WWE's developmental system to prove he had kicked his pill dependency, which he is very frank and honest about in his book, *Walking a Golden Mile*. I have only known Regal since he's been sober, so it's hard for me to imagine him as the wreck he was prior to getting clean. Before I met him, I had heard the stories—how he pissed on a flight attendant and "shot on" (that is, used legitimate moves or holds on) Bill Goldberg in a live TV match, which wasn't true. Being at MCW was Regal's opportunity to prove he could stay sober, and if he did, WWE would bring him back to TV. Not only did he stay sober, but Regal also ended up being the most influential person in my career.

The William Regal I met was nothing like the man I'd heard stories about. He was soft-spoken and funny, and he had a genuine interest in helping anyone who wanted to be helped. Regal took to Brian and me right away when he saw how eager we were to learn. He introduced us to the European style of wrestling, which was heavily based on submissions holds, counters, and advanced mat-based wrestling—something I had never seen before, particularly as it became increasingly more difficult to find European wrestling videotapes would work in a U.S. VCR.

At first the multiple trainers we had in Memphis—including Jim Neidhart and others—were guys under contract with WWE, helping out until they were either brought back to the main roster or let go. At one point, Regal brought in an English wrestler named Robbie Brookside, who'd helped train Regal himself, with the goal of finding Robbie a role as coach in Memphis. That was the first time I'd met Robbie, and, like Regal, he also became a very influential wrestler in my career.

Since I was trying to switch to a less risky style, Regal was the perfect teacher for me. He would go into detail explaining the finer points of basic holds, and why certain counters make sense and others don't, given the intuitive visual intelligence people have about the human body. He opened up a whole new world of wrestlers like Johnny Saint and Mark "Rollerball" Rocco, who were great wrestlers, and the way Regal thought and talked about wrestling transformed the way I thought and talked about it. It made sense to me. However, as eager as Brian and I were to learn the European style, a lot of the other guys were not so keen on it. In the fast-paced, live-TV style of WWE, some saw the mat wrestling and counters as slow and relatively boring. They weren't interested in the specifics of wristlock counters, nor were they receptive to Regal's broader ideas that wrestling should make sense.

There were exceptions, of course, like this one guy named Reckless

Youth, who was one of the more notable independent wrestlers before he was signed by WWE. I heard of him through *Pro Wrestling Illustrated*, where he would get publicity because he was known for having great matches all over the country. Like a sponge, he soaked up what Regal taught, and since he had years of experience on the independents, he was great at integrating it into his matches. The first several months I was in Memphis I ended up wrestling Reckless a lot, which was a great learning experience because I got to try out all the things Regal was teaching us with someone who had a better concept of what wrestling should be than I did. After every match, I would ask Regal what he thought, and he would point out things I did well and things I could have done better. Brian and I had also taken to trying to record our matches, which helped as well.

Unfortunately for us, Regal got called back up to WWE television not long after we arrived in Memphis. He had been there a year and had not only stayed sober but was performing on a whole other level. Regal had a match with Chris Benoit at that year's Brian Pillman memorial show that blew my mind. It was a perfect example of how aggressive mat wrestling could work in the modern wrestling environment. After I saw it, I thought, *Holy shit! That's the kind of wrestling I need to be doing.* Even though we were only in Memphis a couple of months together, Regal became my mentor, and he has remained my mentor ever since. He's the person I go to for advice to this day.

We had a lot of wrestlers—a hodgepodge of people—coming in and out of Memphis while we were there. We had guys like Mabel and the Headbangers, who had already been on TV. We had the Mean Street Posse, who were on TV at the time as stooges for Shane McMahon and were being taught how to wrestle (with the exception of Joey Abs, who already knew how but was down in Memphis anyway). We also had the developmental prospects trying to get their first shot at being on TV, which was the biggest group of us—Joey Matthews, Christian York, Charlie and Russ Haas, Rosey and Jamal (who ended up being Umaga), R-Truth (before he became K-Kwik), and countless others during the year I was there. Another talent down there was Molly Holly, who inadvertently brought a big change to the entire group and procedure in Memphis.

Before the four of us (me, Lance, Shooter, and Brian), I'm not sure who was responsible for setting up the ring, but shortly after we showed up, it became our job, presumably because we were so new to the business and needed to pay our dues. We usually had at least three shows per week, so on those days, we'd get to the building early to assemble the ring and then stay late to tear it down. That continued until Nora Greenwald, who went on to become Molly Holly, came down to Memphis. She had just come from WCW and wasn't going to be in Memphis very long, so she had no reason to be worried about who was handling the ring construction, but when she saw that we were doing it and nobody else was, she offered to help at the end of shows. Shortly thereafter, someone from the WWE talent relations office was at the show, and when he saw Nora helping build the ring, he instantly asked why she was doing it. Terry explained that it was just supposed to be the four of us doing it and Nora had just volunteered. When word got back to the office, they started making everybody—main roster refugees and new faces alike—work on the ring. Needless to say, people weren't happy, especially since MCW was a relatively demoralizing organization in the first place.

One of the reasons Shawn Michaels had put a mask on me back in TWA was that I was not very expressive—a recurring criticism throughout my independent days. Eventually, Shawn and Rudy thought I'd started to develop facial expressions, so they took the mask off me and changed my character. As soon as I got to MCW, they told me they wanted me in the mask again.

The MCW shows we ran usually had very small crowds. We did a Wednesday night show every week in Oxford, Mississippi, at a bar where people didn't even have to pay to see us. The forty-five people who were usually in attendance were there mostly to drink, and in between swallows, they'd watch the show and heckle us.

MCW taped television shows as well. Initially we filmed at a really cool spot on Beale Street, but that didn't last very long. Soon we were

filming anywhere they would let us, like at armories and half-empty high school gyms. By the end of MCW, we were doing shows at gas stations and random locations like that. My favorite place we did television was in a Walmart parking lot, where shopping carts doubled as a guardrail and we all made our entrance out of the RV we all dressed in. This created a semicomical scenario where bad guys were running out of the RV to attack a good guy, more good guys came out of the same RV to chase the bad guys back to the RV, and then the good guys walked back to the same RV moments later.

Another real demoralizer for most of the guys was that very few people were being brought up to the main roster from Memphis. It didn't bother me too much because I'd never really gotten my hopes up that I would be brought up anytime soon. The only time my getting called up to TV was alluded to by WWE was around Royal Rumble 2001, when we were told WWE was looking to start a new cruiserweight division like the one that was popular in WCW. Brian and I were told they wanted to use us for it. Of course, that never happened.

There were certainly good moments as well. In February 2001, WWE renewed all four of our contracts for another year, and I was able to save some money. I earned enough to buy a 2000 Ford Focus and replace my old car, which was breaking down. I didn't have enough to pay for it in cash, so I had to make payments, which turned out to be a big mistake given what would happen a few months later in June. I also bought my first bed after more than a year and a half of sleeping on floors and inflatable mattresses. When I got a bed and a car, I felt like I was living a life of luxury.

The positive moments continued when WWE sent Regal down for a big show and I was able to wrestle him for the very first time. We were reaching the end of having a really fun match, which he was supposed to win. I went to the top rope, jumped off, and gave him a flying dropkick. As I covered him, he told the ref to count three and he didn't kick out. In a completely unselfish act, he let me win. By that point, I had learned a lot from him already, but there is no better way to learn from someone than being in the ring with him. I learned a ton in that match. And not just about wrestling.

In June 2001, shortly after WWE had bought WCW, we went to the training center for what we thought was another normal day. When we walked in we could tell something was up. Terry introduced a guy I didn't know from WWE's talent relations department, and they let us know they were closing down the development territory in Memphis. We were told some of us would be sent to the other developmental territories in Cincinnati or Louisville but, unfortunately, some of us would be fired. They were going to let us know our fate one by one as they called us into the office. I went in third; of the two guys who went before me, one was fired and one was sent to Cincinnati. When I walked in, I knew the score. The man said that although they thought I was very talented, they didn't have any current plans for me and they were going to let me go. Some of the guys who ended up getting fired got angry and threw stuff all over. I was just devastated, left with no idea what to do next.

Under our contracts, if you were fired, you'd still be paid for ninety days. But in order for us to get our money, we had to stay in Memphis and continue working the remainder of the MCW shows. Morale was understandably low, and these shows were the worst I had ever been a part of. Even the guys who were kept on and being sent somewhere else couldn't be excited or in a good mood, because half of the locker room had been fired. There was a lot of backstage drinking (and probably some other stuff I wasn't aware of), and ultimately Memphis went out with a whimper. The last show we had scheduled was in a parking lot of a pawnshop. We were getting changed in the store's restroom when all of a sudden it started raining. Terry decided to just cancel the show. We all went out, loaded up the ring in the rain, and took a group picture in front of the trailer. So ended Memphis Championship Wrestling.

Although I was very, very depressed after getting fired, I was also very fortunate for the opportunities I received while under contract. Former WWE Superstar Charlie Haas and his brother Russ were

really close with Jim Kettner, a top independent promoter out of Delaware who ran the East Coast Wrestling Assocation (ECWA). In 1997, Jim created an increasingly popular annual tournament he called the Super 8, featuring the eight best independent wrestlers from around the country. When the Haas brothers came down to Memphis and saw Brian and me wrestle, they told Jim they thought we'd be great for the Super 8. Charlie suggested that I would be the perfect opponent for Low Ki, who was tearing up the northeast indie wrestling scene and was Kettner's top prospect. When he called and asked me to participate, I gladly accepted. Kettner often worked with WWE to promote live events in Delaware and had a good relationship with the organization. He promised WWE (and me as well) that he would put me in matches where I would have the chance to shine. And, boy, did he.

In the first round, I wrestled Brian; in the second round, I wrestled Reckless Youth (who was gone from WWE by this point); and in the finals, it came down to me against Low Ki. All three of my matches went really well, and the Low Ki match, specifically, got a great reaction, not just because it was the finals but because we were blending hardnosed mat wrestling with stiff kicks and chops in a way that American independent fans weren't used to. The Super 8 received a great deal of coverage, including in national magazines like *Pro Wrestling Illustrated*, so I got a lot of good publicity out of it. Honestly, if I had not competed in the tournament, I would've had a difficult time securing bookings once I was fired, since before the Super 8 nobody really knew me outside of San Antonio and Memphis.

After I got fired from WWE's developmental system, I moved back to Washington—pretty much what I've done nearly every time I don't know what to do. I went back to living with my mom and tried to come up with a new game plan. There wasn't much wrestling in Washington, but I had contacted a company in Vancouver called Extremely Canadian Championship Wrestling (ECCW). They were interested in using me, which was great because almost every weekend, they ran three shows. Jim Kettner still brought me in for his ECWA shows on occasion as well, and I thought that be-tween these opportunities, plus continued word of mouth around the American Dragon, I could essentially avoid getting a "real" job and live off my savings.

Unfortunately, I couldn't. Though I initially planned to have my new car paid off by the end of the year, getting fired made it hard to manage monthly payments and other bills. At ECCW, I was only making $75 Canadian per show (about $45 U.S.), minus the cost of gas for my twelve-hour round-trip drive.

Whenever I worked for Kettner, I made $100, but that was—at most—once a month, and I wasn't getting many other bookings else-where. So I ended up getting two jobs, one at an after-school pro-gram for elementary school kids and another at a combination video store/tanning salon called Video Tonight, Tan Today. Even with an already fairly crowded schedule, I started taking classes at the local community college, too.

I got a big break in October 2001, thanks to Roland Alexander, a pro-moter out of California who ran All Pro Wres-tling (APW). The prior year, he'd organized a tournament called King of the Indies. Based out of the Bay Area himself, Roland used almost ex-clusively West Coast

Bryan wins the 2001 "King of the Indies" tournament
(Photo by Dr. Mike Lano)

wrestlers in his first eight-man tournament. The following year he decided to do something a little different by making it a two-night, sixteen-man tournament and bringing in wrestlers from all over the country, as well as Doug Williams from England. Based on our performances in the Super 8, Roland offered Brian and me a spot each in his elite tournament.

On the first day, Roland matched me up with Brian for the opening round. Since we'd wrestled each other over a hundred times by then, we had a really good match that caught the attention of one ring legend in particular. Nick Bockwinkel, who was among several other legendary wrestlers presiding over the show, approached Roland at the end of the first night. "If you don't put that guy over," Bockwinkel said, pointing directly at me as he suggested I win, "you're crazy." Though it certainly was not the original plan, Roland took his advice—a decision that created a lot of drama and controversy the following day.

Initially, Donovan Morgan, who was the head trainer at the All Pro Wrestling school (the promotion's true moneymaker), was scheduled to beat me in the semifinals and then go on to win the tournament. He was red-hot about the switch, but that wasn't the only thing he was angry about.

On the morning of the second day of the tournament, Roland—immensely impressed with our performance the previous night—offered me and Brian roles as trainers at the APW school. He explained that he needed a new head trainer because Donovan was spending a great deal of time wrestling in Japan. Even though the two of us were relatively inexperienced, Roland said, he believed we would be great trainers. We told him we'd think about it, then went and asked Donovan how the job was—not knowing, of course, that Roland hadn't told him about the proposition. Donovan was furious, though at Roland, not at us.

That night, I wrestled Doug Williams, which was fun because he knew how to do all the European-style wrestling that Regal had taught me. The momentum shifted later on in the semifinals, where I wrestled Donovan. Feeling betrayed and discouraged, he didn't really get into our match or want to do much of anything to make it a memorable performance, which was understandable. It was a short, lackluster match, unlike my final-round encounter with Low Ki, which was essentially a rematch from the Super 8 finals. We wrestled for nearly thirty minutes, incorporating the same elements that made our previous match unique. I won with a submission move I'd started using at the Super 8 as my finish: the Cattle Mutilation, a bridging double chicken wing with my opponent on his stomach. This move became my calling card for the rest of my time on the independents.

Recognizing that a former vegan's use of something called Cattle Mutilation may be a bit unexpected, I figure the origin of the move's name might need some explanation. I first saw the hold at a National Wrestling Alliance (NWA) show called Future Shock '89, a round robin tournament among the top NWA stars of that time, including the Great Muta, who was one of the most exciting wrestlers of that period. All of a sudden, in the middle of a match, Muta pulled out this bridging double chicken wing. It got no reaction and was barely mentioned by the commentators, but I thought it was awesome. I started using it when I was in Memphis, though only a few times as a finish. When I did use it, I called it a "bridging double chicken wing thing." The first time I heard the words "Cattle Mutilation" was when I wrestled Reckless Youth in the Super 8. I told him I'd like to beat him with a full nelson suplex, but given I'd just beaten Brian Kendrick with that submission in the previous round, he told me he thought I should also beat him with Cattle Mutilation. I had no idea what he was talking about. "Cattle Mutilation," he said, "that's what that submission is called." He looked at me like I was a dummy and walked off. I took his advice for the finish, but thought the name was wacky and assumed I'd never hear it again. Shortly thereafter, however, when I wrestled Christopher Daniels, he called it Cattle Mutilation as well. By the time Ring of Honor (ROH) started, everyone called it that. Everyone, that is, except me. I had no idea where the name had come from and hated the imagery, so I stubbornly continued to call it my bridging double chicken wing thing. It wasn't until late 2002 that I finally accepted that the move would always be known as Cattle Mutilation, despite my greatest efforts. Such is life.

Immediately following my victory in the King of the Indies tournament, I was presented with this huge trophy, which I actually got to keep (unlike other wrestling trophies, which are usually just for show and taken back shortly after they're given to you). But more important than the trophy was that this positioned me as a main-event wrestler on the independents. That two-day APW tournament on October 26 and 27 was the inspiration for Ring of Honor , and my win made people see me as a top guy right away, including the people responsible for ROH when it came to be.

After the tournament, Brian and I weren't sure what to do about the APW trainer roles. If nothing else, we were both broke and could use the money. Despite the opportunity, Brian decided not to take it. Before I could decide, I made an important phone call to Donovan to ask if it would be OK with him if I did take the job. He said he was fine with it and encouraged me to do it because it would be a good experience for me. Whether he meant that or not, I have no idea, but the next day, I called Roland to tell him I was interested. I would be earning $350 a week and given a place to stay. Plus, my weekends would be free to take independent bookings. I was sold. I gave notice to my jobs—both the school and Video Tonight, Tan Today—then finished up the quarter at the community college. On January 1, 2002, I moved to Fremont, California, to become the head trainer of a wrestling school.

When I moved down to train at APW, I really had no idea what to expect. Roland gave me the address for where I'd be living, and when I arrived, the house I pulled up to was nice and in a great neighborhood. What I didn't realize was that I would be living with Roland himself, as well as another promoter named Doug Anderson, who was the father of one of the girls in the training program, Cheerleader Melissa. Also in the house was Roland's eighty-eight-year-old uncle Al. We were quite the household. I had a small room on the second floor of the house and, sure enough, I was back to sleeping on the floor.

For a while, the APW wrestling school was immensely profitable—by independent standards, that is. Roland and All Pro Wrestling received tremendous exposure after being heavily featured in the wrestling documentary *Beyond the Mat,* in which two APW trainees received WWE tryouts. After the film came out and garnered some success, Roland was able to charge much higher rates. Whereas I paid $3,900 to train with Shawn Michaels, Roland was able to charge $6,000 per student. Not only that, but he signed new trainees to contracts that required them to pay their complete balance even if they quit.

Each class was limited to twenty students, and before I got there, almost all the classes were full. Their strategy seemed to me to be to work the students to death the first several weeks so that only those who really wanted it would stay. The quitters would forfeit some of their tuition, which didn't seem right to me.

By the time I moved to Fremont, Donovan Morgan and Mike Modest, another one of Roland's former trainers, had opened up a school and promotion called Pro Wrestling Iron in the same area to compete with APW. The rival organization would bash Roland's APW on Internet message boards, which led those in APW to do the same about Pro Wrestling Iron.

The increased competition created a sharp decline in students for All Pro Wrestling, though that wasn't the only contributing factor. I wasn't only in charge of training, but also recruitment. I was responsible for contacting anyone—from nearby and all over the world—who filled out enrollment applications. And Roland didn't just want me to call them once. He wanted me to call them at least every month for a full year. Donovan had done that, and his ability to call people and sell them on the school was one of the reasons APW was so successful. I, on the other hand, was less good at it.

Roland asked me to spend thirty minutes to an hour each training day calling prospective students. I did it at first, but it just wasn't in me to try to sell people on becoming a wrestler, especially when I knew the price tag. I've always thought that if someone really wanted to wrestle, they'd do it and not need to be sold on anything. That is why I'm a horrible businessman.

To be honest, I wasn't that much better at training people to wrestle. I was actually quite good at breaking down the movements of wrestling, but I was bad at motivation. I never needed anyone else to motivate me to work hard at wrestling, to watch tapes, or to try new things. All of that was fun for me, so it didn't ever seem like work. In my classes, I'd start off by showing them something, then opening it up for them to ask what they wanted to learn. That's how I learned, but I was self-motivated. Each session, I told the trainees to come in with three things they wanted to work on the next day, and very rarely did they come in with anything specific. I ended up being a frustrated trainer because I expected them to be self-motivated like I was. For most of the trainees, it seemed like wrestling was something they just wanted to try, not something they were determined to do. I tried to be very encouraging, but to succeed in wrestling, you need a certain degree of passion, and I had no interest in trying to inspire passion in people.

The only student I taught who really succeeded was Sara Amato, who has traveled all over the world wrestling and today is an accomplished trainer for future Divas down at the WWE Performance Center. Prior to my arrival at APW, Sara had already been training with Donovan, but she injured her knee, so she was essentially starting from scratch when I got there. She worked really hard, she was constantly studying tapes, and in general she was *tough*. One time, I was teaching back body drops, and the girl she was in the ring with collapsed under her, causing Sara to land on her shoulder and separate it. She let out an expletive, rolled out of the ring, popped her own shoulder back into place, then got back into the ring to do it again. Another reason I was a bad trainer: I let her try to do it again. She took the back body drop a second time, and when she landed, her shoulder popped out again. Once more, she cursed, rolled out, popped it back in, and was ready to get back inside the ring. At that point, I stepped in and told her she was done for the day, and then I instructed her to go see a doctor. Even though Sara wasn't making the wisest decision to fight through an injury like that, it demonstrated her passion for wrestling. When people ask me what it takes to be a wrestler, I always say passion is the most important thing. Well, passion and luck.

All of that said, I truly enjoyed training people. Teaching forces you to learn your craft better in order to explain it to other people, and at that point in my career, still being so new to wrestling, it helped me a great deal. Plus, I really enjoyed the Bay Area, and despite my doubts about the living situation, it turned out to be fun. Roland, who passed away in 2013, was witty and funny, and he always had something interesting to talk about, mostly wrestling gossip. Doug Anderson was a kind man, who always seemed to be in good spirits.

Living with Roland's eighty-eight-year-old uncle was what made the situation truly unique. Uncle Al had a hard time hearing and seeing. When I first moved in, he was able to dress himself, but after a month or so, Roland had to start laying out his clothes for him. He went from wearing his usual nice pants and a buttoned-up shirt to clothes Roland wore, which is why one day Uncle Al came out confused with basketball shorts over his dress pants.

On Uncle Al's eighty-ninth birthday, we decided to throw him a surprise party, complete with an ice cream cake and tons of decorations. As Roland and I went through the party supply store Roland grabbed two candles, one that was an 8 and another that was a 9. I stopped him and pointed out how rare it is that people live to be eighty-nine. Roland agreed with my suggestion to celebrate with eighty-nine candles. It was just a matter of regular candles or "magic" candles, the kind that don't blow out. Without really thinking things through, we chose the latter.

After training, we invited all the students over to the house for Uncle Al's big birthday bash. We got everybody party favors, like hats and kazoos, and had even found a bunch of paper Batman masks because we thought they were funny and would confuse Uncle Al. Training ran late, so we all got back to the house around 9 P.M., which was about two hours later than Uncle Al's usual bedtime. Since he couldn't hear very well, the noise of us all coming in didn't wake him

up. We quickly set up all the decorations and got to work on the ice cream cake, which we planned on bringing into his bedroom. Not one person—not even Doug, who was a sensible, reasonable adult—brought up that it might be a bad idea to put eighty-nine candles that don't blow out onto an ice cream cake.

We organized all the candles on the cake, which required us to put them very close together. We were less than halfway through when the candles all caught on fire and created an inferno, so high that it left black marks on the ceiling. Of course, what do we all do? We start trying to blow them out . . . which didn't work because they were *magic fucking candles*. I grabbed the cake and tried running it to the kitchen sink to put the fire out with water, while Roland went to wake up Uncle Al so he could see the mess we created. The kitchen faucet didn't work, so as I ran outside, I dropped the cake on the floor. By this point, Uncle Al—dressed only in his boxer shorts and a white tank top—was ever-so-slowly coming out of his room, yelling, "What the hell is going on?!" Sara ran to get a knife and a plate. We cut a piece of the salvaged cake and lit one candle on it, and when Uncle Al emerged, we gave him the cake as we all sang "Happy Birthday." Unexpectedly, Uncle Al started crying. In nearly nine decades, it was the first birthday party he ever had.

8 THE PUNISHER
THURSDAY, APRIL 3, 2014—12:49 P.M.

The leader of the "Yes!" Movement rolls up to an unmarked storefront with zero signage, but a glance through the window gives insight to the battleground on the other side of the entry. Youths are sparring on the mats as Bryan heads past an old-school Superdome fight poster toward a training room where the air is thick and sweat beads fast. Gloved competitors halt their ring session and turn their attention to the five-foot-eight former WWE Champion entering their arena. There, Bryan meets Craig Wilson, a boxer/kickboxer at Power Mixed Martial Arts in Terrytown, Louisiana. As he explained yesterday, Bryan seeks movement and conditioning, not intensity or technique, though both are impossible not to absorb within these walls in Wilson's care.

"I'm there to get my hips moving," Bryan says, "get everything fluid and make everything liquid so that by the time we're at Sunday, I'm not worried about how tight my hip flexors are or anything like that."

Before he can get to strikes and form, Bryan follows Wilson's guidance to do a unique wall stretch as a preamble to the workout that follows. With the WWE warrior's lethal legs outstretched to form a Y, you'd swear it was a modified "Yes!" pose.

They're as uncommon a duo as you'd ever see, with the hulking and deceptively swift Craig Wilson accepting targeted strikes from Daniel Bryan. The fourteen-year kickboxing veteran introduces his Superstar trainee to a few key techniques and combinations—kicks of multiple heights, jab sequences—and pointers on positioning. Bryan pivots around a tall kick bag, delivering a succession of blows from all angles to maximize speed upon each kick reset. It's a sound strategy and certainly a method he may soon put into practice within the squared circle. By the time he's done, the "Yes!" Man's shins and ankles are flushed from the persistent impact, his shirt's darkened with perspiration, and the skin of his bare feet is torn. Bryan is very satisfied. So is Wilson, who comments on the opportunity to work with the WWE Superstar who'll clash with the Game at Wrestle-Mania.

"I know [Daniel's] background. He's a very explosive wrestler, and a great wrestler," Wilson comments. "He's very good as far as technique goes. He's very fast, very nimble. He's going to punish Triple H."

For the kicks—not unlike those levied from Jersey to Mexico and re-fined in Japan a decade ago—to have impact, the "Yes!" Man opts to push forth with further leg training. It's back to the New Orleans Athletic Club, up the stairs to the massive balcony overlooking the pool for end-to-end lunges, following leg presses and other weight exercises.

Bryan jots down his progress in his notebook—the latest among a collection of many he's accumulated over the years. He explains that his earliest workouts were in junior high in his bedroom using his dad's old weight set. Back then, Bryan's attempted bench presses and bicep curls were the limits of his training until he took a weightlifting class in high school. These days, he pops into gyms from town to town around the world to be the best wrestler on the planet.

Shortly after I started training at APW, I got an e-mail from a man named Gabe Sapolsky asking me if I was free on February 23, 2002, for the first show of a new wrestling organization that was starting up. It was called Ring of Honor, and it became the company I was most associated with before I got to WWE.

The inspiration for Ring of Honor was Roland's 2001 King of the Indies tournament, which brought in the top independent talent from all over the place. ROH was originally owned by Rob Feinstein, who owned RF Video, a company that sold wrestling tapes. RF Video made most of its money selling VHS tapes of Paul Heyman's Extreme Championship Wrestling, an extremely popular company among hardcore wrestling fans, but ECW had gone out of business in April 2001. Their idea was to create their own wrestling company using the best independent stars from all over the country, and not just for a one-night thing like King of the Indies or the Super 8, but for a stream of shows that would fill the tape-sales void left by ECW's closure .

In their business plan, it was actually acceptable to lose money on the live shows—which was bound to happen with all the flights they paid for and the higher-paid talent they brought in—as long as they could recoup the money with tape sales. ROH was designed to appeal to a hardcore fan base who was tired of mainstream wrestling and in search of something different. The assumption was that tape traders and ECW fans everywhere would want ROH videos.

The first show was titled Era of Honor Begins, and it was held at the Murphy Rec Center in Philadelphia. That night, ROH officials were very smart in creating a main event that people wanted to see. Eddie Guerrero had been let go by WWE after a drunk driving incident in November 2001, but he was wrestling all over the place after his release to prove he was one of the best in the world. Fans loved Eddie, so he was a great choice for the main event against a popular Mexican wrestler from ECW named Super Crazy. It was something of a dream match. They used Eddie versus Super Crazy to draw people to the show, but the plan was to get people hooked with the younger, hungrier independent talent and build off of us.

On that first show, I was in a triple-threat match against Low Ki and Christopher Daniels. Low Ki had established himself as the hottest young independent talent in the Northeast, and he and I had a history of good matches. Daniels was an established independent

wrestler known for main-eventing all over the country, from Los Angeles and the Bay Area to Chicago and the Northeast. He'd won the original King of the Indies tournament and the Super 8 in 2000; plus, he wrestled on WCW television for a brief time prior to their closing.

Even with an event headlined by Eddie Guerrero and featuring a number of highly talented indie wrestling stars, ours was the match that was going to drive main events forward for the next year. We ended up having a great match, mostly due to the creativity of Ki and Daniels, who'd each been in numerous triple-threats. The finish saw me lock Daniels in the Cattle Mutilation, then, with me upside down and bridging on my neck, Low Ki came off the top with a twisting 450° splash onto both of us. It was a spectacular move, and he ended up pinning Daniels for the win. It was exactly what ROH needed to brand itself as the place to see great independent wrestling.

The first show was terrific, but I honestly didn't think too much of it because lots of promotions had grand ideas and then would go out of business shortly after. They booked me for a couple of events beyond that night, but I didn't necessarily count on it as something that was going to be around. Boy, was I wrong.

A little more than a month later, Ring of Honor had its second show, dubbed Round Robin Challenge. Gabe, who was in charge of booking the matches and stories for ROH up until late 2008, placed the three of us in a round robin tournament, where each of us would have a singles match with the other. The show opened with me losing to Daniels, who then lost to Low Ki in the middle of the show, prior to me facing Low Ki in the main event. If Ki won, he'd win the tournament; if I won, it would essentially be a three-way tie, all of us ending at 1-1.

Ring of Honor shows were *long*, and being in the main event was always tough because every match on the card was trying to steal the show. But Gabe was smart, and for the final match, he booked legendary MMA (mixed martial arts) fighter Ken Shamrock to be the special guest referee to give the main event a special aura. Given

Shamrock's past, Ki and I wrestled a match that was a hybrid of martial arts and pro wrestling. We used legitimate armlocks and knee

Bryan defeats Low Ki in ROH with guest referee Ken Shamrock *(Photo by George Tahinos)*

bars, as well as hard kicks to the legs and head, but then we'd mix it in with the more realistic, hard-hitting elements of pro wrestling. Inspired by the match Regal had with Chris Benoit two years earlier, to give it a more realistic element and make it seem like a fight, we avoided things like hitting the ropes. I ended up beating Ki when he passed out while in Cattle Mutilation.

Out of all the matches we had during that period, to me that one was the best, by far. Overall, this second event—more so than the first—cemented Low Ki, Daniels, and me as top guys in the company. And after this show, ROH became a monthly booking I could count on, which was pretty hard to find in the world of independent wrestling.

Every Ring of Honor match had cool high spots, unlike other promotions, which had a mixed roster with some veteran guys who'd prefer to focus on traditional moves like grabbing a headlock. Everybody who worked on the show was superhungry and wanted to have

the best match of the night. You really had the feeling that everyone was aiming to steal the show and make a name for himself. I didn't really get that feeling in most other promotions.

What made Ring of Honor special were its standards, including its Code of Honor. One of the things ROH wanted was to guarantee its fans that every match would have a clean, definitive outcome. This was essentially in response to how prevalent run-ins were in WWE in the early 2000s. They also required that performers had to shake hands before and after matches, though that rule didn't end up lasting long. Essentially, Ring of Honor stood out from your typical independent wrestling organizations, and it had the talent to show for it.

9 BOTTLE ROYAL
THURSDAY, APRIL 3, 2014—3:48 P.M.

In between workout sets, the well-maned athlete swigs from the ÖKO water bottle pressed up against his beard. He's been toting it all week long—and all 2014, actually—because he stopped using plastic bottles in January as his New Year's resolution. It appears to be catching on, as you can sense from his fellow Superstars, who're seen carrying their own hard plastic bottles around New Orleans. A water container emblazoned with the WrestleMania logo is even part of the roster's hotel-arrival gift bags.

The trend is a small win for a man looking for the biggest victory of his life at WrestleMania.

"I tend to believe that wrestlers can be a particularly wasteful breed," he concedes, *"but I think it's the nature of the volume of travel we do. We've just gotten used to throwing away so much stuff. We go through so many bottles of water in this company. I don't know that I've influenced my fellow Superstars, though I do think I made a contribution with the ÖKO water bottles."*

He adds, "People look at global problems and they seem so incredibly vast. The idea behind the water bottle is that it's a small thing that I can

do, that I can change about myself. You can make little changes, and those little changes become habits, and those habits may transfer to other people."

In early 2012, Bryan was nominated for and ultimately honored by being named PETA's Most Animal-Friendly Athlete. He's had animals around him throughout his entire life—dogs Millie, Mikey, Asparagus, and now Josie, as well as cats Mitten and Chowder—and Bryan sees a vital connection between all animals and the planet, as part of a greater responsibility he acknowledges.

"Protecting wildlife is important, and so is not making everything so homogenized to the point where wildlife and nature can't exist," Bryan asserts. "I feel like, as humans, if we are the keystone species of our planet, we should do our best to keep it alive."

These progressive statements are not what you'd expect to hear midwork-out from a professional wrestler with the grizzliest facial hair in the entire facility.

People are always asking me about my beard, so I figure I might as well address it. I never intended to grow a beard; it just kind of happened. Growing up in Aberdeen is like growing up in a sea of beards. A huge percentage of men work outside or in the mills around town, and it's cold and rainy a good part of the year. Beards help keep your face warm, so most of the men keep at least a short one going.

My dad almost always had a beard. There were times when I'd see him clean shaven, and it would just look weird, as if he had miraculously gone back to childhood. I tried growing a beard several times in my late teens, but I am not especially gifted in the realm of facial hair, and for the most part, attempts at growing facial hair just made me look silly. Despite the length of my beard today, it's never been overly thick; beard density is measured in follicles per square inch, and mine are relatively low.

The first time I started growing a big beard was in 2004. I had just come back from Japan and happened to have left my razor in a hotel room. Since a nice razor was around $10 and I am very frugal,

I decided I'd hold off on getting one until I absolutely needed it. I went on the next Japan tour a couple of weeks later, still without shaving. I was about to shave before the first show when Jushin Liger, one of the best lightweight-style wrestlers in history, told me he liked the short beard. He said it made me look older and tougher. I would have been an idiot if I went and cut my beard right after that.

I tend to go overboard with some things, and not shaving became one of those things. I went six months without using a razor, and my beard became much longer than it had ever been. Shaving my head added to my refreshed look as well. In June 2005, while I was in England, I finally decided to shave it. One of the factors was that my sister's wedding was coming up and I wanted to look presentable for it. Another reason was that in England, I still wore my American Dragon mask, and the beard made the whole thing look pretty ridiculous. The final straw was when we were out at a local bar, where a fifty-plus-year-old, heavyset English woman came up to me and said in a thick accent, "Your beard, it looks like me minge." "Minge" is an English term for "vagina." I couldn't get the image out of my head, and I shaved the next day.

My current beard grew in much the same way. I started by keeping a little stubble, and then I let it grow a little longer to about an inch in length. Shortly after Kane and I formed Team Hell No, I just stopped trimming entirely, and it grew to be pretty long. At that point, I stopped trimming the hair on my head as well, and nobody even noticed at first because everyone was distracted by how thick my beard was getting. A lot of times when you're in WWE, you have to ask for permission to change your look. This particular change in my appearance was so gradual that nobody really noticed until, all of a sudden, there I stood with long hair and this big beard.

Admittedly, sometimes having a substantial beard can present unique challenges. This one time, I was traveling out of Canada, and as I went through security, the TSA agent asked me to lift my chin up. He then combed his fingers through my beard, as if he was checking

for something inside of it, which I thought was really odd. I get a lot of protein shake caught in the beard, and when I'm grappling or doing jiu-jitsu, my beard hair gets all over the mat. Still, I just let it grow. I shampoo and condition it. Those are pretty much "Daniel Bryan's secrets to having a good beard."

10 "CARPET" DIEM
THURSDAY, APRIL 3, 2014—8:19 P.M.

WrestleMania week amps up on the "purple carpet" at the New Orleans Museum of Art for the Superstars for Kids charity auction, one of WWE's many community outreach events during this annual stretch of days leading into 'Mania. Among the guests of honor are a snazzied Daniel Bryan and his stunning fiancée, Brie Bella, who exit their private car into a wall of flashing bulbs and elbow-to-elbow press jockeying for sound bites and struck poses. Like George Romero's undead on a fresh body, an enclave of media and microphones surrounds "Braniel" for rapid-fire responses to questions they've already answered twice over, three reporters back. Still, the couple's enthusiasm is purely infectious. At the edge of the violet walkway stands a six-foot "Twitter Mirror" provided specifically for this major 'Mania event. The two lovers turn toward each other and suck face for social media, the pic capturing their pucker for the WWE Universe to retweet.

Hobnobbing is not what Daniel Bryan does best. This is why Brie is leading the charge on most conversations among the mixed crowd of ring masters (Hulk Hogan), celebrities (Marlon Wayans), and New Orleans officials like Mayor Mitch Landrieu, who specifically approaches the couple.

Landrieu welcomes them, expresses his elation at WrestleMania's emergence in the Big Easy, and invites "Braniel" back to the museum on Monday for a private tour, pre-Raw.

Though coarse and fierce inside the squared circle, Bryan couldn't be softer in his nearly unnoticeable touch-turned-caress on Brie's neck during conversation. If you've seen his in-ring strikes it's like watching a feral animal resting its paw. It's a subtle sign of adoration and demonstrates the simplest form of affection in a soft touch. Before Bryan can say "eco-friendly provisions," the mayor bids them adieu, then moves on to prepare for his party-wide address and the festivities ahead.

The setting of the Superstars for Kids party is up the proverbial alley of the "People's Couple," you could say. The museum location is meaningful not just in the rare art on display, but also in that it calls to the mind's eye visuals from their relationship at its very beginning. Their first social hangout together was a few years ago at the Isabella Stewart Gardner Museum in Boston. She invited him.

"It wasn't a date at the time, but looking back, that was our first date," Bryan says with a laugh. "We started talking after a storyline we shared together. Before then, we didn't really speak much. I've never been someone who talks to the Divas a lot or anything like that."

Two years later, the pair passes through the halls of the NOLA Museum of Art as an engaged man and woman planning a wedding in their not-so-distant, brilliant future together.

"We had so many similar interests," he says. "We had the same sensibility, and we're both kinda hippies."

Try enjoying your night when the guy whose head you plan on kicking in at WrestleMania is within one hundred feet of you. Arriving later than Bryan and Brie, "The Authority" (Triple H and Stephanie McMahon) is done making their rounds on the purple 'Mania-colored carpet and various meet-and-greet scenarios. Now they're mingling with the guests in the distance. "Braniel" focuses on the art and good conversation with the cast of Total Divas, including Brie's twin sister, Nikki, plus their mom and brother. There's no escaping the voice of Steph McMahon, WWE chief brand officer, as it's projected throughout the scene during her *event-wide speech. Tonight, she and the Game concentrate on their corpo-rate responsibilities. Things remain more civil than the lashings, verbal and physical, that have been exchanged on WWE programming in recent weeks, even months.*

"You don't know what people's personal relationships are like, but the appearance is that Triple H and Stephanie's relationship is predicated on power," says Bryan, frankly describing his perception of the corporate couple. "We're just all so different," he adds. "For us, happiness and doing things that are meaningful is more important. They're obsessed with being a power-ful couple. Brie and I are the opposite."

Bryan and Brie keep an eye on the clock. The "Yes!" Man's early-morning international media event compels the duo to call it a night. They exit the marble museum corridors and escape down the staircase to where a black SUV awaits to take them back "home" for the night.

After I was fired by WWE in 2001, my main goal was to go back to Japan and become a regular competitor there. That was actually my ideal situation when I started wrestling, thinking that American wrestlers who could make a living wrestling in Japan had it the best. In my mind, they could go there, do what they love, and then, when they came back to the States, they could walk around unmolested, without having to deal with the hassles of being mildly famous.

The head of WWE talent relations at the time was John Laurinaitis, who had a long history of working with All Japan Pro Wrestling, and shortly after my developmental contract was terminated, he told me he'd try to get me in there. Regal also gave me the number of Brad Rheingans, an older Minnesota wrestler who had the ability to get guys into the other top promotion of the Far East, New Japan Pro Wrestling. Unfortunately, neither of them was able to get me in, and both eventually stopped returning my phone calls.

That all said, I jumped at the opportunity when I was invited to a New Japan tryout in Santa Monica in March of 2002.

The day before the tryout, Roland had flown several of the APW talent, including me, to Las Vegas to attend the Cauliflower Alley

Club (CAC), an annual reunion dinner for retired and active wrestlers. We arrived the day before so Roland could network and several of the APW wrestlers could appear on the CAC's future legends show, the assumption being that it could get some influential eyes on us.

I only remember one thing from that Cauliflower Alley show. I was wrestling Brian Kendrick on the show, and beforehand, we were talking backstage. Brian turned and saw a skinny young wrestler doing a stretch on his back while kicking his legs over his head and leaving them there. Brian walked up to the kid, whom we'd never met before, and casually said, "Hey, you know that's the best way to suck your own cock, right?" The kid was terrified as he watched Brian get down on the ground next to him and demonstrate the motions. With that, Nick Bockwinkel—a wrestling legend and the man responsible for my winning the King of the Indies tournament—entered the room, dressed to perfection. Brian didn't see him come in, so Bockwinkel saw the entire demonstration as Brian told the kid to just "let gravity do all the work." Brian looked up just in time to see an appalled Bockwinkel shake his head in disgust and walk out of the room. I nearly fell over laughing.

After the CAC event, we drove from Las Vegas to Los Angeles, staying with Brian's friend Jordan (who had a Foreman Grill with ants that he refused to kill treading all over it). Brian and I had to be at the tryout at 10 A.M., so we woke up early the next morning and headed to Santa Monica.

The Inoki Dojo was in a large warehouse, and it was the nicest wrestling training center I had ever seen at that point. It was huge. They had amateur wrestling mats on the floor, kickboxing bags, nice lifting equipment, and the coolest thing: an official New Japan Pro Wrestling ring. There were TV cameras and film crews on hand with the intent of airing some of the footage on Japanese television. Seeing the whole production was exciting, even more so because Antonio Inoki himself, a WWE Hall of Famer and the founder of New Japan, was there to watch and evaluate us. Or so we thought. There were around fifteen mostly local independent guys there for the try-out, and we all ran through a series of calisthenics to warm up, followed by a match. Brian and I wrestled each other in the first match, doing our best to impress and busting out our coolest stuff. In the middle of the match, Brian muttered to me, "That motherfucker's not even watching! Look at him!" I managed to look over only to see Inoki holding on to this giant stick, doing what is apparently one of his signature exercises while watching MMA fighter Don Frye on one of the mats. Inoki literally had his back to us to watch Don Frye stretch.

When Brian and I finished our match, all the other wrestlers on the outside clapped. We then took our turn at ringside to see the other exhibition matches and noticed that Inoki didn't watch a single one of them. It turns out they weren't truly interested in scouting or assessing talent at all. They really just wanted the dojo to look full in front of the Japanese cameras. I was bothered we'd wasted our time, but Brian was especially irate. After the "tryout," Christopher Daniels and I were sitting on a couch in the dojo while Brian stood talking to us. Inoki was fooling around over on the cable crossover machine, which actually wasn't fully assembled. It just looked like it was. When Inoki jumped up on the beam to do a pull-up, the whole thing came crashing down on him, weights and all. Everybody rushed over to help him, except for the three of us. Daniels and I remained seated on the couch, and as more people scurried over, Brian loudly said, "Serves that motherfucker right."

Despite my disappointing first experience there, every time the Inoki Dojo told me there was an opportunity for a tryout, I made the trip down. It was a six-hour drive from Fremont to Santa Monica, and the tryouts were always in the morning. I'd drive down at night after I finished training at APW, then find some place to park and sleep in my car until the call time. None of the subsequent trips down there were as bad as the first, possibly because I made sure not to expect much. Even if there was just a minute chance it would lead to an opportunity in Japan, I had to take the chance.

My whole perspective on how I approached the dojo changed when I went there in August 2002 and met a New Japan wrestler named Shinya "Togi" Makabe, who was running the workout. I performed pretty well that day, and at the end of the session, he spoke with every athlete there, through an interpreter.

"You can't come down for just one day and expect to go to New Japan," he said, before pointing at Rocky Romero, TJ Perkins, and Ricky Reyes. "These guys are here every single day. They show their determination, they work hard. And if you want to be successful, you need to work just as hard."

Those words really resonated with me. I was working hard up in Fremont, but nobody was *seeing* that hard work. At that point, I knew what I needed to do.

When I got back to Fremont, I told Roland we needed to talk. I explained that, although I was thankful for the opportunity he gave me, for my career to move forward I thought I needed to move down to Santa Monica and train at the Inoki Dojo full-time. I expected Roland to be angry or at least disappointed, but he wasn't. I think "thrilled" would be too strong a word, but he was definitely relieved. I hadn't been able to bring in many new students to the school, and even though Roland wasn't paying me tons of money, it was enough that it was putting stress on his finances. He thought it was a great idea for both of us. So in early September I packed my stuff back in my car and moved down to Santa Monica.

I found that all of the guys who trained at the Inoki Dojo lived locally. And by "locally," I mean the Los Angeles version of locally. Sometimes it would take TJ Perkins two hours to get to the dojo just because of traffic. Before I moved down, I spoke with Hiroko Inoki (Antonio Inoki's daughter) and her husband, Simon, who ran the place together. They said they'd love to have me come down, but there was an issue as to where I would live. Los Angeles is *expensive,* and though I had been able to save some money working for Roland, a rent of $1,000 per month will bring your savings down in a hurry. That's when I asked if I could live at the dojo. The couple considered it, made some calls, and then told me they thought that arrangement could work. They barely knew me, but I had a reputation for being honest and responsible. Looking back, it's shocking to me they agreed to it, because I was essentially a stranger that they let live in their very nice and expensive facility. From their perspective, I suppose it was nice to know that someone was there all the time to watch over the place.

Initially I slept in my sleeping bag on the wrestling mats, but after several months, I got myself a cot from the army surplus store and put it above the office area. It was just a bunch of plywood up there, but it gave me a little privacy in case I needed to lie down while the dojo was occupied.

Training there was awesome. At first Shinya Makabe—whose advice persuaded me to make the move—was our trainer, and he taught us the New Japan way of doing things. Once he left, an MMA fighter named Justin McCully guided us through practices, mixing up pro wrestling stuff with jiu-jitsu and kickboxing. It was a fun place to be, and we worked hard.

Much to my surprise, I was offered a three-week tour with New Japan in October, only a month after I started training there full-time, joining Ricky Reyes and Rocky Romero, who teamed together as the Havana Pitbulls. I was thrilled. The tour was incredible. New Japan was the biggest wrestling company in Japan at the time, and we wrestled in front of at least a thousand people every night. The high-light, however, was my first time wrestling in the Tokyo Dome.

The Tokyo Dome is huge. At its capacity, it can hold over sixty thousand people for a wrestling show. When I first walked inside I was amazed. The dome-shaped roof is an air-supported structure held up by pressurizing the inside of the building. When we came in, we walked into a vaultlike room. They closed the door we came through—at which point I could feel the pressure change—then they opened another large door to enter the stadium. All of that was done to stabilize the pressure and keep the roof what I called "in-flated." To me, the building was a feat of modern engineering.

In a show called the Spiral on October 14, I teamed with the Pitbulls against Masahito Kakihara, Tiger Mask, and one of my all-time favorite wrestlers, Jushin "Thunder" Liger. Around the time when I was in high school, Liger had come to the United States and wrestled for WCW multiple times, including one high-profile match with Brian Pillman that was incredible for its time.

Shortly before our match, referee Masao Tayama, who spoke great English and was always there to help us out, jokingly gave us some advice: "Don't look at the crowd when you walk down the ramp." I could understand why. The ramp down to the ring at the Tokyo Dome was *long*, maybe a hundred yards, and it was intimidating for three guys who'd never wrestled in front of a crowd anywhere close to its size.

They had a golf cart take us to the staging area where we would make our entrance. All three of us were giddy as schoolgirls—not to mention a little nervous—yet when we walked out, I couldn't help but look out to the crowd. There were over thirty thousand people in attendance, and though probably less than 10 percent of the audience had even heard of the three of us, it didn't matter. I was mesmerized and lucky I made it down to the ring without tripping over my feet. I remember nothing from the match, only that I had a hard time keeping a smile off my face throughout it. A short time later, I ended up living in the dojo and would make several more trips to Japan.

Though I'd previously been completely focused on wrestling, living at the Inoki Dojo forced me to be surrounded by wrestling all the time. There was no escape. Sometimes it was suffocating, but it was undoubtedly good for my development. The Inoki ideal of infusing pro wrestling with legitimate martial arts opened up my eyes to all that was possible with the form, and as a result I was performing better than ever.

In April 2003 in ROH, I wrestled in what—up to that point in time—was the best match of my career. It was against Paul London, who, though relatively new to ROH, was loved by fans because of his charisma, his ability to sell being hurt, and his daredevil style of wrestling. Paul had trained with Rudy Boy Gonzalez down in San Antonio, and we'd discovered we had instant chemistry the first time we wrestled a number of months before. That initial match we had was relatively short, under fifteen minutes, but the fans enjoyed it, and Gabe booked the rematch to be a two-out-of-three-falls match.

Both Shawn Michaels and William Regal tried to instill in me the idea that more so than moves, storytelling was the most important thing in a match. Though I tried to learn as many techniques as I could over the years, I also always focused on different ways of telling stories. Our rematch went over forty minutes, and it was not only the longest match I'd ever had, but also the first time I really felt like I nailed telling a story in a match. I didn't wrestle another match in ROH for seven months, and that was the perfect way to leave.

Unlike Frontier Martial-Arts Wrestling a few years earlier, when New Japan told me they were interested in bringing me back over, they actually did it. I joined them for two more tours in the beginning of 2003. The initial series of shows in March was relatively uneventful, though while on tour, I met TJ Wilson (now Tyson Kidd) for the first time, and I rejoined Scott Norton, who had been on my inaugural tour of New Japan in 2002. Scott, an enormous world champion arm wrestler, was a great guy to be around. Given he'd been a New Japan regular since 1990, he taught us a lot of tricks about surviving in Japan. He showed us how to get to gyms independently, showed us some great restaurants near our regular hotels, and informed us about New Japan's inner workings, politically speaking.

Scott joked that if I had come to New Japan four or five years earlier, he and the other guys would have forced me to drink. Fortunately, there was far less pressure for a teetotaler like me because Scott was the veteran "gaijin" (which the Japanese called all of us foreigners) wrestler, and he had stopped drinking entirely himself. He said to me, "Kid, I can't make you drink, but I can make you drink *this*!" With that, he bought me my first cup of coffee. I was wired for hours.

In May, I went abroad for another short tour of only two or three shows, one of which was at the Tokyo Dome again. This time, instead of being on the main show, we were on a show the day before that had only three matches and was also in the middle of a pachinko tournament, which was a form of Japanese gambling I never quite understood. The setup for our show was memorably weird. Outside the ring there were a few hundred chairs, but there were also a ton of pachinko machines, which took up roughly the space the size of a high school gym—all right in the center of the gigantic Tokyo Dome.

That night, TJ Perkins wrestled first, and then Rocky Romero and I teamed up against Masahito Kakihara and Akira, and I'll admit that wrestling in a stadium that large with so few people felt strange. I almost would have preferred wrestling in the Walmart parking lot from the Memphis days. The match didn't light the world on fire, but it was good considering Kakihara and Akira put forth so little effort. Our opponents didn't seem to even want to be there, like it was a demotion for them to be wrestling on this show the day before the "real" big show. Now, having experienced so much more in my own career, I completely sympathize with them.

When we got back to the hotel, Justin McCully had us meet him in his room. The three of us (me, Rocky, and TJ) stood there as Justin told us how disappointed Antonio Inoki was in the match. Then he slapped us. Each of us. If that happened to me today, I would instantly punch him in the face—which would surely have ended with me getting my ass kicked, since even at that time Justin had already fought at UFC (the Ultimate Fighting Championship) and was a heavyweight.

I was confused and wasn't quite sure what I had done that was so wrong that I deserved to be slapped. Justin explained that the slap was from Inoki because he thought we should have done more of the "shoot" fighting style we practiced at the dojo. According to him, Inoki understood that it was difficult because our opponents were the veterans—and in wrestling, you're taught to listen to the people that have more experience than you—but the slaps were to inspire us to challenge the system. The intent was to transfer his fighting spirit to us, a common custom in his dojo (people lined up to be slapped by Inoki) and the Japanese culture. Truthfully, he could have just said it instead of slapping us, and it would have been every bit as effective.

After the debacle at the Tokyo Dome, instead of flying back to Los Angeles with the rest of the guys, I flew to London for an opportunity to work for longtime English promoter Brian Dixon. For a while, Regal had been pushing Dixon to bring me over, but Brian preferred using bigger Americans because they made such great villains. Plus, with English wrestlers typically being on the smaller side, it would automatically put them in an underdog role that the fans could get behind. I was obviously not very big, and though I'd developed a reputation as a good wrestler, I wasn't a great character that would appeal to Dixon's fan base. Finally Dixon agreed to give me a chance to perform for his company, All Star Wrestling.

For most Americans coming over, Dixon wouldn't pay for their flights. I was no exception. Fortunately, New Japan didn't mind flying me to London, and I figured I'd just stay until I could get another Japan tour or until an American company was willing to fly me back, which I didn't foresee being too big of a deal. Dixon wouldn't get most talent work permits either, and again, I was no exception. When I spoke with him on the phone, he didn't think it would be a concern, and he instructed me to tell anyone who asked that I was just visiting friends.

After landing in England, I had to go through immigration before I could get my bags. The immigration officer asked me what I was doing there, and, as instructed by Dixon, I said, "Oh, just visiting friends."

"What friends?" he asked.

Immediately I started getting nervous because I wasn't a very good liar. I gave him Brian Dixon's name. After he requested his contact information, I supplied his phone number, too.

"How long are you staying?" he asked.

"A couple months."

"Do you have a return ticket?"

"Not yet. I was going to get one."

"How much money do you have on you?"

"About four hundred dollars." (This caught his attention right away.)

"So, what are you going to do for money for the couple months you are here?"

Clearly $400 would not be enough. Had I been a better liar, I could have easily made up something, like I would have money transferred over when I was running low. Instead I struggled to come up with an answer, and by this point I was sweating. The immigration officer could tell.

He brought another officer over, and they questioned me further. During the interrogation, they got my bag from baggage claim, and as they looked through it, they found my wrestling gear. They asked what I was doing in Japan, and I told them.

"And you're sure you're not *here* to wrestle?" they inquired.

"Nope," I said, "just here to visit." Even though I could tell things weren't going well, I was going to stick to my story.

They must've done some research on Dixon and figured out that he was a wrestling promoter. They called Dixon to ask if he knew me. At first he kept with the story that I was just in England to visit, but at some point he changed his tune and stooged me off. When the officer came back, he said, "Just so you know, we're going to deport you. Your friend told us you were going to work as a personal trainer."

They stuck me in a room with a bunch of other people getting deported, and I was the only American. They were all looking at me, thinking I must've done something *really* bad if I was an American getting deported. That wasn't really the case. I was just a twenty-one-year-old without much of a game plan. To make matters a little more stressful, I learned that when they deport you, they don't deport you back to your home country—they deport you back to the country from which you came. They were going to deport me back to Japan! I would have to buy my own ticket back to the States if that's where I wanted to go.

They let me call my mom, and after I told her the situation, she and my sister started researching all the flight options on the Internet. Everything they could find would cost thousands of dollars to get me back to the United States within the time I had, and I wasn't allowed to leave the airport. Flying back to Japan and then getting to the States from there wasn't any cheaper and was a really long way to travel. I was starting to get desperate when I spoke with an agent for British Airways. The whole time we had been looking for a one-way ticket. She decided to search for a round-trip ticket and found one that wasn't available online, direct from Heathrow to LAX for only $500. I couldn't believe how lucky I was.

Shortly after I got back to the States, I got in touch with Brian Dixon. He told me if I still wanted to come wrestle in England I could, and this time he would get me a work permit. I could tell he felt bad about the whole thing, especially because he knew I had a close relationship with Regal. I had purchased a round-trip ticket, so I still had the return flight and since I didn't have any shows booked because I had planned on being in England this whole time anyhow, I told him I would come. I drove my car back to Aberdeen from Santa Monica (I didn't know how long I would stay in England, let alone anticipate a full six-month stay), then flew back across the Atlantic that May.

It surprised me that I didn't have any problems getting into England the second time. When I arrived, the immigration officer took a look at my passport and asked if I'd ever been deported. I told him a brief version of the story, which didn't include me trying to lie to get into the country, and showed him my work permit. Fortunately, I was able to enter, and ever since, I've never had a problem coming in and out of England.

My first day in England was interesting. I had flown into Heathrow Airport and had a show that same night. Brian told me the name of the building and the address, but I was left to my own devices to

actually get there. The show was at Fairfield Halls in Croydon, which is near London. I had no idea how to get there and had no clue how to use the English transportation system. I'd never lived in a place where the public transportation infrastructure was good enough to be useful. If not for the kindness of the random strangers I was asking for directions, I might still be lurking around London today.

When I finally got to Fairfield Halls around 4:30 P.M., I found out Brian had told them I'd be there early and they had a quiet room with a small bed upstairs for me to take a nap. I fell fast asleep and didn't wake up until I heard a knock on the door around 7 P.M. It was Dixon's daughter Laetitia, whom we all just called "Tish," and she very politely told me the show started in a half hour. As I walked down to the locker room, someone informed me that I was part of a tournament to crown a new middleweight champion and that I was going to have three matches, all against guys I'd never met before and knew nothing about.

With very little time before showtime, I got a little flustered. In a rush, I got downstairs and walked around introducing myself. I was saying hellos and shaking hands when I noticed three guys sort of huddled together. Guy #1 was holding Guy #2 while Guy #3 was slapping him. It looked to me like they were just fooling around, so I kept shaking hands, laughed at the scene, and then walked out into the next room.

That night, I went on to win the tournament and the middleweight championship. The coolest part was being presented the title by Mark Rocco, who was famous for being the original Black Tiger in Japan. Rocco was also part of a small group of guys who revolutionized wrestling in the late '70s and early '80s by creating a hybrid of Mexican, Japanese, and English ring styles. If you go back and watch Rocco's matches from that time period, they're still exciting today.

What was unusual about the night, however, was that during the entire show, people kept apologizing to me. I had no idea why; I thought it was because I had to do three matches right after taking that long flight.

"Sorry, Bryan. This sort of thing never happens here," someone would say.

"No worries. This happens all the time in the United States," I'd respond, and go on my merry way.

I later found out they weren't talking about the three matches. After the show, I rode with a referee named Mal to the next town, and he apologized to me again. I explained to him that wrestling multiple matches was no big deal to me since tournaments like this were very popular in the United States and I usually ended up competing in a tournament almost every month somewhere. He stared at me confusedly. Then he realized I didn't know what had happened. He explained that the three huddled guys I thought were fooling around earlier in the locker room weren't. It turns out that Guy #1 and Guy #3 (relatives of a current WWE Diva) were really beating up Guy #2. My understanding is they threatened to throw him out the window of the locker room, which was four stories up. Fortunately, they didn't.

My response was simple: "Holy shit! How did I miss that?!"

Thus ended my first day in England.

Summer is the busiest time of year for Dixon and All-Star Wrestling, which is why I went out when I did. My first show was what they refer to as a "town show," a normal show in front of wrestling fans, but during summer months, most of Dixon's events take place at Butlins. Butlins, which is what the English call a "holiday camp," is a chain of inexpensive seaside resorts with beaches for families who pay an all-inclusive fee for lodging and entertainment (food is extra). These resorts have music acts, magic shows, and all sorts of entertainment, including wrestling. As a result, most of the people who watched the shows aren't actually wrestling fans; they just happen to be there, and wrestling is a fun novelty.

We'd wrestle at the three Butlins locations—Bognor Regis, Skegness, and my favorite, Minehead—twice each, every week. We'd typically do Tuesday, Wednesday, and Thursday, hitting a different Butlins location each day, then we'd go back on Saturday and

Sunday, sometimes doing a double shot on Saturday, performing at two different locations in the same day. Every week, I wrestled a minimum of five shows, oftentimes MORE because there would be town shows and other holiday camp shows thrown in along the way.

When Regal talked to me about this type of show, he said it was important to understand the audience at Butlins: kids. Adults would come, too, but they weren't wrestling fans; they came because their kids dragged them there. Regal has expressed to me that his longevity in wrestling—working through injuries and all—is due to what he learned at Butlins. He learned to entertain and to do so without putting his body in too much danger night after night, given the kids didn't care about big falls or hard-hitting moves. Being entertaining was one of the bigger weaknesses in my game, so I worked on it almost to a fault while at Butlins.

Dixon wanted me wearing my mask again, which was great because it instantly made me more of a character. Though I was originally a good guy at town shows, the theme for the Butlins shows was England versus the United States, with the Americans being the villains. Being the American Dragon, it was clear which side I fell on. I'd carry the U.S. flag to the ring, and at first I just did typical bad guy stuff from '80s wrestling. I soon started to really enjoy myself and get creative. My voice has never been good, but I made it even worse for the act by coming to the ring and singing the American national anthem. I even intentionally forgot words to further rile up the crowd and eventually added to the mix cutting promos on the microphone prior to singing, which helped me get a little more comfortable on one of my other biggest weaknesses. In the ring, I alternated between trying to be a ruthless villain and trying to make people laugh, often in the same match. I'd regularly try to find as many unique ways to get hit in the crotch as possible. My all-time high was getting hit in the balls twelve times against Mason Ryan in Bognor Regis.

English wrestlers, who had years of experience wrestling at places like Butlins, had some really fun comedy spots that I'd never seen before. My favorite was called "The Head, the Hand, and the Bol-locks." The villain would toss the fan favorite out of the ring. When the good guy would try to get back in the ring, the bad guy would stomp his hand, so then he would find a lady in the front row to kiss his hand to make it better. He'd try to get in again, and then the villain would stomp his head, which the same lady would kiss as well. Then the two opponents would basically flip roles; the villain would try to get back in the ring, and the crowd favorite would kick the middle rope, which would hit him in the balls. The villain would then go back to the same lady, gesture toward his crotch, and ask for a kiss. Naturally, the lady would refuse every time, leading to plenty of laughter among the crowd. I kept thinking that one day they'd find the wrong lady who would actually do it, and then it would turn into a completely different kind of show.

Being in that environment added another dimension to wrestling for me; it changed my perception of what wrestling could be and what people want from it, especially in the context of it being more of a "variety show."

The drives between Butlins camps were pretty long, and it didn't make it easy that our home base was in a small town near Liverpool called Birkenhead. Pretty much every drive was over three hours, mostly on small, winding roads that contained lots of roundabouts. I hadn't ever been prone to car sickness, but it would happen to me quite a bit on those drives.

The rides were part of the fun, though, and the guys I met along the way became some of my favorite people I've ever traveled with, like Frankie Sloan (a cousin of Robbie Brookside), who became a good friend of mine and is probably the funniest man I've ever met. If you weren't driving (and I never drove), you might sleep, but even though we all had portable CD players, we would usually laugh and joke most of the trip. We did the drives together, we'd set up and take down the rings together, and if we had a night free at Butlins, we'd go out together. I've rarely gone to bars during my career, but in England it was different. I *loved* going out, mostly because the guys

were so much fun to be with. I obviously wouldn't drink, but I'd find contentment in karaoke, and we'd all go make fools of ourselves on the dance floor.

The English wrestlers also had this awesome system where if you made a mistake or committed a "crime" (common crimes were cock-blocking, making a huge blunder in a match that was an embarrassment to the job, or avoiding setting up the ring), you'd have your case judged by the senior wrestler of the group. If found guilty, you'd be punished by having to run miles. In the middle of a trip, the van would drop off the guilty party on the side of the road and he'd have to get to the van in ten minutes or be forced to run another mile.

All that time together developed camaraderie, and, of course, with all that time came disagreements, too. Yet it was the closest I've ever seen a wrestling locker room come to being like a real family.

In the middle of my trip, I also ended up doing my first show in Germany, thanks to Robbie Brookside. Robbie, whom I originally met when I lived in Memphis, was a good friend of Regal's, and the pair teamed together when they were young.

On Dixon's shows, I occasionally got to wrestle Robbie, though he was mostly matched up against the bigger Americans in the main events because he was a world-traveling wrestler and the biggest star on the show. Still, he was constantly looking out for me, and while I was out there, I always asked his advice before anyone else's. Robbie was another influential mentor for me, not just in wrestling, but in life. Though I recall Regal saying it to me, too, at some point, it was Robbie who first said the following: "Wrestling doesn't owe you a living. If you're not having fun, you can always go do something else. We are lucky to be able to make a living doing what we do." I've tried to always remember that.

Robbie was the champion for an older promoter in Germany who had been running wrestling events for years. They were doing two and a half straight weeks of shows in the same venue, a tent put up in the middle of a carnival, which was a longtime German wrestling tradition. The promoter was hesitant to use me when Robbie brought it up. He, like Dixon, liked using larger Americans or ones who had established names. To him, I was a small, unknown wrestler, and he didn't know if the fans would like me. Robbie was persistent, however, and eventually got me booked on one show, where he and I wrestled a two-out-of-three-falls match for his title. What made it unique for me was that they used the rounds system for championship matches. Ours took place over twelve three-minute rounds.

Earlier, I mentioned the match with Paul London was the best match I'd had at the time. This was the match that surpassed it. Robbie was *hated* in Germany, and though the fans had never seen me before, it didn't take them long to start cheering for me. In the Paul London match, I was the ring general, even though I'd been wrestling for less than four years at that point. In this match, Robby took control, and he was amazing. He told me when and what to do, and everything he instructed me to do was perfect for what the crowd wanted. He was a vicious bad guy and I was a fiery good guy, and when the match ended, even though I lost, the fans cheered me on my way out. When I got to the back, Robbie gave me a big hug, and then the promoter came over to congratulate me on the match. Afterward, he also admitted to Robbie that he had been wrong about me and that I was a great choice for the championship match. When Robbie told me what the promoter had said, he looked so proud. Given how much he helped me, seeing him that satisfied with what we had done was way better even than wrestling in the Tokyo Dome.

I ended up staying in England for a little over six months. Right before I went back to the United States, I wrestled seventeen days in a row, doing twenty-one shows in that time. Sometimes, it would be in front of nearly a thousand people; sometimes, it would be in front of fewer than fifteen. But it was awesome. Truth be told, if Brian Dixon had been able to pay a little bit more, I probably would've never left. The lifestyle really appealed to me. I didn't own a lot because there was no room for it in the suitcase I literally lived

out of for half a year. There was no stress, no pressure, just driving up and down the roads with interesting guys and wrestling. We essentially lived like gypsies. It was perfect.

I try to meet up with Frankie every time I go to England when we run shows there with WWE. I love being able to see Brian Dixon and his family when they occasionally come to the shows, and I'll run into guys like Mikey Whiplash here and there. I love seeing them all. And whenever I go back, I always get this secret longing in my heart for the days gone by when everything was a little more innocent for me. It was the most fun I'd ever had wrestling.

11 EARLY BEARD GETS THE WORM
FRIDAY, APRIL 4, 2014—5:29 A.M.

The streetlights are still bright at this hour when Daniel Bryan gets into a chilled limousine for the earliest scheduled appearance of his week. With little time to eat a formal breakfast, he reminds the car of the fruitfulness of his initial Whole Foods mission.

"This is where a grocery store trip comes in handy," Bryan states. "I had a protein shake, a banana, and vegetable juice."

He shares the ride with Sheamus and the Shield's Roman Reigns and Seth Rollins, all attendees at the morning's international media event at the New Orleans Ernest N. Morial Convention Center—the same site where WrestleMania Axxess, WWE's annual fan festival, is being held. They arrive along with the rest of a larger group that includes Big E, Cesaro, Natalya, and Emma; then the Superstar squad is divided for interview conquering.

Bryan's very-early-morning interviews include discussions with local news affiliates, satellite radio stations, and more at emptied booths on the Axxess floor, many hours before the doors open for the second night of fan festivities. Interviewers rap with Bryan about everything from his

upcoming nuptials and WrestleMania to his indie star days and WWE training grounds.

Daniel Bryan's on-camera interview is brought to a halt by a second buzz in his pocket, like a record scratch on the meet-and-greet music being made by the media on hand. It's the "Yes!" Man's mom. The dual calls are a signal for Bryan's attention, so he politely pauses the Q&A to connect with his mother, whom he's expecting to arrive in New Orleans later in the evening.

He ends the call, "Yeah, I love you, too." Then it's back to countless conversations for broadcast and beyond. It's ordinarily difficult to see the expressions beneath Bryan's beard, but as he exchanges banter with the myriad media personalities, there are plenty of wide smiles visible.

Shortly after I returned from my first trip to England, I did the December tour for New Japan, then drove back down to Santa Monica to resume living in the Inoki Dojo, which had changed while I was gone. Justin McCully must have had some sort of falling-out with them, as he was no longer there. There were now several other guys living in the dojo, having made the same decision I did to move there to train. One of them bought a cot and put it above the office close to mine, which I didn't mind, but it greatly diminished the amount of privacy I had. Simon and Hiroko Inoki brought in more teachers to help us, including two different yoga teachers, a new jiu-jitsu coach, and a Muay Thai coach. With all the guys there and the different classes, it was a great learning environment. I've loved yoga, grappling, and kickboxing ever since.

In 2004, New Japan brought me over for eight different tours, the longest of which was over six weeks. Being there so much allowed me to get more comfortable with the style and get to know the Japanese wrestlers better. In March, I won my first Japanese title, the IWGP Junior Tag Team Championship, along with a masked Christopher Daniels. Chris wrestled as Curry Man, a bizarre dancing character whose mask included a curry bowl on top of his head. The Japanese fans loved him, and I always found it funny that Chris wasn't actually a very big fan of curry.

In May, I wrestled on another Tokyo Dome show, in which I teamed with Último Dragón and Koji Kanemoto to wrestle Tiger Mask, Heat, and Marufuji—my best experience in the Dome. I ended up getting the pin for my team, demonstrating the faith New Japan had in me. That May was also the first and only time I competed in the annual Best of the Super Juniors tournament, a three-week, sixteen-man round robin tournament that dated back to 1988. It was supercool because so many of my favorite wrestlers had done the tournament, including Owen Hart, Chris Benoit, Eddie Guerrero, Fit Finlay, and, of course, Dean Malenko. It's a physically intense tournament, and early on, Chris dislocated his shoulder. We were scheduled to defend our tag team titles in the middle of the tour, so Chris taped his shoulder up every night and continued on. We lost the championships to Gedo and Jado, but the match was great because all the fans knew Chris was hurt and got behind him big-time. Afterward, Chris was able to go home.

As far as the tournament went, I made it to the semifinals—much better than I thought I'd do—where I lost to Kanemoto. I felt like Kanemoto and I had had a really good match, but when I watched it, I realized Kanemoto performed light-years better than I did, and I recognized I still had a lot more work to do. That was one of the many wonderful things about working in Japan. On the United States independent scene, I was almost always the more experienced wrestler and had led the matches since 2002, even only three years into my career. Very few of us had experience working with veterans in the industry. It was almost like the blind leading the blind. In Japan, it was different. The first time I wrestled Kanemoto, he'd been wrestling twelve years. Jushin Liger had already been wrestling for eighteen years against some of the best in the world by the time I wrestled him. It was a wonderful place to learn.

Though I only got to wrestle him a couple of times in tag matches, Yuji Nagata was my favorite person to watch perform. He didn't really do any fancy moves, but everything he did was believable and crisp; plus, he had a great fire, and the fans always got behind his matches.

I made sure to watch his matches every night because there was always something I could learn from them.

Midway through 2004, I had an unexpected surprise that improved my quality of life. Simon and Hiroko Inoki had always been very nice to me, and one day, they asked if I wanted to move into the Inoki Sports Management apartment. It was an offer I couldn't refuse. The apartment, which cost nearly $3,000 a month, was a two-bedroom on Sixth Street in Santa Monica, only a handful of blocks from the beach. It was the most expensive place I had ever lived, and I got to live there for free. Being around wrestling 24/7 at the dojo was good for me for a while, but there were times when I needed a break, and the apartment provided that. I had my own room, so I slept better. I had a full kitchen, so I ate better. I had a place to get away to, so I had time to relax. The apartment was only a couple of miles away from the dojo, too, so on nice days I could ride my bike there. And of course, if I had a free day, I could enjoy the beach or walk on the Third Street Promenade.

At times I had a roommate. One, briefly, was former UFC Light Heavyweight Champion Lyoto Machida, because he was under contract with Inoki Sports Management. There have been rumors that he drank his own pee, but I never saw it. I also lived with Shinsuke Nakamura, who was a young New Japan wrestler training for his first MMA fight. Nakamura and I got along really well, and he ended up being a huge star for New Japan.

At this point you may be dying for some sort of crazy party story— like, maybe I took advantage of this prime location to lure strippers into my place and snort cocaine off their fake breasts—but nothing like that happened. The only perverse thing that I experienced there took place as I walked back to the apartment. A man in a black SUV pulled up beside me and asked if I worked out. I said I did. He asked where, and I told him I worked out at the 24 Hour Fitness down the street. He next asked if I liked it and I said it was all right. Then he asked if he could pay me to let him suck my cock. I said, "No thanks," and that was it. He drove off to find another man to service, and I kept walking back to the apartment.

In between tours, I continued to wrestle on independent shows, mostly for Ring of Honor. Earlier in the year, I won a ROH tournament called Survival of the Fittest, which came down to me and Austin Aries, who'd just started with ROH a couple of months earlier. Gabe Sapolsky, the booker, loved the finals and subsequently booked Aries and me in a two-out-of-three-falls match that August at Testing the Limit. I was talking to Gabe on the way to the airport when he told me he'd advertised that each fall had a one-hour time limit. I thought that was weird, especially since there was no plan for any of the falls to go an hour; it was just going to be like any other two-out-of-three-falls match. But then I started thinking. I envisioned leveraging the significant time limit. We could go to an hour draw in each of the first two falls, then—just when it looked like we were going to a third hour-long draw—somewhere around fifty-five minutes in, Aries would beat me. I called Gabe back and told him my idea. At first he thought I was joking and laughed, but the more I talked to him, the more he realized I was serious. Given the business model of ROH, the most important thing was selling DVDs and tapes. If we did what I had planned, it would be the longest pro wrestling match in modern history, and my justification was that a ton of ROH fans as well as non-ROH fans would buy it, even if they fast-forwarded through most it. Gabe started to come around, and he eventually said I could do it if I wanted to.

When I landed in Philadelphia, I ran the plan past Aries. Gabe had spoken with him earlier, and at first Aries thought he was ribbing him. After he realized it wasn't a joke, it didn't take long for Aries to agree to the concept. My only concern was the live fans and keeping them engaged. Nothing kills a match quite like a crowd that's bored, but I came up with what I thought was a brilliant idea. Since we were on last, we would have the ring announcer tell the fans that it could end up being a long match and that neither performer

would be offended if an audience member decided to head home. That's right, my brilliant idea was to encourage people to leave in the middle of my match. I thought it would be easier to wrestle the three hours if we didn't have to worry about entertaining people live, and I knew the commentary would make it easier for people to watch at home. Unfortunately, people weren't leaving, but they were getting bored, so we improvised and went to our backup plan, exchanging a few falls in what became a seventy-six-minute bout. It is still the longest match of my career, though I've always been disappointed we didn't go the full three hours.

Around this same time, the Inoki Dojo started running some shows. Simon and Hiroko worked with a few other people who knew the promotions side of wrestling very well, and they also sought some of us who trained there for our advice on booking the shows. We sat in several long meetings coming up with how we should book the first show.

Rocky Romero, Bobby Quance, and TJ Perkins had done a long tour of CMLL (Consejo Mundial de Lucha Libre) in Mexico, and Rocky had become friends with Negro Casas, one of the bigger Mexican stars. Since CMLL television programming aired in the Los Angeles area, which has a sizable Hispanic population, we thought bringing in one or two guys like that would be our best bet. From there, we could fill out the rest of the card with those of us who trained at the dojo, along with a couple of fly-ins. Everyone seemed to agree that this would be the best bet and went to work. They booked a Mexican restaurant/nightclub for the show, and it seemed like it would be perfect.

I left for Japan, and when I came back, I found out the idea had changed. Instead of bringing in Mexican wrestlers for the show, they flew in two Japanese wrestlers named Nishimura and Takemura. Nishimura was quite popular in Japan but not very well known in the States, and Takemura was barely known in Japan. The show bombed, drawing about forty-five people and losing around $30,000, I heard. The intentions were good, but it was yet another example of one of the important things in wrestling: You have to know your audience.

Later that year, I continued to try to help Simon and Hiroko by recommending they consider Jamie Noble, a rugged yet immensely talented cruiserweight. I'd wrestled Jamie in early 2003 on WWE's syndicated show called *Velocity*—one of several times I worked for WWE as an enhancement talent. Most enhancement talent were given very little offense since we were there to make the contracted WWE stars look as good as possible. Jamie just wanted to have a good match, though, so we went back and forth, with me getting in considerably more offense than a situation like that warranted. Our short TV match went really well, so in late 2004, when Jamie was released from WWE, I immediately went to Simon and Hiroko. I told them he would be perfect for New Japan and his talent could really strengthen the gaijin juniors division.

The connection was made with New Japan, and Jamie was booked for the December tour. He and I teamed on a regular basis, and though I'd met him before, I got to know Jamie in Japan. He has a great sense of humor, which is made even funnier by his thick West Virginia accent. At the time, he'd recently had a baby boy, and the way he talked about him made my heart melt. We had a great tour together that included a fun Juniors Tag Team Championship match against Jado and Gedo. At the end of the tour, Jamie gave me a big hug and thanked me for helping him. (Since then, he's helped me a thousand times more than I've helped him, as I'll explain later.)

I loved wrestling in New Japan, and when 2004 ended, I envisioned spending the rest of my career there—similar to the way Scott Norton had spent a majority of his—but it wasn't meant to be. That December tour was the last time I worked for New Japan Pro Wrestling.

The beginning of 2005 looked a lot like my 2004: I wrestled every weekend on independent shows and had a New Japan tour booked for February. However, two weeks before the tour was supposed to start, I still didn't have my visa. Simon and Hiroko, who were the ones that actually dealt with New Japan, didn't know why it hadn't

arrived but got back to me about it the next day. They apologized and said I would be on the March tour, which I didn't mind because my body could use the couple of weeks off.

Prior to the March tour, I continued to inquire about my visa, and Simon and Hiroko continued to reassure me it would be there anytime. Ten days before it was supposed to start, they told me I wouldn't be on the March tour either. Admittedly, when it happened the second time, I grew frustrated because living in Santa Monica, it's hard to get independent bookings at the last minute. Independent promotions have limited budgets, so flying an independent wrestler like me—whose experience also earned him a higher pay—from L.A. on short notice wasn't within their finances, especially since they didn't have a long time to promote it. I was able to pick up a couple of ROH shows and a Pro Wrestling Guerrilla booking because they were in the L.A. area, but that was about it.

April was a Young Lions tour for New Japan, so I knew I wouldn't be on that either, but they claimed they wanted me in May for their Best of the Super Juniors tournament. In mid-April, the same thing happened yet again. I had no idea what was going on. New Japan always seemed happy with my work, and I had a good relationship with Simon and Hiroko; everything about this seemed suspicious. After this third disappointment, I decided to go back to England since, again, independent bookings were more difficult to come by. It wasn't much money, but I knew I'd be wrestling and having fun, so I drove back to Aberdeen to leave my car there for the trip and prepared for my journey.

In early May, shortly before the Super Juniors tour, I got a call from Simon, who said that New Japan did indeed want me for that month's tour, but because I was a last-minute addition, they would need to lower my pay by $500 per week. I told him thanks, but no thanks. Even with the pay cut, I would have made more money on the three-week New Japan tour than I would working the entire summer in England. It was one of the few times I made a decision in wrestling because I was angry and felt disrespected. I never found out exactly why all of that happened, though I later learned it had something to do with politics between the Inoki Dojo and New Japan. I was essentially a pawn in a larger struggle. As a result, I never went back to the Inoki Dojo or to New Japan, which is unfortunate because I loved both.

My second tour of England was much the same as my first back in 2003: lots of fun, stress-free wrestling, where I could further hone the "entertainment" aspect of my performance. Also, as on my previous trip there, it was kind of like I disappeared from the planet when I was in England. My cell phone didn't work there, so other than trying to make a monthly call to my family (and that's a very loose definition of "try"), I was pretty much incommunicado. Sometimes on rare days off, I'd go to the library to check my e-mail, and on one such occasion, I had a message in my in-box—from CM Punk, I believe, though I could be mistaken—citing a rumor that both WWE and TNA (Total Nonstop Action) were interested in Ring of Honor's three top guys: Punk, Samoa Joe, and me.

I'd done a few enhancement matches for WWE earlier in the year and knew I was at least on their radar, because I was always given competitive matches rather than just getting squashed. After that e-mail, I became more conscious of getting to the library on days off.

Soon after, Samoa Joe signed with TNA, and they pushed him right away on TV. Punk went the other way and signed a developmental deal with WWE. I stayed in England for four months on this trip without hearing anything more about it. When I flew back to the United States that September, I kind of expected to be offered a deal by one of the two organizations, but when I turned my phone on, I didn't have a single voice mail, and nobody from either company contacted me in the weeks that followed. (To be fair, I didn't call them either. That's that lack of ambition.)

I did, however, receive a phone call from Gabe Sapolsky, booker for Ring of Honor. He didn't reach out to offer me a contract or a ton of money; his offer was something different: my first opportunity to be "the Man," as Ric Flair often described it.

Gabe has admitted he never saw that potential in me at first. He thought I was a great wrestler but lacked the ability to be the guy the company was based around. He saw that trait in Punk, and he saw it in Samoa Joe, who had a nearly two-year reign with the ROH Title. Those guys were locker room leaders, and each of them had a unique charisma. Gabe saw me as a nice, quiet guy, content to just do my own thing.

With Punk leaving for WWE and Joe heading to TNA, Jamie Noble (known as James Gibson in Ring of Honor) won the ROH Championship in August 2005. But not too long after that, WWE offered Jamie a contract to return, which he took, and Gabe was out of options.

"You're the guy we want to build around," Gabe said to me. "But to do that, I have to know that you won't leave for WWE or TNA, or be gone all the time on Japan tours." I didn't have any offers from those larger organizations and hadn't heard a word from New Japan since I left for England, but there was definitely more to consider than that before accepting. Being the ROH Champion was a tough gig. They would rely on my matches to sell DVDs and bring people to the buildings. To go on last and send the people home happy was a considerable challenge because everyone was trying to have the best match on the card, and by the time you went out there, the fans had seen it all. Nonetheless, it wasn't more than a few seconds before I agreed. I vowed I wouldn't go to WWE and that I'd put all of my energy into ROH for at least one year. It was a huge opportunity, but I needed to raise my game.

At Glory by Honor IV on September 17, 2005, I beat Jamie Noble (competing under his real name, James Gibson) for the Ring of Honor World Championship. Even though we didn't go on last, I knew we were the main event. Jamie and I wrestled our hearts out for over twenty minutes in front of the very appreciative fans in Lake Grove, New York. I always loved wrestling Jamie, but this was the first time we got to have that kind of match—the kind of match people would remember. When it ended, after Jamie ultimately tapped out to the cross-face chicken wing, the crowd erupted. He and I hugged, after which I grabbed the microphone and promised the fans that while I was champion, I wouldn't even think of leaving Ring of Honor. Ironically enough, I missed the next two ROH shows—two of the biggest shows in the company's history because they featured a rare appearance in America by Japanese wrestling legend Kenta Kobashi—because they took place on the weekend my sister got married. (To me, some things are more important than wrestling.)

My Ring of Honor World Championship win has always ranked very high on my list of accomplishments. They chose me to be the man, and that hasn't happened very often in my career. It was one of the few times when it was decided I was going to be given the ball and get pushed into the top spot to carry the promotion.

Before I won the title, the ROH fans hadn't seen me since May, when I had a shaved head and a long beard. When I returned, I came back clean-cut, with no beard and neatly trimmed hair. Whereas before I wore black, I came back wearing all maroon, gear given to me by William Regal. I even came out wearing a maroon jacket with AMERICAN DRAGON embroidered on the back. It was a more classic look, inspired by an older generation of wrestlers like Bob Backlund and Billy Robinson, symbolizing that I would be more of a sportsman and less of an "entertainer." Soon I realized that was a mistake.

My very first championship defense was against AJ Styles, and our rivalry was based on a story about who of us was the better wrestler. We both wrestled on the aggressive side, but at the end of the match, fans were supposed to like both of us. We had a good match with a decent response from the crowd, but it wasn't what a title match should be, as far as crowd reaction. The same happened with the next several title matches, none of which lit the world on fire. I knew I needed to change something or my title reign was going to bomb.

It wasn't until I was in the ring wrestling Roderick Strong that I found the answer. The fans in Connecticut were fully behind Roderick, with a few of them jeering me. I started to subtly get

more aggressive, then became less subtle about it. That kind of transition isn't so strange in wrestling, but my thought process changed: *I am the Ring of Honor World Champion, and this guy isn't in my league. In fact, not only is Roderick not in my league,* nobody *is in my league—not anybody in ROH, not anybody in WWE. I am the best and I will prove it every night.*

That night, after I beat Roderick, I cut a promo about being the "Best in the World," and it stuck throughout my 462-day reign. It doesn't sound that great now since people have heard both Chris Jericho and CM Punk claim to be "the best in the world" on national TV. But at the time, nobody had consistently made that claim in years. It legitimized me among the independent wrestling fan base, and I was then a top guy anywhere I went, against anybody I faced. It worked because it was boastful and gave me an attitude; it was also a rallying cry for the Ring of Honor fans. They believed ROH was producing the best wrestling in America. WWE was far too interested in entertainment, and that didn't appeal to this audience, who wanted something grittier and organic. They wanted most of their action between the ropes, not on the microphone or in silly backstage vignettes.

Most of all, they wanted to believe that the wrestlers they watched at Ring of Honor events—at least some of them—were "better" than those appearing on TV programming of larger organizations, so I changed my character to appeal to that desire.

The night of that first match against Roderick was also the first in a series of experiments I was doing on wrestling finishes. A standard wrestling trope was that you beat guys with your "finisher." Some guys have two, but very rarely do people have more than a couple of moves that they will actually beat guys with.

For the more astute fans, matches become more predictable: They know that even if a wrestler hits another with a big impact move, if it's not his "finisher," it won't end the match. I wanted people to think that a match could end at any time. On top of that, though the hardcore fans at ROH very much appreciated wrestling, it was hard to get them to believe that any of it was legitimate, after so many years of WWE saying it was all "just entertainment." We didn't need people to believe the whole thing was real, though, just part of it.

Guys lose their tempers and sometimes things get real in the ring—most people never know it because it just seems like sloppy wrestling. My idea was to create a moment in which the audience would wonder if what they were seeing was actually real. The finish of the Roderick match was something that legitimately happened to us. One night after a show, a bunch of us were hanging out in my hotel room and Roderick was drunk, his behavior growing more and more irritating as he jumped all over the place while I was lying in bed. I told him to get out of the room if he was going to be annoying, so he charged and sprang on top of me. I immediately put Roddy in an omoplata shoulder lock with my legs until he screamed (it didn't take long), and then I let go. Gabe was in the room and saw the whole thing. He thought it was awesome, and later that week, he told me he wanted that to be the finish in our upcoming match. I agreed, although only if Roderick wasn't drunk.

So we did it. In the match, Roderick was chopping me so hard that my chest was bleeding. As lots of wrestling fans who've tried chopping each other know, it hurts. Chops make a loud, visceral sound, and people know they sting. So it wasn't hard for fans to believe that with all the chops Roddy had given me, I was pissed off. Instead of the usual cavalcade of moves before the finish of a big match, we just started elbowing each other in the face really hard until Roddy nearly knocked me out. He went to jump on me and, just like in the hotel room, I instantly put him in the omoplata. Rather than the typical milking of the submission, Roderick tapped out almost immediately, rolling to the floor without selling anything. He was pissed off, I got up pissed off, and then I spit on him and said he was a "piece of shit." People in the arena had no idea what had just happened. It looked as if, in the middle of a normal wrestling match, tempers flared and a fight broke out. That was exactly what I wanted.

Weeks later, our rematch had a different buzz about it, and

Roderick had gained even more support from the fans. The entire match was aggressive and hard-hitting. Even though the scars hadn't healed from the first match, he chopped me until my chest was bleeding again. Finally I beat Roderick by putting him in a crucifix and elbowing him until he was knocked out, an idea I got from a Gary Goodridge fight in UFC. The referee had to stop me from elbowing Roderick after he was knocked out, and, in one night, we created a new way a match could end in ROH: a referee stoppage. The fans didn't understand it at first, and some were pissed off, but you have to take chances sometimes—and this one made my matches ahead much more interesting.

When I competed in Ring of Honor, my character was much different than how I've come to be known in WWE. Within WWE, I've constantly been portrayed as an underdog. In ROH, I wasn't a small guy compared to the other guys; especially those last couple of years when I was the top guy, whomever I was *facing* was actually the underdog. One of the more popular things people would chant over and over again toward my opponent was "You're going to get your fuckin' head kicked in!" It originated in England for soccer and got popular for wrestling in Ring of Honor. My style was more technical wrestling, but brutal, incorporating a lot of MMA movements into what I did, like the repeated elbows or repeated stomps to the skull. Ring of Honor crowds saw me as a badass with a big beard and shaved head.

Ring of Honor opened up 2006 with a hot interpromotional feud with a company called Combat Zone Wrestling (CZW). Each organization had its own passionate fan base, which really contributed to the success of this rivalry. CZW was known for doing extremely violent wrestling that incorporated a great many weapons in matches. By this point, using things like tables and chairs was commonplace in mainstream wrestling. CZW took things a step further. Instead of just putting somebody through a table, they would put somebody through a barbed-wire table that was on fire. They would hit people not only with chairs but with things like long fluorescent light tubes that shattered on impact. I even saw a guy turn on a weed whacker and use it on his opponent. Their fans loved it.

Most of our fans, however, thought it was garbage wrestling and that the CZW wrestlers were vastly inferior to the regulars of Ring of Honor. On the flip side, a lot of CZW fans found technical wrestlers like me boring, and they didn't like what they perceived to be Ring of Honor's elitist attitude. With both companies based in Philadelphia, it was a perfect rivalry.

It started off with some CZW wrestlers invading an ROH show and Chris Hero, one of their promotion's top performers, challenging me for the ROH Title. In return, we invaded a CZW event when we were running a show across town the same night—the first time I'd ever been in the famed ECW Arena in downtown Philadelphia. A bunch of wild brawls broke out, including one in which ROH wrestler BJ Whitmer had a sheet of paper stapled to his forehead. The fans of each company were white-hot for the feud, leading to my match with Hero for the ROH Championship in Philadelphia on January 14.

One of the hardest things in wrestling is getting the fans to care. I've had a lot of good technically sound matches in which nobody cared because there was nothing at stake, just another match where it didn't matter who won or who lost. That wasn't the case with me and Hero at Hell Freezes Over. We had a split crowd—half CZW fans, half ROH fans—who were excited as hell for this match and couldn't wait to cheer on their respective guys. You could absolutely feel the electricity during our entrances. When we started off wrestling, trying to prove who was the better wrestler, the crowd was really into it. But then we kept wrestling . . . for almost thirty minutes. The more we wrestled, the more the crowd became disinterested. The fans wanted a fight, and what ended up being a long, scientific wrestling match should have been a hate-filled brawl.

You need to know when to wrestle and when to fight. That night

in January 2006 was a time when I chose the wrong option. I'd say that match was my biggest failure as Ring of Honor Champion.

In 2006, ROH made a great business decision by running shows in WrestleMania's hosting city the two nights prior to WWE's mega-event. WrestleMania brings in dedicated, hardcore wrestling fans from all over the world every year, so while they were all in town, even people who'd only heard about Ring of Honor on the Internet could come watch a show. It led to big business for ROH, and they've done it every year since.

That year, WrestleMania 22 was in Chicago, one of the cities with the most ROH fans. Our first show, on Friday, had more than a thousand people, and they seemed to really love it, with the exception of how long the show was. Gabe wanted me and Roderick Strong to tease an hour-long draw but have me beat him right before the sixty-minute time limit. It was a great idea, but the problem was that the show started at 8 P.M., and by the time Roderick and I went to the ring, it was already after midnight. The full show had already been going on for four hours! The crowd was tired, and I could see people leaving midway through our match. (I couldn't help but think, *I wish they would have done that for the Aries match.*) Yet we got through it and the crowd gave us a polite applause after we wrestled for fifty-five minutes, ending the show at 1 A.M.

The following night was way better, and we had a record-setting attendance for an ROH show, with over 1,600 people. I wrestled former WWE, WCW, and ECW star Lance Storm, who was coming out of retirement, for the ROH Title in a fun match. Nobody in the crowd left during it, so I considered that a huge success.

When I'd returned from England a year before, I'd moved back in with my mom and enrolled in Grays Harbor Community College in Aberdeen for the fall quarter. Now, in the middle of the winter quarter, Ring of Honor presented me with another opportunity.

I had a chance to go from student to instructor (again) when they offered me the role of trainer at the Ring of Honor School they'd opened in Philadelphia. When it initially opened, the wrestling school's first trainer was CM Punk, but he got signed by WWE. Austin Aries was the next trainer, but then he got signed by TNA. I'd be the third trainer since the school's inception, and despite knowing I wasn't the best trainer while in APW, I assumed that I would be better some four years later after amassing so much more experience.

My apartment would be paid for, and I'd also make a commission on any students who attended. Besides that, my sister had moved to a place in Pennsylvania about ninety minutes from where I'd be living. So I finished the winter quarter at Grays Harbor, and in April 2006, I drove the nearly three thousand miles from Aberdeen to Philly.

Much to my chagrin, I was no better at training people to wrestle in 2006 than I was in 2002. Nobody stuck with the class more than three weeks. I constantly asked my students to come in with things they wanted to work on, and they rarely would. I don't chalk that up to them being complacent, though; it was still the problem of me not being able to inspire them. In a coaching role, inspiring people to want to get better is often more important than teaching them techniques. And I was no good at inspiration.

In summer 2006, I had my first encounters with one of my all-time best opponents, an English wrestler named Nigel McGuinness. Outside of the ring, I enjoyed being around Nigel because he was superintelligent and had a great self-deprecating sense of humor. He and I became exceptionally good friends, and the tremendous chemistry we developed carried over into the ring, where I had some of the greatest matches of my career against him. The most memorable bout was at a show called Unified, which was Ring of Honor's first event in England.

Our contest at Unified was a unification match to merge the promotion's top two titles: the ROH World Championship and the Pure Championship—which, created in 2004, was essentially the same as WWE's Intercontinental Title. In Ring of Honor, the Pure Title and its defenses had unique rules, like limited rope breaks and no punches

to the face; plus, the championship could change hands on count-outs or disqualifications. Nigel was the Pure Champion for almost a full year and had even beaten me, the ROH World Champion, by count-out in Cleveland, Ohio, using the distinct rules to his advantage. Nigel was traditionally a bad guy, but that night in Liverpool, he was incredibly popular with his fellow Englishmen. The crowd was passionately behind Nigel, cheering him on the entire match and booing me every chance they got.

At one point during the match, I grabbed Nigel by both arms and pulled him into the ring post headfirst, causing him to bleed. It was Nigel's idea, but he wasn't sure if he could get the post to bust him open. I suggested blading, but he wanted to do it the hard way. We decided I would pull him in three times, and if he didn't bleed, we'd stop. After three attempts, he wasn't bleeding, but he yelled at me, "One more time!" This time, he slammed his head really hard into the post, and the blood started pouring like crazy. We continued on—the blood adding more and more drama—until finally I did the same thing to him that I did to Roderick. I put him in a crucifix and elbowed him until he was knocked out.

The match was great and sold a ton of DVDs, but looking back, the ends didn't justify the means. Due to the shot to the ring post, Nigel had an enormous hematoma on his forehead, a huge knot of blood that slowly drained down to his eye. He ended up with serious concussion problems because of things like that, although that ring-post spot may have been the most visual example. We've all done a lot of stupid things in wrestling. Some end up being worth it, others not. Even though it was a great match, it wasn't worth what Nigel ended up paying for it.

In August of 2006, I had three one-hour matches within a two-week period, two of them on back-to-back nights. It used to be that the NWA World Heavyweight Champion toured all over the world and worked with the top star in every territory. Sometimes he would win clean, but oftentimes, because the champion would be moving on and the local star would continue wrestling in the area, they would wrestle to a sixty-minute draw. Lou Thesz did it. Harley Race did it. Ric Flair did it. I looked at it as my chance to do it.

Unfortunately, wrestling fans don't have the patience they used to, and, just as unfortunately, I am not as good as my predecessors at going sixty minutes. None of the hour-long matches were bad, they just weren't epic in the way you want it to be. The first one was against Samoa Joe in New Jersey, and I cannot remember a single thing about it. The second hour-long match was against Nigel in St. Paul, Minnesota; it was probably the worst of all the matches Nigel and I had against each other, and he got another concussion, to boot. Everything about it was regrettable. The following night, I wrestled Colt Cabana in his hometown of Chicago—the third and most memorable of the sixty-minute matches, but not necessarily because it was good.

Roughly five minutes into the match, I was pushing Cabana into the ring ropes and, as he came off them, I'd catch him with a head-butt to the stomach. We did it a few times, until he stepped aside on the last attempted headbutt, sending me crashing to the floor. I had previously fallen that exact same way well over a hundred times, and never once do I remember even stubbing my toe. This time, however, I missed posting on the apron with my hand as I fell, and I crashed down, shoulder first.

I knew something was wrong, so I took my sweet-ass time getting back into the ring, hoping I could shake it off. It didn't help. I was lucky I was in there with Cabana, because he can be entertaining without throwing you all around. Still, everything I did hurt. At one point, I was going to give him a diving headbutt off the top rope, trying to gut through it, though I knew I was just going to make it worse. I could have stepped down, but I knew I would look stupid, so instead, I jumped off the turnbuckle and stomped Cabana right in the chest, way harder than I intended. He let out this guttural sound on impact and had a hard time breathing for the next minute, but we were able to get through the match.

After I flew back to Philadelphia the next morning, I went to the hospital. The doctor told me I had partially torn two tendons and, more distressingly, separated my right shoulder—the same one I separated in 2000 and the same side I'd have problems with later on in my career.

I had bookings over the next two weeks, which, for the first time in my career, I had to cancel due to injury. In three weeks, I was scheduled to wrestle Japanese star KENTA (now Hideo Itami in WWE) for the ROH Championship in New York City. Everyone knew I was hurt, because Ring of Honor had covered my injury on their Web site. Given my reported condition and how KENTA was positioned around that time, most people expected him to beat me.

Bryan faces Japanese star KENTA for the ROH World Title in NYC, 2006 *(Photo by George Tahinos)*

In American wrestling, if somebody has a legit injury, you try to mostly stay away from it to avoid further injury. For example, with my shoulder hurt, someone might attack my leg. In Japan, if the fans know you have a real injury, the wrestlers almost feel obligated to treat it like a legitimate fight and attack an injured body part to avoid insulting the intelligence of the fans. KENTA and I took the Japanese route: Instead of protecting it, KENTA kicked the shit out of my right arm the entire match. My girlfriend at the time was in the crowd, and she was literally crying in the middle of the match, with one of the other wrestlers trying to settle her by telling her I was OK. But I was more than OK; I felt alive. With the emotion of the crowd, the physical intensity of the match, and the story that was told throughout, it is undoubtedly one of my favorite matches of my career. When I put KENTA in Cattle Mutilation and he tapped out, the crowd erupted. It was one of those times when the pain was worth it.

After the KENTA match, I did my first tour of Japan for Pro Wrestling NOAH, basically, so that KENTA could get his win back in front of the Japanese audience. I did my best, but with my shoulder getting progressively worse, I focused on trying to make it until Ring of Honor's biggest show of the year, Final Battle. At that event on December 23, 2006, a wildly popular wrestler named Homicide beat me for the Ring of Honor World Championship in front of a sell-out Manhattan Center crowd, our second show in the building. My shoulder was a wreck, but Homicide and I tried to pull out all the stops to make his title win as memorable for the fans as it could be. In the end, Homicide hit me with his Cop Killa, one of the coolest-looking moves in wrestling, then pinned me, as the crowd went nuts. My 462-day title reign was over.

In retrospect, I was proud of the work that I had done as champion in Ring of Honor, and it made me grow as a performer. It was the first time anybody had chosen me to be "the Man"—the *only* time, really—and I can't thank Gabe, ROH, and the ROH fans enough for giving me the opportunity to be the guy to carry the promotion.

After losing the ROH World Championship in December, I moved back to Aberdeen from Philadelphia. Ring of Honor and I agreed they needed a new trainer for their wrestling school and I needed to rehab my shoulder. While focused exclusively on getting healthy, I didn't wrestle again for over three months—the longest time I'd ever taken away from wrestling.

When I was healthy enough to return to the ring, I was thrown right into the fire. Despite not being my best during my first Japan

tour with Pro Wrestling NOAH, the promotion brought me back for a four-week tour in April of 2007. With my shoulder healthy and my body feeling rejuvenated, I made a much better showing after shaking off the early ring rust.

On that tour was the first time I met Ted DiBiase Jr., the son of the Million Dollar Man, a WWE Hall of Famer. Teddy had only competed in sixteen matches before he went on the tour, which reminded me of my first tour with FMW. The big difference was that Teddy was way better this early in his career than I was the first time I went to Japan. As far as having a natural instinct for wrestling, Teddy might be the best I've ever seen. There were definitely times when he showed his inexperience, but 90 percent of it he did really well, and I was impressed. Not only that, but he was also fun to be around. With his Mississippi accent and his southern hospitality, it was hard not to immediately like the guy. Soon after this tour, Teddy signed to a WWE developmental deal, and I couldn't have been happier for him.

By May 2007, it had been over five months since I had wrestled for Ring of Honor, and I was excited to come back, especially because they had made some major changes since I'd left. In early May, ROH announced they had signed a deal to produce bimonthly pay-per-view events. Live pay-per-views were beyond ROH's budget due to the substantial expense of satellite time, so they taped the shows, edited them, and then put them on pay-per-view a few months later. These events were another way to expand the audience, on the assumption that fans who might not want to buy a DVD might be more willing to order a pay-per-view. In addition to the expansion to pay-per-view, for the first time, ROH started to sign talent to contracts in order to make sure the guys they built the promotion around wouldn't leave for WWE or TNA. I happily signed a two-year deal.

The inaugural pay-per-view taping, called Respect Is Earned, featured my return to ROH, and it was back at the Manhattan Center on May 12. Everyone in the locker room was amped up for the opportunity to be on pay-per-view, including me. The fans were really excited, too. I wrestled in the main event, teaming with a 350-pound NOAH wrestler named Takeshi Morishima, who'd beaten Homicide for the ROH World Title, to face Nigel and KENTA. After Morishima and I won, he dumped me on my head for being a dick, and then Nigel clotheslined Morishima in the face, thus creating two potential challengers for the ROH Title. I thought the show was an excellent introduction to the promotion for people who had never before seen our wrestling. It established who all the characters were, who the rivals were, and why the fans should care.

The following month, Nigel and I wrestled each other in the main event of the second ROH pay-per-view, Driven 2007. Toward the end of the match, Nigel and I started headbutting each other without putting our hands up for protection, as if we were two rams butting heads to display our dominance. In the middle of the exchange, I was cut wide open at the top of my hairline and blood poured down my face. The fans loved it.

After I won, fellow wrestler Jimmy Rave took me to the emergency room, where they closed up the cut with staples. I finished up at the hospital just in time to catch my flight home, and I felt good knowing that Nigel and I had put on a great match that the pay-per-view audience was going to love. I had no idea what was about to transpire that would shake the wrestling world for some time.

On Monday, June 25, 2007, I was in the car driving home to Aberdeen from Olympia, Washington, after two hours of kickboxing and jiu-jitsu. I was exhausted and content with about fifteen minutes left in my hour-long ride when I got a call from my friends Mike and Kristof. They were watching *Monday Night Raw*, and WWE had just announced that Chris Benoit, his wife, Nancy, and their seven-year-old son, Daniel, had been found dead in their Atlanta home. I went straight to Mike and Kristof's apartment, and we watched *Raw* together in shock. Chris Benoit had been one of my favorites, and someone I'd patterned my career after. He had wrestled all over the world, getting better everywhere he went, and by the time he

made it to WWE, he was one of the best wrestlers on the planet. Beyond my professional admiration, the few times I met him, he was very kind to me. I was crushed.

WWE canceled the live show and ran a three-hour tribute to Chris that night. They showed some of the biggest moments of his career, interspersed with video packages and interviews with WWE Superstars who shared their very personal memories of him. It was an emotional program to watch, and I ended up leaving Mike and Kristof's halfway through.

The next day, horrific details started coming out, and what was eventually discovered was that Chris had killed both his wife and son, then hanged himself. The Benoit double murder/suicide horrified people, and media outlets picked up on it right away. People tried to figure out why it happened, with speculation that it was caused by "roid rage" or because Chris and Nancy's marriage was falling apart. To this day, there is no definitive reason for why it happened and there probably never will be. But investigations led to the Sports Legacy Institute performing a series of tests on Benoit's brain, which according to Dr. Julian Bailes "was so severely damaged it resembled the brain of an 85-year-old Alzheimer's patient."

The type of brain damage Benoit had is known as chronic traumatic encephalopathy (CTE), which researchers believe is connected to having multiple head injuries. CTE's most common symptoms include depression, cognitive impairment, dementia, Parkinsonism, and erratic behavior, and many experts believe CTE was a significant contributing factor in the Benoit tragedy. Multiple NFL players who committed suicide were found to have CTE as well, and the condition became a major news story in itself. There was a palpable shift in the nationwide awareness of the dangers of head injuries and concussions.

Chris Benoit popularized a wrestling style that was hard-nosed and aggressive, with lots of explosive suplexes and diving headbutts off the top rope. Looking back on it, you can see how easy it would have been for him to have multiple undiagnosed concussions. It was the same style that influenced me and many wrestlers of the new generation; it was action-packed and exciting, with an element of physical violence that was believable. That kind of wrestling is what made me and many of the other guys in ROH stand out from the pack.

When Nigel and I did the headbutts in June at the Driven pay-per-view, it seemed awesome. Two warriors ramming each other in the head until one of them bled. It made for a great visual, and spots like that showed our love for the business and our willingness to do anything for the fans. But when the match finally aired on pay-per-view on September 21, with all the awareness around the dangers of head injuries, it no longer seemed awesome. It seemed stupid and it seemed reckless, which made people question why they supported something that endangered the long-term health of the performers. In hindsight, Gabe told me, he wished they'd never aired it.

After the Benoit tragedy, the perception of wrestling became so negative that many fans no longer cared to watch—especially a company like Ring of Honor, which heavily featured a style similar to the one Benoit helped to popularize. Initially, ROH pay-per-views garnered around ten thousand buys, which was phenomenal for a company whose only exposure was through word of mouth and the Internet. However, with each passing pay-per-view, buys dropped, and after the six-event deal was up, ROH chose not to renew it.

The paradigm of how we should be wrestling was shifting. Some people accept new paradigms quickly. In this instance, I was not one of them. Despite all the concussion awareness and my own acknowledgment of certain dangers, I refused to tone it down. I stopped the aggressive headbutting, but I kept everything else about my in-ring performance the same. In mid-2007, I ruptured my left eardrum during a wild, open-palmed exchange with KENTA in

which one errant shot caught me in my left ear. I never got it fixed, and even now I don't hear as well on my left side. Later in the year, I detached my retina, in another example of my own stupidity.

Takeshi Morishima was still the ROH World Champion when I was booked against him that August at Manhattan Mayhem. At 350-plus pounds, Morishima was a giant compared to your standard ROH star, and, working in Japan, he was used to wrestling bigger guys (whom he had no problem smashing around). In Ring of Honor, Morishima had some great title matches against stars like Claudio Castagnoli (now known as Cesaro in WWE) and Brent Albright, but he proved to be a gentle giant, of sorts. In title matches with smaller ROH wrestlers, he tended to use a lighter touch, almost as if he were afraid of hurting us.

When Gabe booked Morishima and me in the championship match at the Manhattan Center show, we both agreed I needed to do something to turn the big man into the monster he was when he wrestled larger opponents. If he handled me gingerly, it wasn't going to work. I decided—because I'm somewhat of an idiot—that the best way to do that was to piss him off.

Prior to our match, I stressed to Morishima to treat me as if I were a heavyweight in NOAH. He smiled gently and nodded his head, but I don't think he understood. We structured the match so it would be based on me trying to stick and move, not wanting to be crushed by a man that size. My "sticking" comprised kicking his leg; Morishima would attack, and I'd move out of the way and use a Muay Thai kick to the leg. At first I was kicking him normally—hard yet safe—but he wasn't being very aggressive. So then the leg kicks got harder. With the first really hard one, I could tell he thought it was an accident, but as I kicked him harder in the leg, I could see the expression on his face change. He was starting to get mad. I kept with it and kept with it, and when he finally caught me in the corner, he was a giant, pissed-off Japanese monster.

He started clubbing me to the side of the head with each hand in rapid succession, a style of punching popularized by another large wrestler named Vader. Usually when he'd do it to the smaller ROH wrestlers, it would look light as a feather and phony as could be. These were different. In the middle of the flurry, one blow caught me directly in the eye and I dropped. My cheek started swelling, and everything in my left eye was blurry. We wrestled another ten minutes after that, and I was still able to do things like the springboard flip dive into the crowd, but my eye was throbbing and it worried me. I had never experienced anything like it. Morishima continued to bring it in a way that made the match exactly what it needed to be. Afterward, Morishima—a truly nice guy—felt horrible and apologized what seemed like a hundred times, despite the fact that he was limping and had one long, giant welt on his leg from the low kicks. I told him it wasn't his fault and that he did a great job, which he did.

The backstage doctor told me I needed to go to the emergency room right away, and it was at the hospital that I found out I had not only fractured my orbital bone but also detached my retina. Two days later, I underwent laser surgery to have it reattached. I was instructed to take it easy for at least a month, if not longer, to permit my eye to heal. I was told to avoid flying because altitude changes could aggravate it. I had to wear an eye patch to keep the light out and just generally be careful to not put any pressure on it. But other than a little bit of pain from the fracture, I felt fine. So, like an idiot, I demanded to keep my scheduled rematch with Morishima three weeks later. Why? Because I thought it would be a great story.

The rematch with Morishima in Chicago went well, despite the doctor's recommendation. I wore the eye patch—more for the visual than for actual protection, of which it provided very little. In another one of my dumber ideas, for the finish, Morishima gave me repeated clubbing blows to my damaged eye until I sold being knocked out. The 350-pounder made sure I was safe, and luckily I escaped the

match without further damage (though I still have some vision problems in my left eye).

Eye-patched Bryan faces Takeshi Morishima in Chicago, 2007 *(Photo by George Tahinos)*

In 2007, Morishima and I had four matches, and Gabe and I worked together on the story to make sure each showdown built upon the last. I had also learned from the Chris Hero debacle the year before. After Morishima attacked my eye in Chicago, it became a violent and bloody feud. The third match was under twelve minutes and ended in a disqualification because I repeatedly stomped Morishima in the testicles. Usually Ring of Honor crowds hated disqualifications, but they cheered this one because it was a moment of vengeance against Morishima, who, in their eyes, got what he deserved.

My final match of the year against Morishima was taped in December for a pay-per-view called Rising Above, and given the previous match's disqualification outcome, this one was held under "relaxed rules." At under six minutes, this was a short, violent sprint. We were going to war. I bled after Morishima threw a table at my head, and somewhere toward the end of the quick match, one of the

Japanese giant's clotheslines knocked me out. When I watched it, I could see the shift in Morishima's attitude from wild monster to concerned colleague. Our referee, Paul Turner, didn't know what to do; I was out of it, and this was for pay-per-view. He was in a tough position as the official: He didn't want to mess up the booking, but he also wanted to protect me as a performer if I was hurt.

The next thing I remember was being on Morishima's back and using the opportunity to elbow the shit out of his face. The big man didn't have much problem getting back to being a monster after that. The calamity continued as we both attacked the referees who were trying to break us apart. The announcer declared the finish as a double disqualification, but they couldn't ring the bell because I'd taken it and attempted to gouge out Morishima's eyes with the bell hammer, while I wildly screamed out that I was going to "blind this son of a bitch!"

After the match, I was in bad shape. My head hurt, and I couldn't shake the dizzy feeling. Unfortunately, on that same show, Nigel—who by this point was the ROH World Champion after beating Morishima—received a concussion as well when the back of his head hit the barricade in a match against Austin Aries.

Earlier in the year, Nigel had told me I needed to read former WWE wrestler Chris Nowinski's book *Head Games: Football's Concussion Crisis*, which discussed the dangers of concussions in football and other contact sports. It specifically talked about people getting early onset Alzheimer's disease and dementia due to head injuries. Reading it scared the shit out of both me and Nigel. One of the things Nowinksi emphasized in the book is that it takes time for the brain to heal and that in order to prevent long-term damage, it's important to not rush getting back into action after a concussion. Of course, in almost all contact sports, acknowledging that you are hurt and that you have to recover goes against the ingrained mentality. Wrestling is no different.

The following night at the Manhattan Center, Nigel and I were supposed to be in big matches, but we both knew we needed to take

the day off. Nigel, smartly, did. I, however, did not. I wrestled over twenty minutes in a four-way elimination match in the semi-main event. My head wouldn't stop pounding for the next several weeks.

Despite moments like this, I loved being an independent wrestler. One thing I really enjoyed was consistently being able to wrestle new people. A lot of times, I'd go to a show and not know a single person there, including the person I was scheduled to wrestle. Sometimes I'd show up and someone I hadn't seen in years would be there, which would make my day.

On one occasion, I was booked for a rare Wednesday show in the Midwest. I flew from Seattle to Chicago, then had a two-hour drive to the small town I wrestled in that night. My flight was heavily delayed, which set me back a bit in getting to the show on time, so I called and spoke with the promoter. Given my expected arrival time, it became clear that I was going to end up going straight from the car to the ring for the main event. To make matters more interesting, I'd never wrestled my opponent before, and I wasn't sure if I'd ever even met him. I was also going to need to get changed in the car, and in the middle of winter, it was pretty darn cold to be half-naked in your vehicle.

I pulled into the parking lot a solid three minutes before my music was set to play. I walked into the lobby of what appeared to be a VFW hall and stood there in, essentially, my underwear until it was time to go. I borderline dreaded doing the match, because there are a lot of horrible, unsafe wrestlers out there, and I hadn't even talked to the guy I was wrestling by the time my music hit, as I walked to the ring from where the fans came in.

What happened next was a surprise. Without having even spoken, my opponent and I wrestled a good basic match. The longer we went, the more impressed I was. I was a relatively big star on the independent scene by this point, but he didn't even seem nervous. Quite the opposite, really: He was confident that he knew what he was doing and confident that what he was doing was good. His name was Jon

Moxley, and he'd go on to become better known as Dean Ambrose in WWE.

I had another surprise in early 2008 the first time I wrestled Tyler Black, who is also now in WWE as Seth Rollins. Rollins had come into ROH a couple of months prior to our collision, mostly participating in tag matches and even winning the ROH Tag Titles. I had seen his matches, and I respected his athletic ability and poise in the ring. His trunks were too small, but I could look past that. I really looked forward to our match. Truthfully, we needed some new guys fans would accept as main-event talent in ROH, and Gabe thought Rollins had "it."

Gabe knew what he was talking about. In the ring that night, Rollins made an impression on me and the entire ROH crowd. Even though we weren't in the main event, they titled the DVD *Breakout* because of Rollins's performance in our match, and I was happy to be a part of it. After that, he and I ended up having a series of matches, my favorite of which took place in Detroit. He gave me a powerbomb into the turnbuckle and the whole thing broke, adding chaos and unpredictability to the match. Instead of getting flustered, he improvised, and that match was one of the best I had that year.

12 "YES!" FOR THE MASSES
FRIDAY, APRIL 4, 2014—11:04 A.M.

Across the spectrum of media personalities he's encountered, Daniel Bryan's been asked nearly every question imaginable asked in countless languages. He's also been asked to recite lines from the "#SELFIE" song, rapidly rattle off excessively colorful DJ names for shout-outs, and, of course, strike a "Yes!" or three. The tally is fifty-four total uses of the word "yes" in chant by the time he's through—culminating with a nine-time succession along with a gaggle of the morning's media correspondents. It's clear that in any dialect, Bryan's signature word (and its Movement) have strength.

"The 'Yes!' chant gives fans a way to vocalize their feelings about me not getting what, in their minds, I deserve. They want to see me succeed," Bryan details. "In my career, the most important thing I've ever said 'yes' to is following my own dreams, as opposed to the dreams of other people. I said 'yes' to pursuing my dreams of becoming a wrestler, which is mildly impractical for someone who's five foot eight and from Aberdeen, Washington. You've heard it a thousand times before—'follow your dreams'—and it's the only reason I'm here right now."

Yards away, the exhibits are unmanned within the sprawl of Wrestle-Mania Axxess, giving Bryan free rein to explore. In a wide display lined

with mannequins posed in vintage gear like the Heartbreak Kid's signature chaps, Bryan rediscovers a memory from his past. He relives the first pay-per-view he ever watched back on March 31, 1996. WrestleMania XII was an event in which a lingerie-swathed Goldust clashed with "Rowdy" Roddy Piper in a Backlot Brawl and "Big Daddy Cool" Diesel fell to the Deadman. But more importantly, it housed the clash that countless current Superstars claim is their favorite 'Mania bout of all time: Bret Hart versus Shawn Michaels in a sixty-minute WWE Iron Man Match. A former pupil of HBK, the "Yes!" Man has studied this and other classics over the course of his career, which he hopes to redefine at WrestleMania 30. Bryan continues along the display to find images from WrestleMania X and others, recalling instances like the Hit Man's WWE Championship–winning double-duty in 1994. These all serve as inspiration for the contender who may end up in two all-important battles on the Grandest Stage of Them All.

At the end of his explorations, Bryan can't deny the heavy eyes glaring at him from overhead on a series of immense banners featuring WrestleMania 30's top gladiators. Positioned across from one another just as they will be days later on Sunday, a massive Triple H and Daniel Bryan linger atop a long Axxess hall passageway. The only thing bigger will be the actual clash itself.

From where he stands, just forty-eight hours lie between Daniel Bryan and the Game—the "Yes!" Movement and The Authority. He marches out from under the symbolic shrouds and toward the exit.

"I'm very confident in my ability to compete in two matches in one night," he asserts, describing the many single-night tournaments he's experienced in the past. "That kind of accomplishment will make me worthy of all these cheers and the adulation."

On June 7, 2008, I got the first of the two phone calls I ever had from Vince McMahon. I was in my hotel room in Hartford, Connecticut, where we'd just done a show for ROH. At first, when he introduced himself, I laughed because I thought someone was ribbing me. Vince McMahon has a very distinct voice, one that many people are good at imitating. What initially made me suspect it might actually be him was that he said he had been speaking with Shawn Michaels.

Two weeks earlier, Shawn had called me, and it was the first time we had talked in several years. He asked how I was but quickly got to the point. He was in the middle of a feud with Chris Jericho, and they were getting Lance Cade involved in the story because Shawn had trained him. They thought getting me involved, too, would be an interesting twist; I could potentially come in beside Shawn, then turn on my onetime teacher to form an alliance with Chris and Lance. Shawn didn't try to pressure me at all, but he explained it would be a great spot for me to come into, *if* I wanted to go to WWE—something I hadn't even thought of since 2005. He said that he knew, from speaking with William Regal, that I liked the independents and that I preferred being more of a "starving artist." (This was the first time I'd heard that in reference to me, and it kind of made me proud, since I never aspired to be wealthy and it was mostly the artistic form of wrestling that I truly enjoyed.) We had a good conversation, and I expressed that I'd be interested if we could work things out with ROH, with whom I was still under contract.

It was most certainly the real Vince McMahon on the phone. He said Shawn had spoken highly of me, and then he told me he'd like to have a meeting with me in Oakland, California, that Monday before Raw.

I mentioned that I could meet him that day if he wanted, noting that I was in Hartford, Connecticut, which I confused with Stamford, where WWE Headquarters is located. I couldn't understand why he wouldn't just meet me that same day. It was kind of embarrassing, though Vince never pointed out my stupidity, which I only realized when we passed Stamford on the way from Hartford to our show in Newark, New Jersey. That all aside, I agreed to the meeting in California.

In hindsight, I should have just had them fly me to Oakland from Newark. Instead, I flew home from Newark to Seattle, then had to

fly from Seattle to Oakland some six hours later. I needed that time, though. After talking to Regal, I thought I should get a suit to meet with Vince, and all I had was workout clothes, so I went to a department store near the airport. My mom was nice enough to bring me new workout clothes so I could switch everything out. I bought a cheap suit with a cheap shirt and equally cheap tie, packed up my stuff, and headed down to Oakland.

I met with Vince on Monday and was very uncomfortable. Wearing the suit didn't help, as I was awkward in it, which is especially noticeable in the presence of people who wear them so easily. That wasn't the only thing. Almost as soon as he saw me, Vince seemed taken aback that I was the one Shawn had talked so much about. I'm not sure if it was because of my size or just because of how plain I look, in general. And my personality didn't seem to help things. Our conversation went a little something like this:

"Shawn says you're very good," Vince said.

"Yeah, I'm OK," I replied.

"Just OK?" he asked.

"Well, yeah," I very casually stated. "I've got a match tonight if you'd like to see."

Knowing Vince a little better now, I could see how he would have hated that. He wants people who will say, "No, I'm the best!" And not just say it—*believe* it. But except during promos, I wouldn't say that then and I wouldn't say that now. Some people think I'm good, some people don't; I let people decide on their own, which is not a top-guy attitude, at least not to Vince.

We talked a bit longer, and I explained that I was under contract with Ring of Honor but had their full blessing in coming to see him. He asked me if I wanted to come wrestle for WWE (probably because Shawn mentioned the "starving artist" thing), and I told him I had concerns. I said that WWE didn't have the best history of pushing smaller guys like me, and I wasn't as acrobatic as somebody like Rey Mysterio. I think that comment made Vince raise an eyebrow as well. But overall, despite my nervousness—and my slight anxiety about whether or not I was supposed to keep the suit jacket buttoned when I sat down—I thought it went well.

My match that night went well, too. I wrestled Lance Cade, and not only did we have a good little match, but there were quite a few fans who knew who I was and gave me a good reception. It helped that Lance and I had known each other for years, and he did his best to make me look good.

Afterward, John Laurinaitis, who was in charge of WWE talent relations, told me they were definitely interested and that he'd call me that week. Two days later, I went to Mexico for a week to perform in one of its biggest wrestling shows, TripleMania. When I came back from Mexico, I had an ROH show and then left for three months to England. I didn't hear from Laurinaitis until he called, literally, as I checked in my bags for the flight to the U.K. I told him my phone wouldn't work while I was in England, but I gave him my e-mail address so he could contact me if WWE was interested in using me. I checked my e-mail religiously that trip, but I never received a message from him. On the flip side, it would have been very easy for me to have called Johnny regularly while in England, just to check in and see what the status was. But, of course, that sort of ambition was not my style.

I had another great time in England, and I was able to add more shows in Europe during some weekends, just for fun. I wrestled at an anime convention in France, which was surreal, and performed at shows in Germany as well. I went straight from England to Japan on another tour with Pro Wrestling NOAH, which had teamed with Ring of Honor to promote some ROH shows in Japan at the end of the tour that were held in the Differ Ariake Arena, the same building where NOAH had their dojo and offices.

A few of us who had been on the NOAH tour—me, Rocky Romero, Eddie Edwards, and Davey Richards—had a couple of days off before the ROH shows. In years past, on their days off, wrestlers would be out partying or whatever. Then, you had *us*. We decided to have a cookie-eating contest at midnight in the hotel lobby. We

made several trips to this little convenience store to pick up boxes of Country Ma'am cookies, which we'd never seen in the States. The winner of our contest would be whoever ate the most boxes of these ever-so-soft sweet treats.

The only one not participating was Davey Richards, who actually walked in on us after going for a midnight run because he couldn't sleep. He was disgusted. I suspect if old-school wrestlers who had come to Japan before us—like Stan Hansen or Bruiser Brody—saw us, they would probably punch us all in the face. If notoriously tough wrestlers like them ever had any contest, it would've been a drinking contest, not one with soft cookies. But in my mind, there are few things better than a good old-fashioned eating contest . . . even if I never win.

It was at an ROH show called the Tokyo Summit on September 14, 2008, where I won the Global Honored Crown (GHC) Junior Heavyweight Championship from Yoshinobu Kanemaru, who was the title's very first champion and had held it multiple times. During my many tours of Japan, it was the only singles title I had won. Despite holding it for only a month, I was pleased they gave me the opportunity to be the champion, as I was only the second gaijin wrestler to win the title. I ultimately lost the title to KENTA on the following NOAH tour at a show in Hiroshima on October 13. (I consoled myself by eating more Country Ma'am cookies.) I was treated really well by Pro Wrestling NOAH, and it was just another example of why I loved wrestling overseas in general.

When I returned home from the Japan tour, I was shocked to find out that Gabe Sapolsky had been fired from Ring of Honor, and I was devastated. Gabe had been the booker since ROH's inception, and we had a great working relationship. He always listened to my ideas and was honest with me when things were good and when things weren't so good. Unfortunately, the business side of ROH had grown stagnant, and the organization was losing a significant amount of money. Wrestling's popularity had declined, and the amount of people looking for alternatives to the wrestling they saw on television was limited. So Cary Silkin, the sole owner of ROH and the individual whose finances kept it afloat, decided to make a change.

Cary loved wrestling and grew up as a big WWE fan when Bruno Sammartino was the champion. He collected old wrestling posters and magazines and loved showing them to the guys who appreciated them. He would often give me old wrestling magazines, my favorite of which had "Nature Boy" Buddy Rogers on the cover in an iconic wrestling pose.

When Cary decided to replace Gabe, he went with someone he thought would incorporate some of the more old-school ideology he loved. Enter Adam Pearce, an independent wrestler known for his traditional style . He was one of the best bad guys on the independent scene and had wrestled all over the country making people hate him.

Whereas Gabe would book longer shows in which the participants in almost every match tried to steal the show, Pearce wanted shorter shows with the guys on the undercard working hard, but not busting out every trick in the book. Cary was also trying to make budget cuts, and he thought Pearce would be more willing to use fewer performers on each show. Though I honestly didn't think a change in bookers would make the company profitable, I understood why Cary made the change.

Prior to his termination, Gabe was booking me with Claudio Castagnoli (Cesaro) in a feud that was supposed to culminate in December at Final Battle, the biggest ROH show of the year. The match was set up at the Manhattan Center in an incredible moment where Claudio crushed my head beneath a steel chair. When Pearce came on board, he had a different plan. He ended my feud with Claudio right away, which disappointed both of us. Instead, Pearce booked me against Morishima, who hadn't been in ROH all year, in a match called "A Fight Without Honor," a rare match in Ring of Honor where absolutely anything goes. Given our past together, it was a smart move, and the fans in New York City were excited to see it.

My proudest moment as an independent wrestler was ROH's Final Battle 2008. In WWE, there's a stigma about independent

wrestlers that before we got to WWE, we all just wrestled in front of a hundred people at an armory somewhere. Yes, most of us did that. But we also did things like this show. On December 27, 2008, Ring of Honor drew their record crowd of over 2,500 fans to the Hammerstein Ballroom in New York City. We did that without having a television show and without having any big-name wrestling stars from the past. It was us. All of us. We created something that fans wanted to see, and though Ring of Honor may be a niche product, we were able to garner a huge amount of fan support based on the quality of our wrestling and the fans' belief that what they were seeing was important.

Ring of Honor moved the show from the Manhattan Center to the Hammerstein Ballroom, a larger room in the same building. In the main event, I wrestled Morishima in our bloodiest and most violent match yet. It was a true grudge match, culminating with me giving Morishima the crucifix elbows to the face—with a chain wrapped around my arm—then putting him in Cattle Mutilation. The crowd erupted when I won, and it was a great finish to a great show.

With all of my health issues starting to add up, I decided to give WWE one last attempt and gave myself all of 2009 to get signed. If it didn't work, I was going to cut back on my independent dates and resume going to school, changing the focus of where I put my energy.

By 2009, I'd really started to enjoy kickboxing and submission grappling, but unfortunately, there weren't any places to train in Aberdeen. I would drive an hour to Olympia, train kickboxing in one gym, then drive over to another gym to train jiu-jitsu. I tried to do it a few times each week, but when I was exhausted from traveling, the last thing I wanted to do was spend two hours in a car just to go train. If I was going to change my focus at the end of the year, I was going to spend the next year doing what I wanted. With this in mind, that January, I moved to Las Vegas.

On my days off from wrestling, I wanted to focus on martial arts. I didn't move there to party. In fact, as a city, I don't care much for Las Vegas at all. All the tourists, gambling, and flashy lights—none of that is my thing. However, Vegas is also the home of UFC, and with that, there are a ton of great MMA gyms there. After trying out several of the options, I ended up settling on Xtreme Couture, owned by former UFC Heavyweight and Light Heavyweight Champion Randy Couture. I was lucky I did.

I started training four days per week on days I wasn't wrestling or traveling. The gym was only ten minutes from my house, and I could train kickboxing at 9 A.M. and then go straight into submission grappling for two hours after that. No long drives and no trying to fill time between classes.

Neil Melanson was the head grappling coach of Xtreme Couture at the time, and he soon started noticing how often I was coming in. After about six weeks of training, Neil asked me what my deal was and if I was interested in fighting. I wasn't, I just enjoyed it. Plus, I was interested in using more legitimate martial arts in my wrestling style. When he realized I was a pro wrestler, he thought it was awesome. He loved wrestling during the Attitude Era and had even considered doing it himself. Neil's a big dude, around six foot five, and thickly muscled. One could easily imagine him being very successful in the wrestling world. Neil also knew a lot about the history of pro wrestling and its transition from a real athletic competition to the entertainment that it is today. From that moment on, Neil showed me cool stuff he thought would be good for pro wrestling.

I kept training hard and could feel myself getting better. Soon I stayed after class with Neil and helped him, too, with some of the things he was working on. Neil would tell me exactly what he was trying to do, and I would try all sorts of different ways to defend against it. If I did something that really stumped him, he'd have me do it again and again until he figured it out. If he was grappling somebody else and something that opponent did gave him problems, he would have me do that as well. Watching the way he approached learning was inspiring, and all the while, I learned more and more as well.

One of the things I excelled at was a shoulder lock called the omoplata, the same move I used against Roderick Strong in Ring of

Honor. But when I got to Vegas and trained with grapplers who really knew what they were doing, they were able to get out of it. Neil showed me how to stop a guy from rolling out by pulling up on his head while I had the shoulder locked in. He called the move the LeBell Lock after Gene LeBell, under whom Neil had trained. I still use this hold today, although now it's known as the "Yes!" Lock.

Another cool thing about training with Neil was that it put me in with this strange lineage of catch wrestling: Strangler Lewis trained Lou Thesz; Lou Thesz trained Gene LeBell; Gene Lebell trained Neil; and Neil trained me. There you go! I am directly linked to Strangler Lewis, the greatest pro wrestler of his era!

A little while later, Neil introduced me to Gene, a colorful old man who could still rip your head off today. He was in Ronda Rousey's corner in a fight before she made it big. Neil and I went to the show and afterward briefly met up with Gene and his wife, and it was a pleasure meeting them. I was honored to meet Gene and even more honored that he vaguely knew me. By that point, I was using the LeBell Lock on WWE TV and even had the announcers calling it that, which I think he appreciated.

Also in January, Ring of Honor struck a TV deal with HDNet, a station owned by the famous billionaire Mark Cuban. HDNet focused heavily on the 18–35 male demographic, showing a lot of MMA, and they hoped the more athletic style of wrestling that ROH featured would appeal to the people who regularly watched the station. For ROH, there was hope that being on TV would expose the product to people who normally wouldn't see it, and originally we had a great time slot on Saturday night.

The first TV shows were filmed at the old ECW Arena, and seeing the small building undergo a metamorphosis with the HDNet production crew was incredible. It obviously didn't look as polished as WWE, but for an independent wrestling show, it looked great. They took me on a tour of the production truck, and we got to work with the folks producing television.

Ring of Honor also brought in Jim Cornette and a former WWE writer named Dave Lagana to help format the show. Adam Pearce had never written TV before—it was a totally different animal—but they did a good job, and the show was vastly different than either TNA or WWE. For the hour-long program, there would be some short interviews, but the focus was always on the matches. Since the show was only sixty minutes, viewers didn't always see their favorites every week. I, for example, would typically do a match only once every three episodes, doing short interviews or run-ins in between.

Unfortunately, the TV show didn't increase business for Ring of Honor, as far as I could tell. Attendance was stagnant, and I'd heard DVD sales were the same. Though the show never really took off, it was a great introduction to wrestling-TV production. Whereas before I could wrestle for however long or short I felt the match needed to be, the times for matches on television shows needed to be concise. If I had twenty minutes to perform, it meant the match, the entrances, and the aftermath all needed to take place in twenty minutes or less. If you didn't hit your time, they would either have to edit your match or cut something else from the show. Admittedly, I went over time on a couple of my matches. It took me some time to figure out how long things would actually take, but I tried to learn quickly. The first time somebody's interview got cut because my match went overtime, I felt horrible.

My ROH contract was up in May of 2009, and until then I hadn't contacted anyone from WWE. As soon as my contract expired, I called John Laurinaitis to let him know. It was the first time I'd ever called someone in WWE to try to get a job. I left a message but never heard back from him. In June, Brian Kendrick—then known as *the* Brian Kendrick—was doing a story in WWE in which he was looking for "*the* Tag Team Partner." He gave me a call saying he wanted me to be that person. He told me WWE knew I could wrestle but wasn't convinced I could talk. Brian's idea was for me to

fly out to an event and shoot some interviews with their people, just to show them I could do it. But since this was something just Brian and I wanted to do, and not WWE, I had to fly myself to the show.

The next week I traveled to Oakland, ironically, to the same building where I had the meeting with Vince the prior year. Brian and Regal picked me up before the show and gave me a brief rundown of what I needed to do. Brian introduced me to Steve Lombardi, a.k.a. the Brooklyn Brawler, who was and still is pretty much in charge of what's called the Pretapes Room, where most prerecorded interviews took place backstage. (Whenever you see Sheamus wishing you a Merry Christmas or see Kane promoting the next show in Munich, Germany, odds are it was filmed in this room.)

We worked with Brawler recording several interviews, some with Brian and me together and some by myself. Brawler gave me some good insight into what else WWE would like to see from me promo-wise, and I gave those a shot. We all thought the interviews came out great, and as a result, Brawler put in a good word for me with Laurinaitis, who actually approached me later that night to say he heard everything went really well. When I left Oakland, I was feeling optimistic, but a few weeks went by and I heard nothing. Then, unfortunately, on July 30, Brian was fired from WWE. I felt bad for Brian and also figured that with him gone, WWE would no longer have any interest in me.

In the summer, the lease on my apartment was about to expire, and I was still unsure of what might be next with WWE. Instead of committing to being in Vegas for another seven months, I started looking for rooms to rent on Craigslist—which in itself is a weird experience—in order to save money and prepare to move back to Washington. When going to check out this one guy's place, I was wearing sandals—pretty standard fare when I'm relaxing. The renter immediately asked me if I wore sandals all the time, to which I replied that I did, and he then asked to see the bottoms of my feet. I thought it was weird, but I showed him, and when he saw a little bit of dirt, he told me I couldn't rent the room unless I stopped wearing sandals. He was a neat freak and didn't want his floors dirty. Eventually I ended up finding a room to rent for only $500 total per month from a nice guy named Nathan; my childhood friend Mike Dove also rented a room there about a month later, which was great. The best part was that I only needed to give Nathan one month's heads-up if I was going to move out.

Toward the end of the summer, I'd pretty much thrown in the towel and accepted that WWE wasn't interested in signing me, when Johnny finally called me in late August. Having just come back from grappling training with Neil, I was a sweaty mess when I answered the phone. He offered me a contract—not a developmental contract, which most new signees get, but a regular talent contract. Earlier in the year when I resolved to get to WWE, I told myself that if they offered me a developmental deal, I'd turn it down, so I was relieved they weren't going to try to send me to Florida Championship Wrestling (FCW), their developmental system, where people sometimes got stuck for years. Luckily, my contract ensured that I'd pretty much go straight to the main roster . . . or so I thought. I thanked Laurinaitis as I got off the phone, superexcited.

I found out shortly thereafter that WWE had offered Nigel McGuinness a contract as well, which was great. We had helped build each other on the independents, and now we'd get that same opportunity in WWE. All we had to do in order for it to be official was go through WWE's standard medical screening in Pittsburgh.

When I landed, Nigel picked me up, and with us was another WWE signee who was also there for a health screening. We didn't know her, but she was a Playboy Playmate of the Year who knew next to nothing about wrestling. I'm not quite sure she had even seen any wrestling before, either, but it didn't matter. She was nice, and all three of us were pretty happy on our way to meet the doctors.

I've always prided myself on being a fairly honest person; Bri says I'm too honest, sometimes. On this occasion, though, when the doctor asked if I'd ever had any surgeries or major injuries, I just said no. I made no mention of the detached retina, no mention of the

shoulder issues, and no mention of the concussions. I told them I was perfectly fine. For some reason, I've always found it easier to lie to doctors than to normal people.

Nigel took a different approach. He was completely honest with the doctor (minus, maybe, the concussions), mostly because he thought he had no need to worry. Earlier in the year he'd torn his bicep, and instead of getting surgery, he took time off to rehab it, just like I did with my shoulder several years earlier. He came back to wrestling when his doctor told him he was ready to go and the bicep was all healed. Nigel disclosed all of this to the doctor at the medical screening, assuming it would be fine. But it wasn't. Before they would sign him, they wanted him to do more testing on his bicep. I wasn't exactly fine either. I'll explain shortly.

The first person I called after WWE reached out to offer me a contract was Cary Silkin, the owner of Ring of Honor. I let him know what was going on and thanked him for all the opportunities ROH had given me. Shortly thereafter, ROH booked what they called the Final Countdown Tour, a series of six shows that were supposed to be the fans' last opportunity to see me and Nigel compete in Ring of Honor. This would be the perfect ending to my time with ROH, and I had just one other project I wanted to see to its end before heading to WWE.

Previously, fellow indie star Colt Cabana and I had discussed doing a documentary on our lives as independent wrestlers, inspired by Robbie Brookside, who filmed a similar documentary that aired on British television in the 1990s.

We had big plans initially; we wanted to rent an RV and drive all over the country doing shows. But with my Japan tours and long distances between shows (like one weekend in Philadelphia and the next in Los Angeles), we settled on documenting a ten-week tour. When I got contacted by WWE, Cabana had everything set up for the filming, and though he was actually worried I would cancel the shoot, I thought the addition of me signing with Vince McMahon's organization would make the documentary even more interesting. We were moving forward with what we called *The Wrestling Road Diaries*.

Cabana started the trip in Chicago with an Englishman named John, who hopped on for the ride and filmed the whole thing. Together, they drove 750 miles to Philadelphia—the site of the first two Final Countdown Tour shows—to meet up with me and Sal Rinauro, an independent wrestler from Georgia, whom Cabana and I love because he's hilarious, kindhearted, and always in good spirits.

Over our ten-day trip, we wrestled on seven shows, from the famed ECW Arena to a garage in Connecticut and even an amusement park in Ohio (where I wrestled almost five straight minutes with my butt exposed—on purpose), then ended with a big Ring of Honor show in Chicago. Along the way, we did seminars at two wrestling schools, visited my sister while she was pregnant with my first niece, and, in general, just had a great time.

The only thing that put a mild damper on the whole thing was a call I got from the doctor in Pittsburgh. According to the tests I'd taken, I had really high cholesterol and, far more concerning, severely elevated liver enzymes. The doctor asked me if I drank a lot, and I told him I'd never had a drink in my life. He also asked about steroids, and I'd never used them either. Since blood test results already ruled out hepatitis, a disease of the liver, those two are the most common reasons to have elevated liver enzymes. The third most common reason was cancer. I was scared to death. Plus, WWE couldn't officially sign me until I'd been medically cleared.

With that cloud hanging over my head, I nonetheless finished the rest of the trip. At the last show in Chicago, I wrestled Austin Aries in a match I truly enjoyed. Then, after the show was over, I said goodbye to Cabana, Sal, and John. It had been a really fun trip.

When I got back to Vegas, Nigel and I were both still waiting for our WWE contracts to go into effect, and they had me doing all sorts of tests: MRIs, more blood tests, and even a colonoscopy, which was miserable. I went into my final ROH show not knowing if I would

actually be leaving. Before the show at the Manhattan Center, ROH promoted an autograph signing for both me and Nigel as the last time fans would get to see us. As we signed, we joked with each other that there was a good chance we might be back a lot sooner than people thought. We laughed about it, but we were both legitimately nervous.

My last match for ROH was on September 26, 2009, and fittingly, I wrestled Nigel in the main event. It was a difficult task. We wanted to do justice to the matches we'd had before, but we also wanted to stay safe, which is easier said than done in wrestling. When Nigel caught me on the springboard dive into the crowd, the back of his head hit a chair. All of a sudden, he was loopy and probably concussed. We continued on and tried to give the audience one final classic match. I'm not sure we quite reached that, but the fans reacted like we had, all the same. When the match was over, all the ROH wrestlers and employees surrounded the ring as Nigel and I said farewell to Ring of Honor. The crowd gave us a standing ovation, a demonstration of appreciation for all the hard work we'd done to entertain them over the years. I got pretty emotional about it. I still do. When you have that many good memories, it's hard to walk away.

Soon after that, WWE advised Nigel that they wanted him to get bicep surgery before they would sign him. Not only could Nigel not afford the surgery, but he was receiving a different, conflicting message from his own doctor, who kept telling him that his bicep was healed already. Nigel refused the surgery, and WWE rescinded their contract offer. He ultimately signed with TNA, and after doing really well for a year there, he ended up needing to stop wrestling entirely because of his health.

As far as my health, doctors never found out why my liver enzymes were so high (and remain high today). They ran all the typical tests, and all the results came back clean. Once I had passed all the tests, my medical paperwork finally went through, and WWE pushed through my contract on October 2, 2009, almost ten years to the day of when I had my first match.

13 FROM PRO TO BRO
FRIDAY, APRIL 4, 2014—5:23 P.M.

It's awkward, at first, to see Daniel Bryan and the Miz seated so far apart—almost intentionally—at a conference room table just prior to meeting the ten winners of the WrestleMania Reading Challenge. The former NXT Pro and Rookie pair has a turbulent history, dating back to Bryan's WWE debut in early 2010. Yet Miz and Bryan keep it more than cordial and even chat about the "Yes!" Man's upcoming marriage.

Recently wed to former WWE Diva Maryse, Miz asks the right questions and shares something of a "bro" moment with Daniel at the table. "The Awesome One" then switches gears to talk shop, specifically WrestleMania. The NXT connection raises an interesting truth about the competition's first season.

"When I first heard about NXT, I thought, 'I'm a ringer for this, right?' It turned out that it wasn't the case at all," says Bryan, who finished with a record of 0-10 under Miz's tutelage. "By the end, I saw NXT's headline stars as Wade Barrett and David Otunga—those were the two guys 'they' really liked out of the group. I did not foresee me being the first one of us to main-event WrestleMania."

The unexpected "bro-down" ends as the Reading Challenge sweepstakes

winners rally for their private Superstar signing in the room next door. The anxious young readers light up when both Daniel Bryan and the Miz make their entrance. One girl repeatedly squeaks, "OhmygodDanielBryan!" until he comes over to meet her.

"You want to inspire curiosity and inspire kids to be able to learn on their own," Bryan says. "Anything you can do to get them to read as many things as possible, that's just all the better. It's a step forward."

The winners line up for autographs and interrogation by Miz, who demands to know what book each youngster read to win the gift of his presence. Bryan turns the tables on the Awesome One moments later when Miz tries to start his own mock "Yes!" chant. Of course, Miz brushes off the response by this very exclusive crowd, but does acknowledge Daniel Bryan's big match at WrestleMania, actually encouraging the kids' cheers for his former NXT Rookie. Read between the lines of the Miz's message and discover what might signify that Bryan has the support of the WWE locker room.

When WWE offered me a contract, I came in with low expectations. Several of my friends had wrestled in WWE and expressed their frustration with the lack of opportunities. Brian Kendrick actually quit the company in 2004 because he was so unhappy there, then came back, only to get fired before I signed. Colt Cabana spent nearly two years in the developmental system, the whole time only getting a couple of appearances on TV. The only independent guy at that point who had had any major success was CM Punk.

I also knew I had to change my style. I was used to wrestling twenty minutes every night in matches that made me popular with the independent wrestling fans. Most WWE TV matches are under five minutes. If you're not winning the short match and you don't get interview time, it's hard to establish yourself as a character, much less get the fans to care about you.

Wrestling longer matches always challenged me, both mentally and physically. It inspired me to be more creative, which was important because wrestling is my primary artistic outlet. It didn't boost my confidence at all when William Regal warned me, "Your wrestling career is what you did before this. Anything after is just a bonus." I tried to look at it that way and told myself not to expect much; just come in, save money, do my best with whatever I was given. That attitude has served me well through the dips I've had with WWE. Still, when you love something so much, it's difficult not to get a little frustrated.

One of my early frustrations, before WWE even knew what they wanted to do with me, was the issue of my name. I'd always been known as the American Dragon, but sometime in 2002, Ring of Honor booker Gabe Sapolsky told me he thought we should start using my real name as well, so it didn't sound so much like a cartoon. I finally stopped wearing the mask at that point, so "the American Dragon" could just become more of a moniker. I liked the idea, and it didn't take very long for me to be booked as Bryan Danielson almost everywhere I went, with two exceptions: New Japan (they didn't want to confuse fans to whom I was introduced with this name during my first Far East visit) and All Star Wrestling (England was the last place where I still wrestled under mask to make me more kid-friendly).

However, before I started in WWE, John Laurinaitis called to inform me that I needed to come up with a new name, something WWE could license and own. When he told me it couldn't be my real name, I argued that I had a decent following as Bryan Danielson and that a lot of guys in WWE used their real names, including John Cena.

"Well, we don't do that anymore," he said. He wanted me to come up with a list of ten names.

The first person I called was William Regal, whom I asked for some input. We both liked the name Buddy because it was fun and it was my dad's name. We next came up with some absurd last names to go with it, most notably Peacock, based on an English wrestler named Steve Peacock. I thought of using my middle name, Lloyd, so that went on the list as well. Then Regal brought up the idea of using Daniel because he thought it was a strong name. With that, a

lightbulb went on in his head, and he came up with the name Daniel Bryan. Regal thought it would be a great idea because anybody who'd heard of me on the independents would easily be able to tell that it was the same guy. It sounded weird as I said it, but all the names sounded weird except my own anyhow. I put it on the list, along with Buddy Peacock and my favorite, Lloyd Boner.

After I was officially signed, WWE just told me to wait and they'd call me when they were ready to use me. So for two months I waited in my rented room in Las Vegas, spending my time kickboxing, grappling with Neil, and trying to get in the best shape possible. During that time, WWE never contacted me or informed me of any plans. I wanted to be proactive—especially while I was receiving my first weekly paycheck in years—so I called them every two weeks to check in and see if they needed me to do anything.

In December, I traveled home to Aberdeen for Christmas. Thinking there was no way WWE was going to call me up until after the first of the year, I indulged in ten days of Christmas gluttony. Sugar cookies, pumpkin cake, cinnamon rolls. Nothing was off-limits. That, of course, was when WWE called: the Saturday after Christmas.

To put it mildly, I was concerned. After eating all those sweets and barely working out for ten days, I felt like the fattest man alive. How much damage one can do in that amount of time is debatable, but it didn't matter, because it affected my confidence. To make matters worse, I was still ailing from my third staph infection of the year. Plus, I hadn't wrestled in months—a critical detail since, as the old wrestling saying goes, "The only thing that can get you in shape for wrestling is wrestling."

When I got to the show that Monday, I was actually relieved to learn I wasn't doing something to air on TV. I wrestled Chavo Guerrero in an untelevised match before the show. That match against Chavo was only the second time I'd ever gotten "blown up"—a phrase used in wrestling for when someone gets *really* tired in a match, to the point that it affects performance—in my ten-year career. The first time was my forty-minutes-plus match with Paul London in 2003, when I weighed my heaviest at 205 pounds. With the combination of eating horrible food, not wrestling for months, and my nerves, by the end of the seven-minute match with Chavo, I was sucking wind. Everyone told me it was good, but I didn't feel my best. And if I was going to debut on TV, nothing less than my best was acceptable.

With that in mind, I asked to go spend a week down at FCW, WWE's developmental program in Tampa, to shake off the ring rust and get back into wrestling shape. After only a week there, where I mainly wrestled Low Ki, I felt infinitely more confident. My plan was to ask to go there one week each month until they were ready to have me start on WWE programming. But right before I was about to leave Florida, seven other guys and I were pulled into an office by the trainers, Dusty Rhodes, Norman Smiley, and Tom Prichard (Dr. Tom). They gave us the good news that we were all being called up to TV. WWE was debuting a new show called *WWE NXT,* a hybrid of wrestling and reality TV that was going to replace the ECW program that aired on Tuesday nights. They didn't have a lot of details, though we were told it would be some sort of competition/reality show. At first it didn't feel real, but the next day, they had us shooting all sorts of pictures and videos for the show. We were all excited for the opportunity, especially some of the guys who had spent years in developmental without getting their break.

The way they explained it to us, we would only wrestle on Tuesdays each week, and there was no way all of us could wrestle every show. I wanted to stay sharp and wrestle more frequently, so I talked to Dr. Tom and made the decision to move down to Florida so I could wrestle on the FCW shows as well. I drove the 2,300 miles from Vegas to Tampa in three days, which included a minor breakdown in Texas that set me back some hours. I got there just in time to move my stuff into a room I rented from Evan Bourne, then, not long after, we all flew out for the first NXT taping.

Shortly before the premiere on February 23, 2010, we were given a little more info on the show. We were going to be called "Rookies," and we would each have a "Pro," somebody who had been in

WWE for a while and was assigned to teach us the ropes in the big leagues. WWE revealed the Pro and Rookie pairings online, which is how I found out my Pro would be the Miz. Even though the whole thing was fiction, the fans who followed me on the independents were outraged. I had years of wrestling experience and had become relatively well known as an excellent wrestler, whereas Miz had way less experience and struggled with credibility among the hardcore audience. Originally I wanted Regal to be my Pro because of our

history, but I quickly realized being paired with Miz gave me a built-in story.

We had an interesting dynamic because Miz was everything I wasn't. He was good on the microphone and carried himself like a star. We both thought the concept of Miz—this arrogant, overbearing Hollywood egotist—trying to turn a bland independent wrestler into a WWE Superstar would be a great story to tell. I even tried to make myself look more generic to fit in. I cut both my beard and my longer hair and avoided using my nicely designed ring gear, instead wearing plain maroon trunks and gear. As it turned out, WWE decided not to leverage any of that detail in the story, and I just made myself look uninteresting. Chalk that up as a lesson learned.

Initially I felt lucky to have that entertaining contrast with my Pro, but I was also fortunate that Miz actually wanted to be there participating in NXT because, when we came in, most of the other Pros didn't. At the time, WWE Superstars didn't typically work on both

Monday (Raw) and Tuesday (SmackDown). You were typically on one or the other, not both. The selected Pros who were used to going home on Tuesday after Raw were pissed because they had to spend an extra day on the road, and the ones who were there for Tuesday night's show were already aggravated because it took them away from focusing on their own segments for SmackDown.

The Miz didn't complain at all. Instead, he saw it as an opportunity and spent time with me to find ways we could make our partnership stand out. He genuinely wanted what we did to be good. The more I saw how hard he worked, the more I respected him. I also learned a lot from him on how to navigate the political waters in WWE. He's also somewhat of a perfectionist; if he wasn't content with what we were doing, he would talk to as many people as he could to get it changed. Sometimes he was successful, sometimes he wasn't. But watching him handle it all was really helpful in familiarizing myself with the world of WWE.

Although he didn't have as much wrestling experience as I did, I recognized all that he had been through. He was mildly famous for being on MTV's *The Real World*, which helped him get signed with WWE, but hurt his reputation among fans and wrestlers alike. When he first started, Miz went through a period where he was almost exclusively relegated to hosting various WWE segments like the Diva Search. Backstage, he was kicked out of the locker room because, supposedly, he accidentally spilled crumbs over someone's bags and didn't clean it up. His gear was literally thrown out into the hallway, and he wasn't allowed to change in the locker room for months. Despite all this, he didn't quit or give up. Even though there was a portion of the locker room that still felt he didn't belong, Miz's hard work and ability to get under the crowd's skin was making the right people take notice, and by 2010, he was *really* on the rise.

As I mentioned earlier, the inaugural episode of NXT went really well—so well, in fact, that I thought for sure I was a ringer for the show, a natural favorite. It turns out that wasn't the case at all. On the second episode, they had me heavily tape my ribs from the match

with Chris Jericho the previous week, in which I did a suicide dive onto Jericho and hit my ribs hard on the announce table, instantly bruising me up. WWE.com covered it, and the moment was replayed during my entrance, so it was fresh in fans' minds. That night in week two, I wrestled Jericho's Rookie on the show, Wade Barrett, who beat me in three minutes. There was an embarrassing moment when I slipped trying to do a springboard into the ring, but Wade covered it perfectly by immediately hitting me with his finish and pinning me. At the announce booth, Jericho helped out the situation as well, because he was on commentary and claimed that I slipped because of my damaged ribs, then took all the credit for Wade's victory.

After the match, without warning, Chris started beating me up and put me in his submission hold, the Walls of Jericho, essentially a modified Boston crab. I didn't know it was coming, and it wasn't preplanned; Chris was on commentary, and Vince directed him over the headset to do it. For most of the season, we Rookies had no idea what was going to happen on each show, but there were times when the Pros didn't know either.

The next few shows fell in line with the story I expected. Miz and I teamed together, and he ended up getting pinned because he and I were arguing. The following week, Miz wasn't there, so he scheduled me in a match against the Great Khali, a seven-foot-one, 350-pound Indian giant, which was my punishment for causing him to lose. I lost the match, but as long as I put up a good fight and showed heart, it didn't matter. It was all about the story between Miz and me.

Also around this time, I realized that moving to Florida was a complete waste of time. FCW was only able to book me on a handful of shows because of the number of people with developmental contracts who needed the experience. The matches I did have were mostly multiperson tag matches with the other seven NXT Rookies, so I'd only be able to get in the ring for a couple of minutes. The last match I did for FCW was the straw that broke the camel's back. We were doing a four-on-four tag match, and due to some sort of confusion or mishap, I didn't even get tagged into the match. After that, I spoke with Dr. Tom and decided I needed to move back to Las Vegas, where I'd be able to at least stay in shape with my grappling and kickboxing and keep my kicks sharp. Instead of driving myself across country, I paid my friend Kristof to drive my car back— and, like what happened on my drive *to* Florida, my car ended up breaking down on him as well. Fortunately, Kristof got it fixed and into Vegas just in time for me to move into my new apartment— perfect timing, actually, because NXT was being taped in my city that following Tuesday.

A week after my loss to Khali, things took a turn for the worse. We were in San Jose, California, for Miz's second week in a row of not being on the show, and they had me teaming with Michael Tarver against Darren Young and David Otunga. I learned of the match from producer Mike Rotunda, who told me I was scheduled to lose in order "to keep up the losing streak gimmick." I was a little taken aback. I'd lost every match on NXT so far, but there were reasons for each loss that advanced the story with Miz and me. With him not there, they just decided to turn the story into a losing streak. WWE had tried this several times with other wrestlers previously, and it never really worked; they would usually just forget about it, and the fans would just start seeing the guy as a loser. I started getting a little worried.

The next day, I had my first (and, really, my only) experience of disrespect by another Superstar, while headed from San Jose to Phoenix for my first-ever WrestleMania with WWE. All of us who performed on the SmackDown and NXT tapings were on the same flight, including the NXT Rookies. The eight of us were sitting in booths near a food court at the airport, along with Regal. Ezekiel Jackson, a muscular, 300-pound guy who had only been wrestling for a couple of years, came up to us and said, "Which one of you *rookies* has an aisle seat?" He had a middle seat and wasn't happy about it.

"I do," I said.

"Not anymore you don't," he responded.

I could see what was going on, but still replied, "What do you mean?"

"I'm taking it," he said.

The previous night (the "losing streak" thing) already had me frustrated, and I didn't feel like taking any shit.

"No, actually, you're not," I said. "And actually, had you asked nicely, I would have gladly given you my seat. But since you didn't, I'll just give it to somebody else."

Jackson was infuriated, but just as he was about to respond, Regal chastised him. "Do you even know who you're talking to?" he said. "This man is like a son to me and has more talent in his little finger than you have in your entire body." With that, Jackson left, and I gave my aisle seat to someone else and took his middle seat.

After that, my WrestleMania week was a blast. We had a handful of appearances, though not many. I had one signing where I replaced Evan Bourne, who was pretty popular at the time. He had a line of substantial size when I replaced him, and when the announcement was made about it, the crowd's disappointment was audible as half of the line left.

I ventured around the city using public transportation, trying to find the best vegan food. Ring of Honor was doing their yearly shows in the vicinity of WrestleMania, so I went to one of them, hitching a ride with some fans who were going as well (including one who is a radio DJ in Philadelphia and interviews me regularly today to promote upcoming shows). On Sunday of that weekend, we actually got to participate in WrestleMania XXVI—not in any big way, but we still got to go out there. On the pay-per-view preshow, there was a big battle royal, and since we were considered Rookies, they sent us out to the stage to watch "so we could learn." The winner of the battle royal was Yoshi Tatsu, a Japanese wrestler I competed against once in New Japan when he was a young boy. I guided him through that match, and it mildly amused me that I was now out there pretending to learn from him.

On that show I actually did learn from, and was emotionally

touched by, Shawn Michaels's retirement match against the Undertaker. It was by far the best match on the show. Not only that, with a crowd of seventy-two thousand people and the atmosphere being simply electric, it might be the most memorable match I've ever seen live. I watched it from the stands so I could take in the entirety of it. Shawn Michaels trained me, and there I was, my first WrestleMania and his last.

For the NXT after WrestleMania, they advertised the first results of the Pros Poll, a legitimate vote by the WWE Pros ranking each of our abilities to be WWE Superstars. Since they just had the Pros write down their genuine thoughts on our standings, I ended up being ranked number one, despite not having won a single match. I can imagine the fans were very confused, given the idea that winning and losing is supposed to matter. The Pros Poll was important because you were eliminated from the show if you came in last. The first one, however, was just a demonstration; no one would be eliminated until week twelve of the competition, we were told. Still, I felt confident that no matter how many matches I lost, as long as the voting was legitimate, I would do fairly well on the show.

The following week, WWE changed plans entirely on what NXT would be, and they essentially turned it into a joke. Instead of making it a vehicle for us to exhibit our skills as wrestlers, they decide to fill the show with silly challenges that have nothing to do with wrestling; we carried kegs, ran obstacle courses, and jousted like the American Gladiators in a contest called "Rock 'Em, Sock 'Em Rookies." In the middle of one challenge, we had to run upstairs and drink a big cup of soda as fast as we could. (Originally it was supposed to be us eating a hot dog, but since I was vegan and they couldn't find any veggie dogs, it was switched.) Since I don't usually drink carbonated beverages, it took me almost sixty seconds to complete that task alone. That's right, on a show that was regularly viewed by one million people, NXT viewers were subject to a full minute of watching someone try to drink a soda. Now, *that* is quality television.

The only reason to care was that if you won the challenges, you got points, and by the time we did the first elimination, whoever had the most points was immune to being ejected. But the challenges were so inane and demoralizing that by the end, we all treated them as a joke—except, that is, for Skip Sheffield (later known as The Ryback), who demonstrated an undeniable will to win even the most idiotic game.

On top of the challenges, the commentators consistently kept putting us down, especially Michael Cole. Any little mistake in the ring or on the microphone would be called out instantly, and the audience would be reminded of how we were "just rookies." I was persistently ragged on for being a "nerd," ostensibly because I had wrestled on the independents so long and had a decent-sized following on the Internet. Instead of us doing things to make us more popular, we were treated like fools. It's hard for me to imagine the Undertaker ever becoming the legend he is today if, when you first saw him, he was falling off greased monkey bars while the announcers told you he was stupid for trying to be a dead man. Then again, it's possible WWE never saw the potential in any of us to be that kind of star.

Not only were we presented in ways that made us look like schmucks, we were also segregated from the rest of the locker room. Despite all eight of us being under contract with WWE, we had to change in a separate dressing room, which usually wasn't a dressing room at all. They would put up pipes and drapes to cover up a little hallway, with no bathroom or shower. One time, our designated changing area was amid the lunch tables set up for the local crew guys to eat at during breaks. We had to hold up towels over ourselves while we changed so people eating their food didn't have to see our dicks.

Even though my character ended up being a nerd who lost every match (I finished NXT a resounding 0-10), I tried to stay positive. This one week midway through the season, after he came out of a TV production meeting, Arn Anderson told me the only way I'd ever get a real opportunity was if the fans got behind me. He told me he believed in me and assured me that the fans can tell when someone is the real deal.

One week prior to the first elimination, in another unscripted interview, Matt Striker asked each of us at the end of the show who we thought should be eliminated. Most guys pinpointed Michael Tarver because of his bad attitude, but since I'd lost to him earlier in the night, it didn't make sense storywise for me to say him. Since I had lost to everyone else on the show, it didn't make sense for me to say any of the others either. So, thinking it was the right, humble good-guy thing to do, having not won a match, I said I should be eliminated. Afterward, Miz told me I shouldn't have even put that perception in the fans' minds. I was facing an uphill battle as it was. To me, it seemed logical; plus, I figured there was no way I'd place last in the Pros Poll and get eliminated.

When it was time for the first elimination the following Tuesday, we were told to line up by the ring before the show started, again without being told what was going on. Striker came out and reminded the fans that the previous week he asked us who should be eliminated. Michael Tarver had said himself as well, with his justification being everyone was safer without him around. Striker then said, "WWE management feels that if a Superstar does not believe in himself, then how can anyone believe in the WWE Superstar?" And with that, he told Michael Tarver he had been eliminated by management.

After Tarver exited, Striker walked slowly down the line toward me. They replayed the video of me saying I should be eliminated, and I knew what was coming: Striker announced that I was eliminated as well. As I slowly walked up the ramp to exit, a million things were going through my mind, but the one that kept sticking in my brain was that WWE did this to prove a point. All the things I'd heard from guys like Colt Cabana about WWE's negative feelings toward independent wrestlers seemed to be confirmed. Given that I'd been the flag bearer for independent wrestling over those last few years, it all of a sudden made sense why they would mock me on the show, despite me being one of the best performers. Then I thought they might just fire me after this and I'd go back to the

independents as a failure. When I walked through the "Gorilla position" (the space immediately on the other side of the curtain, named after Gorilla Monsoon), I was informed I'd have an interview with Striker after the commercial break and that I should just answer however I felt was right.

The interview started off fine with a fairly harmless question from Striker about whether I thought the whole thing was fair. I knew Matt was fed his questions by producers and probably Vince himself, but the second question was insulting. He asked, "Do you regret leaving the independent scene, where you were a big fish in a small pond, to ultimately drown in the sea that is the WWE?"

Fuck you. In no way, shape, or form did I "drown" in WWE. I was booked as a loser and was still the most popular guy on the show. This only confirmed to me what I thought coming up the ramp. But I answered relatively calmly.

"Well, that's funny, because 'Daniel Bryan' never wrestled on the independent scene," I said. "If you go on and YouTube 'Daniel Bryan,' all you ever see is WWE. But there was this guy, man, he was out there, he was kicking people's heads in; people called him the best wrestler in the world. He was a champion in Japan, Mexico, and Europe. And do you know what his name was?"

Before I could say it, Striker cut me off, saying, "What's next, for this guy?" I could practically hear the yelling in his earpiece, but I continued on. I downplayed the skill of "Daniel Bryan," saying that guy couldn't even beat rookies. And then I said it.

"'Daniel Bryan' might be done, but *Bryan Danielson*—God knows what's going to happen to him."

When I said my real name, it actually got a reaction from the fans. It got a reaction from Vince as well; apparently, he threw his headset. I was in the frame of mind that if I was going to get fired, I was at least going to plug my own name before heading back to the independents. But because NXT wasn't quite live (it was on an hour delay), they made me redo the interview, and Striker asked different questions. When the show aired, however, they played the original on TV. Vince must have changed his mind in the meantime.

It seems to me that Vince's perception of me is always changing. It's actually strange to think about what somebody else is thinking about me. I've never really worried about it, but when one man can change the whole dynamic of your career, you tend to wonder. When I first started on NXT, I got the distinct impression that Vince didn't like me. After the first episode, Jericho came back and told Vince he thought I was great in the ring, but otherwise, Vince's reaction to me was "Ugh, but he doesn't even eat meat!"

Then I thought he just liked to pick on me. Shortly after NXT started, all eight NXT Rookies joined about six other Superstars each week before TV for what they called "promo class," which was led by Vince himself. Vince would call people up to the front and have them cut promos on random subjects. You had ten seconds to think, and then you just had to go. Afterward, he'd ask other people in the room what they thought of your promo, and then he'd give you his own opinion. He was *very* hands-on.

From our very first class, it seemed like he singled me out. He had me cut a promo on a table, and it was rotten. I got nervous because I'd never done anything like that before and it was in front of many people I respected, like Rey Mysterio and Fit Finlay. Every promo class, he called me up—sometimes more than once—but with each class, I grew more confident and I got better. One promo class, he decided to make us the teachers. First, he had Big Show go up and teach, then Matt Hardy. Between the two of them, they pretty much said everything that Vince had taught us, and they called up different people in the class to do promos as well. Neither of them called me up, so when Matt was done, Vince stood up and told me to go teach the class. It was a horrible position to be in. At least Matt and Show were veterans in WWE. Nobody wanted to be taught by a guy on NXT who wasn't even known as giving a good promo. Regardless, I went up and tried to keep it short, not repeating anything

Show or Matt had said. I pretty much just told everyone how important I thought it was to be yourself, then work from there to identify your strengths and weaknesses. When it was time to call somebody up to cut a promo, I named Vince. His topic: "How great Daniel Bryan is."

Vince stood there in front of the class, silent. Then he looked me up and down, judgingly, before his face turned to various levels of disgust, amping it up as he went along. Vince never said a word for about a full minute, and then he said he was done. He went to sit back down, and I stopped him, requesting he stand up front while the class critiqued his promo. I first called on Big Show, who put it over the moon. The next person did the same. And they were right. It *was* great, and the whole room was laughing. I excused Vince to go sit down, but then he said there was a lesson there. He taught us about the importance of facial expressions and how to say something without saying anything. It was really good.

The last time Vince called me up front in promo class was one that included everybody on the roster. When I was called upon, I accidentally knocked over my bottle of water, spilling it all over the floor. I was embarrassed, but then he started asking people how that incident made them feel about me. (Most said it made them feel sympathetic toward me.) Next, he asked me a series of questions—definitely not the usual class protocol of having me cut a promo on something random. Vince made a statement, then said nothing. I asked if there was a question there, and he said there wasn't, so I just stood there in the front of the room, with neither of us saying anything. I thought he was trying to embarrass me, but then he asked, "What are you doing right now?"

"Nothing," I said.

"Close," Vince said, then asked me again, "What are you doing right now?"

I was clueless. "Close to nothing?" Miz let out a groan in sympathy, as if he'd been rooting for me to respond with the right answer and I completely blew it. Vince chuckled.

"No," he said. "You're *using* the silence." And with that, he excused me to sit down.

On my way out the door, Vince pulled me aside and said, "You know I'm doing this for a reason, right?" I lied and told him I did, but, more importantly, that was the first time I thought he saw more in me than I knew. Even today, he will occasionally bring up how much better my promos got after that experience. And they truly did.

After I was eliminated from NXT, WWE told me they would call me when they needed me, which they guessed wouldn't be until the season finale. Plans change rapidly in WWE, though, and they called me back to be on the show the very next week to initiate a story with Michael Cole, stemming from all the times he put me down on commentary. It was the first time on NXT that I was able to prepare for promos—using the instruction I learned in promo class—and it was by far the best talking I'd ever done. We went back and forth verbally, and ultimately physically, as I ended up tackling Cole into the barricade as he ran away. We combined this with a continued rivalry with Miz, and it turned into good television. WWE liked it so much that they ended up using our story to turn Cole into a heel on *Raw* as well.

The final episode of NXT ended with Wade Barrett winning the season and, as part of the story, earning a spot on the main roster. Even though I didn't win, I was confident that WWE would continue to feature me, given how well the stuff went with Cole and all. As I sat with the eliminated Rookies in the front row, watching the final episode, I was thrilled NXT was over, and I looked forward to moving on to the next step, whatever that would be.

14 MATTERS OF THE CHART
FRIDAY, APRIL 4, 2014—7:15 P.M.

His previous chatting with Miz foreshadows an important discussion awaiting Daniel Bryan when he returns to his hotel room to find his fiancée . . . plus Nikki and "Mama Bella." Serving as the couple's wedding party planner of sorts, Brie's mom insists that the two—both with significant championship matches in two days—commit to their final seating chart for their approaching event.

Bryan shares some unfortunate news about an important relative being suddenly unable to attend, then grabs a seat on the sofa between Brie and his future mother-in-law. Mama Bella makes her case for the seating arrangements she prepared but advises the pair to review and adjust for their big day. Table 1 is slated to seat guests from the WWE roster; table 2 will house the cast of Total Divas. Resting across from the trio of Bella clan members on the couch is a short stack of mixed papers, a FedEx envelope, Bryan's full WrestleMania Week itinerary, and a publication: YES! Magazine. *Yes. Correct.* YES! Magazine.

"It's an unbelievable magazine," Bryan emphatically declares, as he shows off the special revolution issue. "It's about powerful ideas, practical

actions, different ideas on how to change the world. And they're actually based out of Seattle. My favorite magazine is YES! Magazine."

Overwhelming (and unintentional) irony aside, Bryan's three-year readership of the publication isn't the limit of his interests in eco-consciousness.

"One thing I want to do is build an Earthship Home," he adds, advocating their use of solar panels, rainwater filtration, and general reuse. "That's a home built out of recycled material—used car tires and stuff like that. It's a completely sustainable system, completely off-grid. I found out about that through YES! Magazine."

Reading isn't presently an option, however. There's tons of chatter in the room with three lady Bellas, and, much the way he may be on Sunday night, Bryan finds himself outnumbered . . . and he feels just fine.

The Monday after NXT was finished, all eight of us Rookies were brought to Raw in Miami. We had no idea why. We still had to dress separately from everyone else in the locker room, in a dirty draped-off space next to the catering area. Midway through the day, Laurinaitis pulled us all into Vince's office, where we waited until Vince and Michael Hayes, a former wrestling star and one of the top match producers in WWE today, came in. Vince told us they had a plan, but it was of the utmost importance we not tell anybody outside of those in the room. If we did, it would ruin it, and if they heard of any of us telling anybody, that person would be fired. We were going to do something that had never been done before on WWE television.

It would happen in the main event, in which John Cena's opponent was to be picked by the fans whose choices were Rey Mysterio, Jack Swagger, and CM Punk. They thought Rey winning was a pretty sure thing, but when you leave things up to the fans, you never know what you're going to get, and Punk ended up winning the vote. I'm not sure how much Punk was briefed on what was going to happen, but after all eight of us got into our ring gear early in the day, if anyone asked why we were dressed, we just told them we had to shoot some photos. We lied to everybody, including people we trusted. I even lied about it to Regal.

While Cena and Punk were wrestling, the winner of NXT, Wade Barrett, came strolling down the ramp. Shortly thereafter, the rest of the Rookies, including myself, came through the crowd and jumped over the barricade. Punk had the Straight Edge Society with him, so we beat up his associate Luke Gallows, and Serena ran off. Punk got out of the ring, and we beat him up, too. Then all of us hopped on the apron and stared down Cena, the biggest star in WWE. We all slowly stepped into the ring, and the eight of us surrounded him. That's when the mayhem ensued and the Nexus was born. We all beat up Cena, then got out of the ring to destroy everything in sight. We tore apart the ring, exposing the wooden beams underneath; we beat up security, we cut up the mat, we tore off the ropes, and we ripped apart the mats on the floor. We created chaos, and in the process, we even beat up ring announcer Justin Roberts, stripping off his jacket and shirt. Vince and Michael had told us directly that they wanted a "gang-style beatdown," and that's what we gave them.

Keep in mind that I hadn't been in WWE very long. I knew some of the rules, like no bleeding, and I knew it was a PG company, but I didn't know what exactly was PG and what wasn't. In the middle of this "gang-style beatdown," I saw Justin Roberts lying there, no shirt on and tie still around his neck. In moments like this, I always thought violence was good for believability, so I grabbed the long end of his tie from behind and pulled it back. Hard. The cameras picked up on it right away because it was a great visual: Justin on his stomach, being choked by the tie around his neck, his face turning purple. Some people thought he was just selling goofy, but he wasn't. I don't trust nonwrestling people to sell very well, especially when it comes to a big, important angle, so it's better to be a little rough, as long as you don't hurt them. I pulled on the tie so hard it left long red marks on his neck.

Amid the melee, somebody from the production crew came to me

on the side, saying, "No choking! No choking!" I stopped and heard it just in time, because I was about to choke somebody else with one of the cable wires at ringside. When we broke the ring, Heath Slater grabbed one of the ring ropes and was about to wrap it around Cena's neck, but John whispered, "No choking!" to him as well.

Inside the ring, we were all given a moment to shine, with each of us hitting Cena with a signature move, mine being a simple kick to the head as he rested on his knees, execution style. Prior to this whole fiasco, Cena pulled me aside and said the most important thing isn't the move, it's what you do before the move. Looking back, I assume he was probably thinking of some sort of hand motion or something. Instead, I looked him dead in the eyes and screamed, "You're not better than me." I then spit in the face of WWE's biggest star and kicked him in the skull.

When we got back through the curtain, everybody thought the beat down was awesome. Then somebody shouted, "Who was choking Justin Roberts?!" They couldn't see because the camera was focused exclusively on Justin's purple face.

I stepped forward and said, "Uh, that was me."

"And who spit on John Cena?!" they asked.

"That was me, too," I responded.

Apparently choking and spitting are two of the things not allowed within the PG guidelines of WWE programming, but I had no clue. Of course, we didn't *need* the choke, nor did we *need* the spit, but elements like that showed our disdain and added to the brutality of the whole thing. The fundamental reason our characters did all of that was that we were pissed off after being treated like jokes for an entire season of NXT, and I just did the most violent and malicious things I could think of. The parameters of PG never crossed my mind.

I apologized to everyone and made a special point to apologize to Justin and Cena. Neither of them seemed to care, and part of me thinks Justin thought it was pretty cool. I'd known him since 2002; he loved wrestling, and I think he was happy to have had such a memorable part in the moment, despite the marks on his neck.

The Nexus attack happened on Monday, then Tuesday we all went to SmackDown but didn't do anything on the show. As I walked down the halls at SmackDown, I passed Michael Hayes.

"Daniel, what did you learn last night?" he asked.

"No choking, no spitting, "I replied.

"That's right. It's OK to make mistakes as long as you learn from them," Michael said.

I thought I was in the clear.

That Wednesday, WWE booked me on an FCW show down in Florida. Miz was on the show, too, and as we sat in the locker room talking about the whole thing, he reassured me not to worry about it. He said they would all forget about it by next week.

Two days later—June 11, 2010—I got the second and last call I've ever received from Vince McMahon. I didn't know it was him at first because it came from a blocked number, but as I answered, I had a sinking feeling that it wasn't good news.

When I picked up, I knew right away it was really Vince, and this time there was no feeling that it was a rib. He said, "You know, Daniel, I'm sorry I have to do this. I feel really bad, but we have guidelines as far as what's PG and what's not PG, and unfortunately, you broke those guidelines. I'm sorry, but we're going to have to let you go."

As far as firings go, it was actually not too bad. It was way better than the first time I got fired when I lived in Memphis. I appreciated that he called me himself, and there wasn't anything mean or malicious about it; it was completely different than what you would expect if you've seen Vince fictionally fire someone on television. He further explained that he *had* to do it to set an example. He didn't *want* to do it. It was actually quite endearing.

My reaction to being fired was different than even I would have expected of myself. I felt liberated, as if an enormous burden had been lifted off my shoulders. I thanked Vince for the opportunity, and after he expressed his regret one last time, I responded, "Don't be sorry. I'll make more money now this year than I did with you guys, so don't be sorry for me at all." It was a weird thing for me to

say, because I'm not overly money-driven, but all I saw was opportunity. There is no better time to be fired than after a hot angle like the Nexus's debut, especially because I essentially got fired for being too violent. And a lot of independent fans hated the sanitized version of wrestling that's required to be PG. I knew they would see the whole thing not only as an injustice but also as proof that the only place they could see the kind of wrestling they liked was on the independents.

I don't know how soon after the incident Vince knew he was going to fire me. He may have been under pressure, considering the company's many sponsors and partners who rely on WWE being PG-rated. Plus, there are all the kids watching the show. I learned that Vince didn't tell too many people before he did it. I called John Laurinaitis after I got off the phone with Vince, just to clear up what this meant as far as me wrestling for other promotions going forward, but he didn't answer the phone. Ten minutes later, Johnny called me back, and he was shocked by the whole thing. He told me Vince had called him about thirty minutes earlier and asked for my number (he didn't say why) and had just then called him back to tell him that I was fired. It was a very uncommon circumstance; Laurinaitis was usually the one responsible for calling and letting talent go.

The comment I made about the money must have really reverberated with Vince, because Johnny asked me, "Did you tell Vince you were going to make more money on the indies?" I told him I did. And it was the truth. There is a lot that people don't understand about our lives as WWE wrestlers. For one, when we sign our contracts, we are guaranteed a certain amount of money, called your "downside." With the exception of top guys, usually it's not very much, and my contract was for substantially less than I made working on the independents. In WWE, the idea is that if you are booked most of the time, you will make far more than your downside, but since I wasn't on many shows, I only made the minimum. It was by no means a struggle to get by, but I wasn't saving as much money as I had hoped. Also, in WWE, the wrestlers are responsible for paying for their own hotels and rental cars, whereas on the independents, all of that was taken care of. WWE takes care of those expenses for anyone under a developmental contract who's brought up on the road for TV. I was actually the only member of NXT not on a developmental contract, but I was lucky to be able to jump in with the other guys.

Anyhow, Laurinaitis told me Vince said I could start working independent dates as soon as I wanted, as long as it wasn't for television or pay-per-view. That was all I needed to hear. As soon as I got off with Johnny, I called Gabe Sapolsky, who was booking shows for both Dragon Gate USA and Evolve. When he picked up the phone, I said, "Gabe, we're going to make a lot of money." (As a side note, what I considered a lot of money, some people would laugh at. It's all relative. If I showed Steve Austin how much I made during the time I was fired, he would not be impressed. My family, however, was *very* impressed, and so was I.)

Gabe and I were both very excited. We discussed some ideas, and Gabe later got me hooked up with a graphic designer to quickly create a new T-shirt and launch a Web site that would basically be a vehicle to sell the shirts he was going to design. I had never been one to try to sell much merchandise when I was on the independents. I hated producing it, and I hated sitting out by a merchandise table trying to sell it. I knew, though, that if I didn't do it, I'd miss out on the opportunity. In the span of a couple of hours, I turned into a full-blown capitalist.

I put Gabe in charge of dealing with other promoters who wanted to book me. Given the circumstances, I could charge a lot more for appearances and bookings, but I didn't want to haggle with promoters, so I left that to him. To start, Gabe booked me for the upcoming shows he had, then we decided to talk again the next day to figure out where to go from there.

By the time I got off the phone with Gabe, WWE had announced my firing on WWE.com. All of a sudden, I got what felt like a million calls and text messages, including ones from Regal and Shawn Michaels. Regal, especially, gave me some great advice (yet again),

which was to make sure I didn't publicly disparage WWE. He had no doubt that if I kept my nose clean, within a year or two I'd be back, though I wasn't sure I even wanted to be.

In the wrestling world, my firing seemed like a big thing. At least, it was the most talked-about thing that had ever happened in my career. Within days, my schedule for the next three months was full: three shows per weekend, every weekend, for far more money than I had ever made before. For a full week, I lay low and just tried to appreciate the calm before my schedule got crazy busy.

Ten days after I was fired, the Web site was up, and I couldn't believe how fast the shirts were selling. It was actually quite stressful, because I decided to ship them out myself to save a little money, and the shirts weren't going to be ready for a few days. I sold two designs: a gray one that said TEAM BRYAN on it, and a maroon shirt with my bloody face "Obamiconned," a picture taken out of a Mexican wrestling magazine. Underneath my face, instead of saying CHANGE like Obama's campaign poster, it said VIOLENT. It was perfect.

My first show, two weeks after being fired, was in Detroit for a company I'd previously worked for called Chikara, itself a family-friendly company. Before I was announced for the show, they had fewer than a hundred tickets sold, and after the announcement, they ended up selling several hundred. The event was held at a swap meet, with no bathroom or shower in the dressing room, no bottled water or catering. I felt right at home. When I came to the ring, instead of throwing streamers into the ring—a Japanese custom that had been adopted by American independent wrestling fans—they all threw neckties.

After the show, I went out to the merchandise stand to sell the shirts and 8x10s, and I was genuinely moved by the support a lot of the fans gave me. They were more pissed off than I was, seeing the whole thing as unfair and "typical WWE." The way they cared for me warmed my heart.

From there, I was off to the races. I had two shows back-to-back the next day in Cleveland, and the following weekend I wrestled several shows in Germany. Somewhere in there, WWE had its Fatal 4-Way pay-per-view, and I received texts from multiple people telling me the live crowd was chanting my name throughout the show, even during the main event. I didn't care. I was already past it. I was excited to be back on the independents and elated to be back working with Gabe.

Before I was signed by WWE in 2009, Gabe and I were talking about starting a new wrestling promotion together. We only talked about it a couple of times, but in that short window, I also came up with a name: Evolve. My concept for the whole thing was based on the idea that wrestling had, for the most part, become a parody of itself. Even in places like Ring of Honor, they kept the same tropes that had been going on in ROH for years. Same in Japan. Same in WWE. There hadn't been much of anything brought to the table that was new to help wrestling evolve, and we were going to create something different that would, hence the name. Of course, with my signing, I never got to be a part of it when Gabe started Evolve in January 2010.

In Evolve, the wrestling would be different, the interviews would be different, and the production would be different. Gabe sent me a DVD of the first show, and when I watched it, I felt the main event—Davey Richards against Kota Ibushi—was excellent. Now that I was no longer with WWE, Gabe and I could get back to collaborating on the project.

But it wasn't just Gabe and me who wanted to bring Evolve into the future. Paul Heyman was interested as well. Paul always has a lot going on, and this period was no different. TNA was in talks with him about working for them, but he would only go if he would have complete control. TNA was also interested in signing me, but I would only consider it if Paul was going; otherwise, I'd rather be on my own. The more it looked like Paul wouldn't be going to TNA, the more he talked to Gabe and me about Evolve. Heyman is a genius,

and his ideas for marketing and promotion blew my mind. We talked about it a lot, but unfortunately, it never went anywhere. We were all pulled in too many different directions.

The first Evolve show I did was in a tiny building in Union City, New Jersey, which gave the whole experience a Fight Club atmosphere. The following night, I returned to the famed ECW Arena in Philadelphia to wrestle for Dragon Gate USA. The throwing of ties during my ring announcement had caught on everywhere, and this crowd probably threw more neckwear than anybody anywhere else. That night, I had the best match I'd have during my return to the independents, against a Japanese wrestler named Shingo Takagi. The arena was hot and humid in July, but the fans didn't care and neither did we. Shingo and I wrestled almost thirty minutes, and the audience was loud the entire time. It was my first time back working with Gabe in a long time, and it was a blast, even if it didn't last long.

If I may digress, I know some fans have fond memories of Pro Wrestling Guerrilla, so here are some quick stories. I was PWG Champion for a relatively short amount of time, yet it was important in the sense that it was a regular booking that I could count on to help me get exposure. The bigger PWG shows, which had a lot of tape or DVD marketability, were important because if you had a really strong performance that people liked, they'd talk about it and you'd get more bookings. There was also Internet exposure through various videos we'd release.

I've done some really wacky promos, but the "American Dolphin" one I did in PWG with Paul London, who'd previously been in WWE, got a good deal of attention and a lot of views on YouTube. Paul was taking improv comedy classes then, so he was saying the most random stuff (such as renaming the American Dragon as a water mammal, as part of the "Hybrid Dolphins" along with him and Roderick Strong). I'd instantly start laughing whenever he'd insert one of his zany lines. In recording it, we'd gotten to the fifth or sixth take, and the limiting factor in each of those takes was how much I was laughing, because Paul is hilarious. The final product that you'll find online is the one where I laughed the least while shooting. My laughing actually got people asking me if I was stoned when it was recorded. I certainly was not stoned, but as for the other parties involved, I have no idea. More important than that, I knew that promo really worked because after the video hit YouTube, I was doing a show in Germany and instead of fans clapping or cheering, everybody just *buzzed* at me—something Paul and I encouraged fans to do at the end of the clip. It shows how the Internet was changing wrestling back in 2009.

During this period, Chikara—an independent promotion in Philadelphia—gave me one of the coolest experiences of my career up to that point: being in the ring with Johnny Saint. It was me, Claudio Castagnoli (Cesaro), and Dave Taylor against Johnny, Mike Quackenbush, and Skayde Rivera. Johnny had been wrestling for more than fifty years at the time and wasn't competing in many matches. Even in his sixties, though, he was still awesome. He's an incredible English wrestler who did things in the ring throughout his career that guys can't pull off today. Lots have tried to replicate his style of technical wrestling, but they can't. As much as you can learn a move, you can't learn the physical fluidity that he possessed. When I first met Regal in 2000, he told me that if I was interested in technical wrestling, I had to watch Johnny Saint. I had even bought a VCR that played different formats so I could watch Saint on old British wrestling tapes. Those were the lengths I'd go to in order to learn something new, because our generation of wrestlers doesn't always have an opportunity to wrestle veteran guys to learn from.

Before our six-man tag with the English legend, I had known Claudio from Ring of Honor. We'd done shows together in Germany, and since he can speak German, he'd help me out. Over time, we got to know each other just by being at so many shows together. It was a very gradual process, not unlike my most enduring relationships with a number of wrestlers—particularly those who've shared my path from Ring of Honor to WWE, like Cesaro, Seth Rollins, and Sami Zayn, who are all very close with me.

Jimmy Jacobs and I still occasionally talk because I consider him a genius. Despite not seeing him for a really long time, I feel closer to Nigel McGuinness than to people I see as friends in WWE. I still consider Nigel one of my best friends because he's a good person and we went through a lot together. I'm not sure why it is, but even though I've been with WWE for more than four years, I don't feel I have as close bonds with WWE people as I do with Ring of Honor people.

Speaking of WWE, the first week of August 2010, Regal's advice became prophecy. My then-girlfriend and I were at the veterinarian's office with a tremendously overweight beagle we were going to foster. The beagle's previous owners were an elderly couple, but the husband had passed away and the woman had moved into a nursing home. The facility permitted the dog, but, unfortunately, the woman wasn't in a state to be able to take her pet out for walks, so she kept the beagle happy by feeding her tons of treats, which created the fattest dog I'd ever seen. Her belly hit the ground as she walked, and she was barely fit enough to walk outside to go to the bathroom without getting exhausted. Eventually the beagle was placed in a rescue center until we agreed to foster, which would only be until the center found her a permanent home. In the middle of the vet's examination of this fat dog, I got a call from John Laurinaitis. It was so unexpected I didn't even think to excuse myself from the room.

Laurinaitis told me WWE wanted to bring me back and in a big way. They were doing a seven-on-seven elimination match for the main event of SummerSlam, WWE's second-biggest pay-per-view of the year, and they wanted me to be the surprise seventh member of John Cena's crew against the Nexus, the group consisting of the former NXT Rookies. The opportunity was hard to turn down. However, there were some logistical issues. I explained that I had a good number of independent shows booked already. Johnny said that was great, perfectly fine; I should honor all of them, except the ones I had the weekend of SummerSlam.

Also, since I felt like my value had increased following my release, I shyly asked for a pay raise—which I'd never done in my entire career. In Ring of Honor, every so often, they would just offer me a pay raise, often in thanks for my hard work, but also acknowledging that I was becoming more valuable. I made my request, and Laurinaitis paused for a minute, then said, "I think we can do that." Thinking back on it now, I asked for such a minute raise, I'm sure he was taken aback by how little it was.

As I agreed to come back, Johnny emphasized that my re-signing and return was supposed to be a complete surprise. I couldn't tell anybody . . . but I did. I told my family, just so they could watch, and I called and told Gabe. So many of his plans revolved around me, and I owed it to him. He was both disappointed that we would no longer be able to work together and happy for me, personally, that I was getting an opportunity to go back to WWE in such a good spot. Gabe was also thrilled I'd be able to finish out the bookings I had with him for the next month, and so was I.

Other than that, I told no one. Under the guise of a "family issue," I canceled the bookings I had during SummerSlam weekend. I also stopped taking any new bookings, which was challenging because I had been in contact with New Japan, and they e-mailed several times during that period asking for my dates of availability. I didn't know what to say that wouldn't tip my hand about rejoining WWE, so I didn't respond. Laurinaitis told me, "We just can't have this getting out to the dirt sheets," and I did my best to make sure it didn't. I didn't even tell William Regal, which was the hardest part.

My return to WWE was a very well kept secret. I flew into Los Angeles that Sunday morning of the event on August 15 and checked into a different hotel than the one where the rest of the talent and crew stayed that week for all of the events leading up to Summer-Slam. WWE hired me a private car to take me to the Staples Center, and I didn't arrive until well after the pay-per-view started. They told me to wear a hooded sweatshirt and nondescript clothes so that no one would identify or notice me as I was hurried from the car to a private locker room.

When I arrived backstage, I was told to hang tight, so I just waited.

Shortly thereafter, all the guys in the match were brought back to the room. With the exception of a few guys on John Cena's team, I don't think anybody else knew I was in the match. Jamie Noble was one of the producers for the match, and he had already worked with a couple of Nexus guys to go over things the "surprise seventh man" might want to do, but those things were generic enough that most of them didn't put it together until they saw me. I wasn't going to actually be *in* the match very much, so I just had to work out a couple of things with some people.

Despite the pressure of being in the SummerSlam main event, I wasn't worried about the wrestling part of it at all. What made me most nervous was the reaction I would get coming out. I was pretty concerned that when Cena announced me as the final member of the team, the crowd would have an anticlimactic reaction. Cena's team consisted of mostly established stars; Bret Hart, Chris Jericho, and Edge were all on the team, and usually surprises are supposed to be big. Prior to being fired, I'd lost pretty much every match on TV and was portrayed as a nerd/loser by commentators. I assumed the casual WWE fan would be like, "What?! Why on earth did they choose *this* guy?!" The concern weighed heavy on my mind before the match.

They wanted me to continue wearing my hoodie so no one would see me as I walked to the Gorilla position for my entrance, which I thought was a little excessive given it was only moments before the match. After the match, I learned that WWE.com revealed that I was the seventh guy minutes before I came out. Given all the secrecy the entire day, I thought that was pretty funny.

When John Cena announced me as the surprise member for his team, in no way did I get a megastar reaction from the Staples Center crowd, but it wasn't the apathetic reaction I had anticipated either. I'd say it was more like polite applause that rapidly shifted in my favor when I started the match and I got a quick submission on Darren Young, who tapped out to the LeBell Lock. The match was structured so I wasn't in the ring much, but each time I was, I looked great. I didn't come in for a second time until well after twenty minutes, but I came in like a house on fire, and after I hit a suicide dive to the floor, the crowd started chanting my name. It had worked. I then submitted Heath Slater, again using the LeBell Lock. In one night, I was instantly made more important than I had ever seemed during my entire time on NXT.

A few moments later, Miz, who wasn't in the match, ran in to hit me with his briefcase because he was fictionally upset that he wasn't chosen as Cena's seventh man instead of his onetime Rookie. Miz's actions led to my elimination from the match, which was great for me because it also easily led into a story with Miz going forward. I considered it a very successful night. Well, for me at least.

After I was eliminated, it came down to Cena against Wade Barrett and Justin Gabriel, and Cena beat both of them. The Nexus had created a lot of interest, and the group needed a win to solidify themselves as a force to be reckoned with. They didn't get the victory when they needed it, and after SummerSlam, they went from being dangerous guys with an edge to just another faction of bad guys.

The night immediately after SummerSlam, we taped two episodes of *Monday Night Raw* because the Raw crew was headed overseas. I was feeling good about the pay-per-view, and I was eager to engage in the new story with Miz. The first Raw went really well. Even though I lost a quick match to Nexus member Michael Tarver, it was due to Miz's interference and resulted in a brawl between Miz and me. During the second taping, I had to run out and attack Miz in the ring. I thought it went well, but when I got back through the curtain, Vince was furious. He said, "That was horrible!" and then sent me back out into the arena to do the same thing, in front of the same crowd.

It was a taped show, so the production team could edit in the better one. This was the first time in my career I ever had to redo something in front of a live crowd. It was embarrassing, made me feel terrible, and, in my mind, justified any of my detractors who looked at me as the independent guy who couldn't do the big league stuff right. The second attempt, they said, was much better, but it didn't

cast away that feeling of failure. That's the way wrestling goes: One day you're high, one day you're low, and at the beginning of each day, you never know what to expect.

That September in Chicago, I had my first WWE pay-per-view match at the next major event, Night of Champions. It was also my first title win in WWE, as I beat Miz for the United States Championship. We had a good little match, but nothing great, and I knew they had me win just so they could get the U.S. Title off of Miz. They had big plans for him in the near future—winning the WWE Championship and being in the main event of WrestleMania—but they needed to detach the title from Miz. I knew the title win didn't mean much as far as how much WWE wanted to push me, but it was still a great opportunity. At the time, both the U.S. and Intercontinental Championships were consistently defended on pay-per-view, and more shows than not, I would at least compete in a match. It was hard to get much wrestling time on Raw with the show being only two hours, but I was confident I could gain some steam if I could get a solid match on pay-per-view every month and wrestle at least ten minutes.

After I won the United States Title, I asked to change my entrance music. I had been coming out to this hard, generic metal-type music that didn't fit me at all, and music is a huge part of the presentation. Admittedly, I've always had questionable taste in entrance music. Coming out to "Born in the U.S.A." in my first match was a Shawn Michaels decision, so I can't take "credit" for that one. When I had a big beard and a shaved head in 2005, I wore a giant crushed velvet cloak to the ring and entered the arena to the "Imperial March" from *Star Wars*. But during my last several years on the independents, the song I came out to was instantly recognizable and, to hardcore fans, became synonymous with me: Europe's "Final Countdown."

I was in Japan in 2004, looking through a music magazine that listed the hundred worst songs of all time. Lo and behold, "Final Countdown" was number one, voted as the worst song ever. I loved that song, but hadn't heard it in a long time. Despite the horrible lyrics about leaving Earth for Venus, as soon as I reheard the horns blaring at the beginning, I knew it would be a great entrance theme. It didn't take long after I started using the ballad for the entire audience to sing along with it, even before it reached the chorus: "It's the final countdown!" Unfortunately, WWE couldn't use "Final Countdown" without paying an exorbitant rights fee, so I suggested using a piece of classical music, Richard Wagner's "Ride of the Valkyries," which is in the public domain and can be used freely. One of my favorite old-school Japanese wrestlers, Yoshiaki Fujiwara, came out to it, and it was badass.

Once I suggested it, I thought it would take a few weeks to get it cleared and approved. Not this time. That same night on Raw, I was wrestling Edge, who had already made his entrance. Right before I walked out, WWE producer Billy Kidman was on a headset in Gorilla and told me, "OK, you're coming out to new music." I was just about to ask if it was "Ride of the Valkyries" when it hit. The version of the song they played—there are many different ones—was not what I was looking for, though. This one was very . . . *soft*. When I walked through the curtain, I could see an entire arena filled with confused faces, some people with their mouths wide open. Edge was visibly laughing in the ring. Miz was on commentary with Michael Cole, and the two of them were having a field day calling me a nerd. It wasn't quite as badass as Fujiwara. We altered it a little bit, and now it's become my thing. It was a rough go of it at first, though.

For the next few months, I was in this interesting position where I would do Raw TVs, pay-per-views, and some live events against Miz, but then would go do my remaining independent shows, where I relished the opportunity to bring in new fans based on my exposure in WWE. During this stretch, I worked my final match for Gabe at a Dragon Gate USA show in Milwaukee: It was me against Jon Moxley (Ambrose) in a crazy brawl all over the tiny building. There are few things in wrestling that add drama to a match like

blood, and because I knew it would be my last opportunity to add that sort of drama for a long time, I took full advantage and bled that night for my send-off. Generally speaking, it was strange going back and forth from the independents to WWE. I was very well respected on the independents, and the fans saw me as a badass submission wrestler who would kick people's heads in. Yet in WWE, I could tell management didn't think very much of me; they didn't really listen to my ideas, and they were constantly trying to portray me as a nerd on television.

The next WWE pay-per-view was Hell in a Cell, where I wrestled the Miz and John Morrison in a triple-threat submissions-only match. Despite neither opponent ever really using submission moves, it turned into a solid match. I felt good walking through the curtain, and then all of a sudden I was getting yelled at again. Alex Riley had come out to help the Miz during the match as we were all fighting on the stage. I went after Riley and ended up throwing him off the stage; unfortunately, he landed on a cameraman named Stu. They were livid. Not only was it dangerous for Stu (and could potentially open up a lawsuit), but in the process, he also dropped the camera—and those cameras are *expensive,* worth more to the company than either me or Riley, at that point. We both got an earful that night and more the next day. At Raw, Riley and I were pulled into Laurinaitis's office and shown the tape. Somehow, they thought we did it on purpose to get ourselves over. I already had the issue after the Nexus attack in 2010, and the last thing I needed was something like that, where I again upset WWE management.

Stemming from this incident, I started to regret coming back to WWE and fell into a bad mental place where I hated every second I was there. When I was inside the ring was the only time I could get out of the funk, but every time I walked back through the curtain, I went right back to where I'd started. Nonetheless, I kept my mouth shut, kept working hard, and hoped that the way I felt would soon change. It did, but it took a long time.

Leading into the WWE Bragging Rights 2010 event, where Raw

Superstars wrestled Superstars from the rival SmackDown brand, I was directed to go out and challenge Intercontinental Champion Dolph Ziggler to a champion-versus-champion match on pay-per-view. It was rare mic time; plus, I'd ultimately get to perform with Dolph, one of the better wrestlers in the company, so I was excited. Then I was told what they wanted *after* I challenged Dolph: He and I would get in a little scuffle, and while we were on the floor, a bunch of Divas would come out to dump confetti on Vickie Guerrero, who was Dolph's manager at the time. OK, whatever. The thing was, after Vickie ran out, they wanted me to get into the ring with the Divas, get supershy like I didn't want to be any part of it, then bust out into a dance while the Divas all danced around me. I hated the idea. Nevertheless, I put a smile on my face as we went through rehearsal, and I did my best to make it entertaining on the show. Meanwhile, on commentary, Michael Cole continued to mock me, declaring I'd never been on a date in my life. He was just playing his character (who randomly hated me); however, to me, Cole's comments were indicative of how the company perceived me: just some nerd who was lucky to even be on the WWE roster.

Dolph and I had a good match at Bragging Rights, and I had another strong pay-per-view outing against Ted DiBiase Jr. the next month at Survivor Series. That November was the first time I'd gotten to work with Teddy since we were in Japan together after he'd only performed in sixteen matches. He was good then, but had gotten way better in the ring, and after Survivor Series we wrestled each other on all of the live events, which was a lot of fun. In between all that, I went on my first WWE European tour: two straight weeks of shows every night, and I got to wrestle Regal almost every show. It was the first time Regal and I had been able to wrestle since 2001, so we went out and had proper wrestling matches every night, incorporating lots of European-style wrestling. It was a blast, and for a while, doing those kinds of matches lifted my spirits. Even if I was a geek on TV, I'd be able to go on the live events and wrestle however I wanted.

YES!

After having four good pay-per-view matches in a row, I thought WWE fans were starting to realize that I could be counted on to provide really exciting matches they could look forward to. However, the match with Teddy was the last pay-per-view singles match I had for over ten months, and my story shifted entirely.

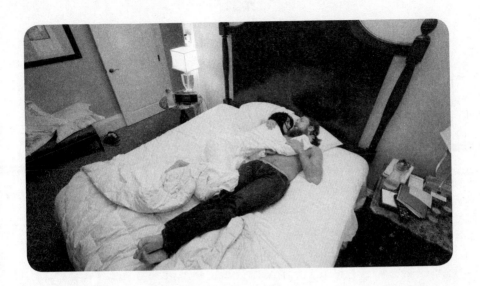

15 BED, BEARD & BEYOND
SATURDAY, APRIL 5, 2014—8:49 A.M.

It's very still on this Saturday morning in the hotel bedroom of a future husband and wife, both one day removed from two highly anticipated championship matches at their profession's most magnificent event.

The quiet scene sharply contrasts with what Daniel Bryan is most known for: explosiveness, intensity. The drama of Total Divas *is nowhere in sight. A bare-chested Bryan and his bathrobed Bella lie hushed, exchanging only short statements before Daniel departs.*

After several moments, the two sit up and Brie reaches for the hairbrush on a nightstand littered with burned tea-light candles. She brushes her fiancé's mane until the clock clicks close to Bryan's call time. It's time to go to work.

On the Raw after Survivor Series 2010, I was told my new story wasn't with any of the male wrestlers, but rather with Divas, specifically the Bella Twins, Brie and Nikki, who would be vying for my affection. That doesn't sound too bad, right? Two hot twins each trying to get with you should make you seem cool. But that wasn't the story. In this case, they were actually in competition with each other to see who could sleep with me first because they both thought

I was a virgin (not *vegan*). I was an oblivious geek who was befuddled by any woman's interest in me. That was the story.

Needless to say, I didn't like it. I didn't know the Bellas very well at the time, but I didn't understand why the company was working so hard to make me look like a loser. My negative attitude at the time didn't help matters either. If it had happened a couple of years later, like when I was paired with Kane as part of Team Hell No, I think it would have been very entertaining; by then, I had developed into a better entertainer and was more open to silliness. Over the two-month story with Brie and Nikki, I warmed up to it and tried to do the best I could with it. Looking back, if I had embraced it more, I probably could have gotten more over with it and made it popular with the fans, despite the horrible premise.

This horrible premise is how Bri and I came to be together.

When I started with WWE, I pretty much avoided the Divas, unless they came up and talked to me. I had a girlfriend, wasn't interested in the party culture, and was pretty much just business when I was at work. Even after my girlfriend and I broke up that October, I didn't have much to do with them. Being in the story with the Bellas forced us to interact more, both on television and at live events.

At first I couldn't even tell them apart. (This was before Nicole got fake boobs. These days, telling the difference is easy.) I would be talking to one of them about what we were doing that night, then walk away, and the other one would come up to me shortly after, and I'd be superconfused as to whether it was the Bella I had just talked to earlier or not. Eventually I was able to tell the difference, and getting to know the two of them was the most fun part about being involved in the story together.

It was also interesting to see the differences in their personalities. It was clear to me that Nicole was the more domineering one, and some of the things she would say to Bri would make me feel bad for her. Not that Bri couldn't dish it out, too; they would get in these sister fights in the middle of work, where they would say the meanest things I'd ever heard two people say to each other. Then, literally two minutes later, they would be doubled over laughing about something else. It boggled my mind. When you share a womb with someone, I suppose you have a different kind of relationship.

Though at first I was bothered by my portrayal, soon the three of us were having a lot of fun on live events. We tried out a bunch of different entertaining entrances, including one where the girls went out first with their arms out pretending to be airplanes, then they'd stop and present me, and I would also come out pretending to be an airplane. I thought it worked great with the music, but when we tried it on TV, Vince hated it. Back to the drawing board. We did another entrance for a while where all three of us came down to the ring and I'd squat by the apron as they each stepped off one of my legs onto the apron, where they would then hold the ropes open for me. The first time we did it, I could tell they were nervous, and I thought it was because they were worried they would fall or something. It turns out it was because they weren't wearing any underwear. Such is the life of a Bella Twin.

At the time, I was wrestling Teddy on the live events, and we were having really fun matches. He was coming into the ring with a Diva

as well—Maryse—so between the two of us and the three girls, we came up with some entertaining stuff. My favorite was a spot where I would put Teddy up on my shoulders to airplane-spin him as many times as I could (which was usually around thirty rotations). He'd be so dizzy that he would try to pin the referee, and I'd count to three and he'd think that he won. Maryse would get in and yell at Teddy, then Bri would come in and slap her, and then Nicole would give Maryse the airplane spin, before we'd go right into the finish. The crowd usually loved it, but we had to put a stop to it when a producer told us those kinds of shenanigans weren't fitting for a United States Championship match.

The three of us working together made it easy to become friends with Bri and Nicole, and soon we'd be laughing and joking together at shows and appearances. Oftentimes after our match, I'd be sitting watching the rest of the show on a monitor and Bri would come sit by me. We'd get in these wonderful conversations about the environment and diverse belief systems and all sorts of different fun stuff. There aren't a lot of eco-conscious wrestlers like me in WWE, and during our conversations, I found out that Bri actually wrote an eco blog on WWE.com for a short time but stopped after getting so many hateful responses. We bonded together while everyone else, including Nicole, made fun of us for being hippies.

Despite all the talking we were doing, Bri and I had recently gotten out of serious relationships, and neither of us was interested in dating. For the two months that we did the story together, we were merely friends, yet the more we talked, the more I looked forward to seeing her. Soon I borderline expected that she would come sit by me at the monitor, and when it took her a while to get ready, I'd casually go looking for her backstage.

My story with the Bellas ended on the Raw episode before the 2011 Royal Rumble in January. While competing over me, each of the sisters had kissed me, but there was no way to really push forward the story of them trying to sleep with me on TV in a PG manner, so WWE ended it. On that Raw, the Bellas lost a tag match and came looking for me in a backstage segment. When they came into my locker room, I was making out with another Diva named Gail Kim, who I then revealed was my "girlfriend."

The Bellas said, "We thought you were a—"

"Vegan? Oh, absolutely, I don't eat any meat," I interjected, not allowing them to say "virgin."

That was the big climax to the story. Then the Bellas and Gail got into a kickass backstage brawl, and as I tried to pull Bri off, she slapped me in the face. Earlier, in preparation for the scene, I told Bri she could hit me as hard as she wanted as long as she didn't slap me in the ear, since it was the same ear I ruptured in a match with KENTA years prior. We had to do the scene multiple times, and every single time, she slapped me in the ear—not on purpose, mind you, just in the heat of the moment with so many moving parts in the brawl. Bri later confessed she was a little bothered watching me kiss Gail in the segment. Even though that's not why she hit me in the ear, that's when she knew she had a crush on me.

The Royal Rumble took place in Boston that year, and Bri was going to the Isabella Stewart Gardner Museum before the pay-per-view event. She knew I loved museums, so she invited me to go with her. I picked her up at her hotel, and she told me all the great things she'd heard about the museum. When we got there, it was beautiful. There was a courtyard garden in the center of the place with three floors of galleries surrounding it. While we were on the second floor, Bri was pointing at a painting, and one of the workers came in and chastised her with a strong "No pointing!" I'd never heard of such a thing, and we had a good laugh about it. We never made it to the third floor because of time constraints, but we had had a great time, despite the whole pointing thing. Though neither of us considered it one at the time, today we think of the Isabella Stewart Gardner Museum as the home of our first date.

We actually didn't start dating until a couple of weeks later. It all began with a show in Victoria, British Columbia, where we had to take a ferry back to Vancouver after the show. While we waited for the ferry, some sort of all-female high school dance team got off their bus, saw our Divas, and did a little dance. It was like that movie *Bring It On*—the high school team seemed to be challenging the Divas to a dance-off. I immediately told Bri and Nicole, "You don't have the guts to have a dance-off with these chicks," and that was all they needed to hear. All of a sudden Bri, Nicole, Maryse, and Eve Torres started battle-dancing these teenage girls right on the spot. It went back and forth with one team doing a dance, then the other. It got crazy when Nicole did the worm on the wet ground, and with that, it became clear the Divas were the true winners.

After we got back on the ferry, I went to sit by myself on the lower level, needing some peace and quiet. Bri was with everyone else on the second level—including Miz, who was in one of his talking moods and yakking away, which I couldn't handle at the moment—and she started texting me to come up and visit. I invited her to come sit down with me, but she didn't know how to devise an excuse for leaving the group and coming down to talk with me. (Not that she told me that, at the time.)

Two days later, Raw was in Anaheim, California, on Valentine's Day, and after the show, Teddy, Sheamus, and I were driving to San Diego, where SmackDown was taking place the following day. Bri and Nicole weren't on SmackDown, but Nicole lived in San Diego, so Bri was staying with her for a few days, and she texted me during the drive, inviting me out to dinner with her and her friends after SmackDown. Bri told me to bring Teddy and Sheamus along as well, but after the show, the guys were tired and just going to head back to their rooms. I decided to go and meet up with Bri and her friends for dinner, and after that, we all hung out at Nicole's place. When I was ready to leave, Bri walked me back to my car, which was parked kind of far away, and then I drove her back to the front of Nicole's.

And this is where Bri and I have a major dispute as to what actually happened.

My version: We were in the middle of talking in the car when Bri quickly wrapped up with "OK, well, I should go. Talk to you later. Bye!" and then sprinted out of the car, closing the door behind her.

Bri's version: She felt like we were talking forever and I wasn't making a move to kiss her, so she gave up and said good night.

In general, I'm very patient, and Bri sees that as slow in a lot of ways. After all that, I was driving back to my hotel thinking about what a fun night we'd had, when Bri sent me a text that said something like, "Wow, I thought a gentleman would have the courtesy to give a lady a kiss good night." I instantly responded, "Don't tempt me. I'll turn this car around right now." Which I did. Several moments later, I was back at Nicole's place. When I pulled up, it was raining, and Bri hurried through the rain to come out the gate. I got right out of the car, went up to Bri, and grabbed her and kissed her. We didn't say anything, just kissed in the pouring rain.

It was February 15, but we still observe Valentine's Day as the anniversary of our first kiss.

The next week, Raw was in Fresno, California, and it was the first time we *attempted* to have sex. Bri and I decided for the time being not to tell anyone about the kiss or that we had an interest in each other. I'm a very good secret keeper, so I didn't tell anyone. Literally, no one. After Raw, Teddy and Sheamus invited me to go out to dinner with them, but I said I was going to stay in and relax. It was an innocent lie, because I'd actually planned to go out to dinner with Bri. When she came to get me, though, Teddy and Sheamus spotted her picking me up. They pointed at us in disbelief from their car and started laughing. They had us caught, but after that, they drove off to dinner. I thought they were leaving us alone.

After dinner, Bri and I came back to my room and started doing the adult stuff—I will spare you the details. We were naked and about to do our thing when all of a sudden we heard the sound of the door handle turning and then the door popped open. Bri jumped under the covers as Teddy and Sheamus barged into the room, inebriated as can be, with the "Ahhh, fella!" and all that. This was one

of the rare moments when I got really, really mad. I let out an angry "What the fuck?!" and butt-ass naked, from the end of the bed, I went to up-kick Teddy in the face. As if in slow motion, a drunk Teddy—with his ridiculous reflexes—sidestepped the kick like he was Keanu Reeves in *The Matrix,* then moved his head right back to where it was to look at me all confused. Meanwhile, Sheamus had sat down on the bed next to Bri, who was under the blanket, and was patting her on the head. Within a few minutes, I was able to get them out of the room, but sat there confused as to how a night that started so great could end like this. After that, Bri and I gave up, and ended up just going to sleep.

The following day, Sheamus told me the whole story. They knew my room number, lied to the front desk about losing their key, saying it was their room, and just hoped I didn't lock my door. I *never* locked my hotel room; I was naïve like that. Needless to say, Bri and I have locked our hotel doors ever since.

16 WORD OF HONOR
SATURDAY, APRIL 5, 2014—9:22 A.M.

The "Yes!" Man's psyched for his VIP Axxess event, now four years after his very first WrestleMania Axxess in 2010. He ends up encountering NXT's Sami Zayn (in his first appearance of this kind), and the two talk their way up the ramp into the loading area of the Ernest N. Morial Convention Center. There's tremendous history between both stars who gained their pre-WWE fame in Ring of Honor.

"Personally, [Bryan] represents to me what he represents to millions of people already, which is an unconventional hero that has really defied the odds," Zayn boasts of his friend. "He means as much to me—as the one spearheading the movement for the little guy—as he does to every kid who sees himself in Bryan. I'm still a kid who sees himself in him as well."

It's been ten years since Bryan and Zayn first met in 2004, and Bryan's opportunity at WrestleMania—the dream stage for these warriors—is a powerful symbol to his friend and fellow entertainer.

"Professionally, I've always looked up to [Bryan] and always tried to catch up with him," the tenacious NXT grappler concedes. "For him to break this barrier, he's paving the way for guys like myself." He adds,

"Daniel Bryan is smashing those boundaries, and now, more than ever, anything's possible for me and countless people like me."

Several moments after the impromptu Ring of Honor reunion, an anticipated "Yes!" chant serves as Daniel Bryan's entrance theme during his arrival at his Axxess signing. Among the first jubilant members of the "Yes!" Movement he meets is young Hunter. Despite his name, he's actually not pulling for the "other guy" at WrestleMania. He's one of the biggest little supporters Daniel Bryan has.

"He's the best wrestler ever," Hunter says after his encounter with the bearded star.

Danielle from Long Island, New York, shows off her special manicure for the Show of Shows with fingertips supporting the Shield, AJ Lee, and Daniel Bryan by way of a YES inscription on her thumb. There's also an eight-month-old baby girl in a Bryan goat-face top who can't help but lock her eyes on the Superstar's face up close.

"Signings are great," Bryan says. "It's an opportunity to meet the fans. We have great fans. They're pretty awesome. It's all about seeing the way that we touch people."

While Bryan scribbles out his autograph, Zayn prepares to compete in a live match at the center of Axxess, just ahead in the distance. If he has anything to say (or do) about it, the young NXT upstart may follow in his fellow Ring of Honor alumnus's footsteps and perch in his seat not too far from today.

I hadn't been doing much on TV once the story with the Bellas ended, but I was still United States Champion, and that gave me hope of being able to get on the card for WrestleMania XXVII. That said, I was delighted at Elimination Chamber 2011, the pay-per-view immediately before WrestleMania, when I found out the plan was for me to wrestle Sheamus on the biggest show of the year. We even had a writer assigned to us, Jen, who would help us craft our story in the six weeks leading up to the event.

Even though I was the U.S. Champion, Sheamus was a far bigger star than I was. He had already won the WWE Title by this point, and the previous year he'd wrestled Triple H at WrestleMania XXVI. For the 2011 edition, they actually asked Sheamus whom he'd like to wrestle, and the two top options were me and Rey Mysterio. Sheamus chose me. When he told me that, I chuckled and thanked him, but I also told him he'd probably made a mistake. If he elected to wrestle Rey, he would be guaranteed to be on 'Mania, because Rey was a veteran who'd earned his spot already, and WWE would feel almost obligated to put him on the card. If Sheamus wrestled me, there was no guarantee our match would make it. Sheamus didn't worry about it, though, because in his experience, when WWE told him something like this was going to happen, it did. My experience hadn't been like that, so from the very beginning I was skeptical, despite assurances from all sorts of people that we would get an opportunity to shine.

And at first it seemed like we might. When we started crafting our story for the show, we knew we weren't going to get a lot of time to build it. WrestleMania season is a notoriously hard time to get on TV, so we designed a simple story, and for the first several weeks, our ideas were actually being executed. We wrestled a short match where Sheamus lost by count-out after he hurt his ankle. The next week, we did a title match where Sheamus declared if he lost he would quit WWE. He won that match along with the championship, and from there, we were setting up my rematch to happen at WrestleMania.

Shortly after I lost the title to Sheamus, we were talking to Jen about the following week's plans when I asked, "What are the chances of us *actually* being on WrestleMania?" She said, "Oh, I think a good eighty percent." I took that as being a good thing. Sheamus, not so much. Until that moment, I don't think he even considered the possibility that we wouldn't be on WrestleMania.

The Monday before WrestleMania XXVII, Raw was at the Allstate Arena in Chicago, and there was a big talent meeting before the show to talk about the busy week ahead. We were all handed packets that had lists of the vital information we would need: hotel

and gym info, contact info, and the schedule of our appearances. It seemed like a normal meeting, until John Laurinaitis announced there had been a rehearsal added for some people on that coming Wednesday night. The rehearsal was for the preshow lumberjack match . . . between me and Sheamus. In front of all our fellow wrestlers, that was how we found out our match would take place, not on WrestleMania, but rather *prior* to the pay-per-view.

I turned and looked at Sheamus across the room, and he just buried his head in his hands. I was upset, but I'd kind of figured something like that might happen, especially because Miz told me a similar thing had happened to him in the past. What did make the pay-per-view was an Intercontinental Title match between Cody Rhodes and Rey Mysterio. Their build was similar to ours, and it was the same tier of match, but they made it onto the show and we didn't. I knew Sheamus should have chosen Rey.

After the meeting, Sheamus and I talked. We were both very angry, not only about the move to being on the preshow but also because they just announced it in the meeting without warning us. We were determined to go out there and show everybody up, preshow be damned. However, once we got to the rehearsal, the match changed again. Sheamus and I would only get to wrestle about three minutes before the lumberjack match got out of hand and it turned into a giant battle royal, with Great Khali winning. The whole thing was thrown together that week to give everybody a chance to work in front of the largest crowd of the year.

This was my first WrestleMania week as a real WWE Superstar, not as a Rookie from NXT, and it was filled with signings, media, and appearances. We were told not to say anything to the fans or media about our match being on the preshow. I was miserable all week, and it didn't help when people would tell me they were looking forward to our match or they thought Sheamus and I were going to steal the show. I knew they'd all be disappointed.

WrestleMania XXVII was held at the Georgia Dome in Atlanta, before seventy thousand people. It was the largest crowd I'd ever performed in front of, and afterward I didn't remember any of it. Shea-mus and I did the best we could in the three minutes we had, but by the end of the night, I'm sure not a single one of those people even remembered we were on the show.

After our match, I watched the rest of the show, yet I barely recall any of it, except thinking during the endless, horrible Michael Cole–Jerry Lawler match that surely they could have cut some time from that to get us on the pay-per-view, as we had advertised. But Wrestle-Mania is a spectacle, not a wrestling show, which is why Snooki of *Jersey Shore* fame was on the show and we weren't. As Regal explained to me when I signed with WWE, "Wrestling is what you did before this. Anything you get after is a bonus." Despite the advice, I sat there disheartened. It was one of two WrestleManias I spent watching the show with my eyes glazed over.

Several weeks after WrestleMania XXVII, WWE held what used to be its annual draft. Raw and SmackDown were completely separate crews, and there would be very little interaction between the two. If I were on Raw, very rarely would I wrestle somebody on SmackDown, and vice versa. Your brand also determined your schedule; the Raw crew worked Friday, Saturday, and Sunday live events, then did TV on Monday, whereas the SmackDown crew did live events on Saturday and Sunday, went to Raw on Monday if needed (which I seldom was), and then did the TV taping on Tuesday.

For the 2011 draft, I got moved from Raw to SmackDown, and I was thankful for the switch, because I'd hoped TV time would be easier to come by on SmackDown. On Raw I would be scheduled for a seven- or eight-minute match, and then somebody's interview would go over on time, cutting my match down to two or three minutes, if it still happened at all. Teddy and Sheamus were also drafted to SmackDown, so our riding crew would be able to stick together. Overall I was pretty optimistic.

It ended up being a great move. In my first SmackDown match, I wrestled Sheamus in a nearly ten-minute match. I lost, but I've always felt that if given time in my matches, I can get over, win or lose.

I just needed the time to have a good match, and I was getting it. Almost every week, I'd have ten minutes to go out and wrestle, and slowly—again, win or lose—I felt like I was winning over the fans.

The May pay-per-view was Over the Limit in Seattle on my birthday. Miz was the WWE Champion at this point after beating John Cena in the main event of WrestleMania. I pitched hard to do a title match with him at Over the Limit, with the concept of Miz, cocky and overbearing about being the champ, giving some scrub an opportunity to challenge him for the championship. I figured it would kind of be like the movie *Rocky*, especially being among my hometown crowd of Seattle and it being my birthday. That idea was shot down pretty quick. Instead, I did the preshow match against Drew McIntyre. Regardless of the fact that it was on the preshow, it was the first time I got a real hometown-hero, starlike reaction in Seattle—and the first time I'd ever gotten that kind of reaction in WWE.

Bryan and mom, Betty, before the 2014 WWE Hall of Fame Induction Ceremony

Being that it was a pay-per-view, Superstars from both Raw and SmackDown were there, including Bri, who wasn't drafted and had stayed on Raw. We weren't able to see each other very much, so the night before, we got a hotel in downtown Seattle and had a really nice, romantic dinner. After Over the Limit, Raw was in Oregon, and my mom's house was on the way from Seattle to Portland, so Bri followed me there, where my mom prepared a nice meal for us and made me a vegan birthday cake. She also made Bri one of her famous pumpkin cakes—my absolute favorite; Bri loved it and took the leftovers to Raw the next day for the other Divas. After the birthday dinner, Bri left for Portland and I stayed at my mom's because I wasn't needed for Raw, but as I went to bed, I felt truly lucky to have had such an amazing birthday.

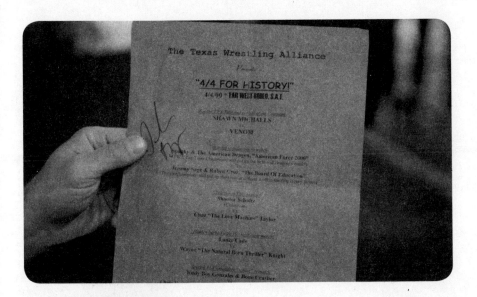

The Texas Wrestling Alliance

"4/4 FOR HISTORY!"
4/4/00 • FAR WEST RODEO, S.A.T.

SHAWN MICHAELS
VENOM

Spanky & The American Dragon, "American Force 2000"

Jeremy Sage & Ruben Cruz, "The Board Of Education"

Shooter Schultz

Chaz "The Love Machine" Taylor

Lance Cade
vs.
Wayne "The Natural Born Thriller" Knight

Rudy Boy Gonzales & Bone Crusher

17 TEXAS THROWBACK
SATURDAY, APRIL 5, 2014—10:39 A.M.

As the line of fans progresses, the man who could soon be the new WWE World Heavyweight Champion signs glossy 8x10s, posters, people (for real), shirts, replica titles, and even one-sheet programs from his past.

Trey Gonzalez from Oklahoma City totes a Texas Wrestling Alliance match card from ten years ago yesterday that features Bryan as the American Dragon competing as a pupil in Shawn Michaels's Academy. The throwback surprises Bryan as he autographs the heavily creased paper. Meanwhile, simultaneous to the signing, HBK participates in a live fan Q&A at Axxess. He's asked about the thirtieth edition of WrestleMania and the match he's most looking forward to seeing, a show stealer. He names Bryan's bout with the Game.

Soon afterward, the "Yes!" Man exits the event and settles into his vehicle from WrestleMania Axxess just outside the building's rear loading dock. Bryan uses the few minutes in transit back to his hotel to examine a few unexpected gifts from WWE fans at the event, as well as unwrap some other presents. He smiles when holding a handmade construction paper booklet with marker drawings of himself with purple hair. He's surprised by an early birthday card from another WWE Universe member,

several weeks before the date on May 22. Bryan is also absolutely moved by a gift-wrapped box that contains twin antibacterial towels for future hikes with his bride-to-be. It's a wedding present based on a comment Bryan recently made in an interview, and the thoughtfulness overwhelms him, particularly when reading the message inscribed on the card.

"Your love is an inspiration," writes Bibo Reyes.

The gesture is an inspiration to Bryan.

My first major opportunity to break through to the next level in WWE came in July 2011 at the Money in the Bank event in Chicago. There were two Money in the Bank matches, one for Raw and one for SmackDown, and the winner of each got a contract to compete for the main championship on their brand whenever they wanted, which usually meant when the champion was in a vulnerable position. No Money in the Bank winner had ever failed to become champion at this point, so it was a big deal.

Kane, Sheamus, Cody Rhodes, Wade Barrett, Sin Cara, Justin Gabriel, Heath Slater, and I were all involved in the match, which also included ladders, tables, and a briefcase. It's one of wrestling's more hazardous stipulation match types so we had a rehearsal the night before.

When we got to rehearsals, the most challenging element of putting the match together was WWE not knowing who they wanted to win. They knew Alberto Del Rio was going to win the Raw Money in the Bank, and they kind of wanted Barrett to win it on our side, but they worried the story of Wade winning would be too similar to Alberto's victory, so they were still considering me and Cody, too. Jamie Noble was one of the producers for the match, and he pushed hard for me to win it, just because it would make the story on each brand so different.

We arrived at the building the next day, and they still didn't know who the winner would be, so we planned out a scenario where it came down to Wade, Cody, and me, and once we found out the finish we would adjust from there. When the production meeting was finally over, I got the good news that I was winning, yet they *still* weren't a hundred percent sure that I was who they wanted. I was informed it still might change, so I didn't get my hopes up—especially since the last time I was in Chicago, we had the meeting where Sheamus and I found out we were on the WrestleMania preshow, and that memory was still strong in my mind.

There were eight men in the Money in the Bank ladder match, and that's *a lot* of moving parts when it comes to climbing up ten to fifteen feet on a ladder to grab a briefcase. Not only do you have to worry about safety, but there's also the concern of living up to the expectations of previous Money in the Bank matches, which have a history of being some of the wildest, craziest, most exciting matches in WWE history. And everyone has to play his part, which adds another level of stress. If someone gets hurt, not only do you feel bad for him, but it throws off everything else; the match can just fall apart. The same is true if someone forgets his part, which is why it was kind of amusing when Heath Slater was struggling to remember certain elements of the match. Right before we walked out, he said, "If I forget something we can just call it out there, right?" Immediately Kane, who had been in plenty of matches like this before, was like, "NOOOO!! We can't! That's why we had rehearsal, and that's why we all had to remember our spots. If something gets messed up, then it messes up everything else!" Heath mumbled in response, and I could tell he was worried.

I had my own concerns going into the match, first and foremost being that I'm terrified of heights. When I'm doing normal wrestling stuff, like going to the top rope, it's not a big deal because I'm used to it. As soon as you get me trying to maneuver around way up high on top of a ladder, I get pretty nervous. Apart from the height thing, I was also worried about actually getting the briefcase off the clip that keeps it hanging above the ring. We went through it a few times, and I was probably only 50/50 with getting the briefcase loose. Lastly, I was worried about the crowd reaction to my win. I had gained steam from where I was several months before, but in no

way was I a red-hot locomotive. I saw myself as someone the audience liked, but I was not sure they liked me enough to be ready for that kind of opportunity.

Luckily, everything I was concerned about went fine. When I went out in front of the sold-out crowd, my fear of heights disappeared. I also managed to unhook the briefcase, even though I didn't do it properly. At first I couldn't get it loose, so I just took the hook off as well, which clanged around when I celebrated with the briefcase. And finally the Chicago crowd reacted just fine. They were excited it was a good match, and they seemed happy I'd won. It all went so well that the worst part of the match for me was trying to get down off the ladder when it was over.

True to form, Heath did actually forget something; he kicked out the wrong ladder at the wrong time, and ended up having to

take a bump from the top rope to the floor off a much higher ladder than anticipated. Still, somehow no one was hurt, the fans liked the match, and I was now the holder of the all-important Money in the Bank contract.

In August, Bri and I had three days off, so we decided to take a vacation together to Yellowstone National Park. It was the first vacation of my adult life, and by this time I was thirty years old. We stayed in a small cabin outside the park, with just twenty feet between where we were and a beautiful river. We went horseback riding, whitewater rafting, and on a beautiful tour where we were just a few yards from a herd of bison. In the serenity of all this natural beauty, I realized I was in love.

Everything with Bri was going great, but wrestling . . . not so much. After I won Money in the Bank, it seemed like I was going to get a bit more TV time, and at first I did. My subsequent pay-per-view appearance was a singles match with Wade Barrett at SummerSlam—my first one-on-one since Survivor Series the year before. Even though I lost, we were given a decent amount of time, and I thought I was back on track.

I thought wrong.

I started being used less and less on SmackDown. For a while, I was having competitive 10-minute matches, but then it devolved into either losing every week in under five minutes or, even worse, not being on the show at all. There was a real down period where I wasn't on SmackDown for six weeks in a row. I talked to writers and pitched stories to get back on the program, but everything got shot down and met by a general indifference. When I left the independents, I knew I had to be prepared for situations like this in WWE. I had to focus on just coming in and doing my best—if something big happened, great; if not, I had to just keep a positive attitude and save my money. As it turns out, though, it wasn't much more money than I was making on the independents, and trying to have a good attitude is easier to say than do when you're really passionate about something yet feel you're not being given a chance. Having won Money in the Bank, I knew they would have to do some sort of story with me eventually, but whenever I asked about it, nobody seemed to have any answers, and it felt as if they just wanted to forget about it. I started to have a feeling that I would be the first person to try to cash in my guaranteed World Title match and lose, although that could have easily just been paranoia.

I felt very discouraged, and Cody Rhodes, who remembers my state at the time, refers to this period as a time when I was "Depressed Dan." The only thing that would bring me happiness was having a good match. Therefore, the saving grace for that entire period—and the thing I've always enjoyed about WWE—was being able to wrestle on the live events. Even though I wasn't doing anything on WWE programming, on the untelevised events, I could go out there and do whatever I wanted, and just wrestle to my heart's content.

But in late November, after what seemed like several long months doing nothing, I was injected into a story with Big Show and Mark Henry. Mark was the World Heavyweight Champion and was having a pretty awesome reign. They did a story where Big Show was trying to get me to invoke and "cash in" my Money in the Bank title match contract on Henry when he was down, but I wanted to wait until WrestleMania and be in the championship match on the biggest show of the year. Big Show kept urging me to do it, though, and right before I did, Mark Henry got up and gave me the World's Strongest Slam. This led to a series of matches with Mark and me, including a steel cage match in my first SmackDown main event. There was also a moment when I actually did go down, cash in the contract on Mark (who was already beaten up), and for a moment held the World Heavyweight Championship. However, it was announced I couldn't claim the title because Mark Henry "wasn't cleared to compete" due to an ankle injury, and the title was taken away.

All of this felt like I was just a prop to further the story of the two giants. I didn't mind, because I was being thrust into the main-event angle after doing nothing for so long. Plus, WWE didn't seem to have any idea about what they were going to do with the whole Money in the Bank situation for SmackDown. Then, shortly before the Tables, Ladders, and Chairs (TLC) pay-per-view on December 18, Mark got hurt. I hadn't been booked on the previous pay-per-views—and not just "not being on the show" type of not booked, but "not even being in the city, sitting at home" type of not booked. At the previous pay-per-view, Survivor Series, Mark wrestled Big Show, and the two big men did an incredible superplex off the top rope; when they landed with all of that weight, the ring collapsed. Both of them were down, and the fans were chanting for me to come out and cash in the contract, but I wasn't there. I was at home in Las Vegas. It was looking like I wouldn't be at WWE TLC either, but at the last minute, I got booked at a Kmart to do a signing with Kelly Kelly before the show.

It had only been earlier that week when Mark got injured, so WWE didn't have a lot of time to figure out what they wanted to do with the World Heavyweight Championship going forward. Henry was booked in another title match against Big Show that night, which was a chairs match, and there was a thought to just have the giant win it. After my signing, I came to the building, not expecting to be doing anything. I was just chatting and goofing around (at one point, I was browsing the Internet for the best paper airplane design, as I recall). It was relatively close to showtime, and well after ticketholders were allowed in the building, that a referee came by and told me Vince wanted to see me in his office. I walked in and saw both Big Show and Mark Henry sitting along with Vince, who invited me to have a seat as well. He started walking me through the plan: Big Show would win the match and the title, then Mark would lay out Big Show by hitting him with a DDT. As Mark was getting out of the ring, I would run down with a referee, cash in the Money in the Bank contract, and—without doing a single move—pin Big Show to become the new World Heavyweight Champion. I sat there waiting for the punch line or for Vince to tell me what the next swerve was going to be, but it never came. Then he stood up, extended his hand, and said, "Congratulations." I couldn't believe it. I stood up and thanked him, Big Show, and Mark Henry, and as I was walking out, Vince told me to make sure nobody knew.

Moments after the meeting, I put my gear on, with regular workout clothes over it. I figured it would look a little weird that I had my gear on that late in the night, but like when we did the surprise Nexus attack, I just told anyone who asked that I had to take some photos with my new gear. I didn't even tell Bri. She and I were sitting in the production office backstage watching the show, and shortly after Big Show and Mark Henry's match started, I excused myself to go to the bathroom. Bri did, too, and as soon as she went into the Divas' locker room, I headed straight toward Gorilla position, right before the curtain. I stood there with my workout clothes still on, until the match finished and Mark was about to deliver the DDT to

Big Show. I quickly took off my sweatshirt and my workout pants, and just as I did, my music hit. I bolted out from backstage with referee Scott Armstrong and did exactly what we had planned. Big Show was already on his back, so I didn't even need to roll him over. Within a matter of twenty seconds from exiting the curtain, I was the new World Heavyweight Champion. Vince's only direction for me after I won was to "celebrate like you won the Super Bowl." So I celebrated like my life depended on it. It wasn't like I had to fake it, either.

Bryan celebrates his first World Title in WWE, TLC, 2011

I never told Bri I was winning the title that night. After she went to the bathroom, I expected her to go back to the production office looking for me, but she didn't—at least in my version of the story. (Yet another time where we remember it differently, but since it's my book, I will tell it my way.) I remember Bri telling me that Alicia Fox came up to her and excitedly said, "Oh my gosh, I can't believe Bryan won the title and you didn't say anything!" Bri was like, "Bryan did what?!" and then rushed over to see me. She still argues that she saw me win, but like I said: my book.

That night in Baltimore, it felt like a real changing of the guard in WWE. CM Punk was the WWE Champion at the time and pulled all of WWE's title holders into a room to take a picture. Punk had the WWE Championship, I was World Heavyweight Champion, Kofi Kingston and Evan Bourne were WWE Tag Team Champions, Zack Ryder was the United States Champion, Cody Rhodes was Intercontinental Champion, and Beth Phoenix was the Divas Champion. We were all young and hungry, and it seemed like we would be the new group of stars who would take WWE into the future. That didn't end up being the case, but it sure felt like change had finally come to WWE after years of having the same guys at the top.

Despite being the new World Heavyweight Champion, I didn't see it as any sort of guarantee or even vindication. Just like winning Money in the Bank, it was more of a circumstantial thing, where I just happened to be the best option at that point. It was a far cry from Gabe calling me and telling me he wanted me to be "the Man," the guy they wanted to build the company around. But it didn't matter. It was an opportunity, if even for only a short time, to show them what I could do.

18 TIED UP AT THE MOMENT
SATURDAY, APRIL 5, 2014—5:11 P.M.

The lobby of the Roosevelt Hotel is starting to fill up with Superstars and Legends in evening wear as they prepare to head to the 2014 WWE Hall of Fame Ceremony. Several floors above, Daniel Bryan is slipping on his suit jacket and wrestling with his feelings about his tie. It's the color, really. To Bryan, it's a little too much on the purple side. To Brie, it's the perfect shade of blue for her fiancé tonight. (Hint: She bought it.) Mid-debate, the stunning Bella slides on her stiletto heels and convinces the "Yes!" Man to say just that to the neckwear. What's more important to Bryan is that tonight he will watch his childhood favorite join an exclusive grouping in the Hall.

"Other than WrestleMania itself, the thing I'm looking forward to the most is Ultimate Warrior's Hall of Fame speech," says Bryan of 'Mania week.

A late Saturday night arrival in New Orleans adds a guest to "Braniel's" Hall of Fame crew: Daniel Bryan's mom, Betty. A social worker from Aberdeen, Washington, the "Yes!" mom has traveled to the Big Easy for the definitive Daniel Bryan bout on the Grandest Stage of Them All. Tonight, she gets a glimpse into what may one day be in store for her son,

which is enshrinement in WWE's Hall of Fame. Overwhelmed and hum-
bled by the pleasantries of those she encounters, Betty beams as she joins
Bryan through crowds of Superstars, Legends, and more. The mom and son
(in a decidedly indigo tie), plus Brie and her family, head toward the bus
heading to the Smoothie King Center for a momentous night in the WWE
Universe.

Regardless of the circumstances, winning the World Heavyweight Championship was cool, just from an "I've been a wrestling fan my whole life, now look at this" perspective. I felt very fortunate because even though what we do is fiction and entertainment, standing out in front of thousands of people holding a giant championship that, in theory, signifies that you're the Man, the whole thing is pretty amazing.

Regal was really happy for me, but also told me to use being the champion as a way to develop a better relationship with Vince. Being the driving force in stories for SmackDown, it was important to know exactly what Vince wanted from me and to start getting comfortable going into Vince's office to get any questions I had answered.

Things may have been different when Vince was younger and on the road more with the talent, but nowadays, it's intimidating for the younger guys to go in and talk to him. I always imagined him sitting in his office as if it were some faraway castle tower, annoyed with any peons such as me that would knock on the door and want to talk. But that was just my mind going into fantasyland. The first time I knocked on his door after I became champion, he seemed genuinely happy to see me.

Once we started talking, I asked him what he wanted from me as World Heavyweight Champion. I had been a good guy since I started with WWE, but as a character, the way I cashed in the Money in the Bank contract was cheap and a little slimy, and lent itself to turning bad. I just needed to know which way he wanted me to take it.

Likely because me winning the title hadn't been the original plan, Vince wasn't sure, but his direction was to let my character take shape organically; we'd allow the fan reaction to determine which direction I would go in. The one thing he did want was for me to be the happiest guy in the world as champion; every time I went out, I had to treat it as if I had won the lottery. "In this instance, there's no such thing as too over-the-top," he said. You don't have to tell me twice.

That's how and why I started using a very simple yet emphatic word: Yes. I used the term as a way to show how happy I was to be World Heavyweight Champion, an idea I actually got from one of my favorite MMA fighters, Diego Sanchez. As he walked down to the Octagon for his fights, he'd hammer down his fist and with a serious, intense face, he'd yell "YES!" Apparently, for him it was about positivity, but I saw it as great showmanship and almost covertly annoying.

I started by occasionally "Yes!"-ing during my entrance, and then after I'd win a match, I'd scream "Yes!" again. From there it evolved rapidly, to the point where I was "Yes!"-ing the entire way down the ramp in celebration of being champion. I started pointing my ring fingers in the air as I did it, the gesture moving in sync with my yelling. I added a side trot in order to "Yes!" on the move. People started to see my overt enthusiasm as irritating. Also, I was put in a story where AJ Lee would valet me and I would be mean to her. It didn't take long for me to turn into a smarmy little asshole the fans wanted to see get beat up by monsters like Big Show and Mark Henry.

For the first time, I was given opening promo segments and main events on SmackDown. Week by week, the better I did, the more trust Vince put in me to go out and carry the stories. I'm not sure if he thought I could pull it off at first, but every week I'd go in to talk to him, and every week he would say how pleased he was with my performances, giving me suggestions here and there, as well as tips on how to evolve as a WWE Superstar.

I turned into this very beatable champion, and I'm not sure people expected me to walk in to WrestleMania XXVIII with the title—an aspect I truly I liked about my character because it added drama to the matches. On the pay-per-view before WrestleMania, for example, I defended the championship inside the Elimination

225

Chamber—a massive chain-link steel enclosure with glass pods containing opponents on each ring corner—against five other Superstars. The odds suggested any champion was in jeopardy, but especially me, given my beatable character. It came down to me and Santino Marella as the final two match participants, and even though Santino was predominantly a comedic character, people actually believed he could win the title. When he hit me with his signature move, the Cobra, a hilarious faux-ninja move where he pokes you with his hand closed outward like a duck, people went crazy and thought he was going to win it. If Daniel Bryan could do it, why couldn't Santino Marella? I ending up beating him and retaining the title, and the closing minutes of that match with Santino were my favorite part of my World Heavyweight Championship run.

The first time I noticed the audience "Yes!"-ing with me was a SmackDown we were filming in Seattle shortly after that Elimination Chamber 2012 pay-per-view in February. Despite doing an untelevised backstage interview designed to get the people in attendance to boo—something along the lines of "I love the city of Seattle [yay!] but I moved away because I hate the people [boo!]"—the crowd still cheered me when I came out because I'm from the area. When I turned to my left, I saw a large row of people, each and every one of them holding up a homemade YES! sign. And as I got closer to the ring, they started "Yes!"-ing when I did. Then the whole section started doing it, then half the crowd. It was infectious. Initially I thought these Seattle fans would be the only people to do it, because I'm their hometown guy. But after that aired, I started seeing more and more pockets of people throwing their arms in the air and yelling "Yes!" I thought it would fizzle out as soon as I lost the title. Boy, was I wrong.

When Sheamus won the 2012 Royal Rumble, I was positive he and I would be paired up at WrestleMania. A year after getting bumped to the preshow match, we were both looking at the match not only as an opportunity for redemption but as a chance to steal the show. We didn't care that John Cena was wrestling The Rock or that the Undertaker was taking on Triple H in a Hell in a Cell match. We were confident we would outperform them all and tear down the house. Unfortunately, we didn't have enough time to tear down much of anything.

I first heard our match might be shorter than we expected from Chris Jericho. I had anticipated Sheamus and I would get at least fifteen or twenty minutes of wrestling time because we were in the World Heavyweight Championship match, a really good spot on the card. A couple of weeks before the show, however, Jericho came up and asked me if we were having a really short match. I told him I didn't think so and explained that nobody had talked to me about time yet. Chris knows a lot. He regularly goes in and talks to Vince and is constantly in the writers' room working on what he's doing, and while doing so, he keeps his eyes and ears open. Chris told me he saw a match listing with times on it, and saw that we were only scheduled for eight minutes. I was blown away. With entrances down the long ramp and a championship introduction, that equated to about a three-minute match!

Arn Anderson was the producer for our 'Mania match, so I immediately went to him and asked him if he knew anything about what kind of time we'd have. He said he didn't know for sure, but he thought roughly twenty-five to thirty minutes, which, after entrances, would be right about what I figured. A week or so later, Arn found out the true plan and pulled me aside. He looked beside himself as he told me the bad news: AJ and I would kiss, distracting me, then Sheamus and I would have a one-move match at WrestleMania XXVIII.

I was instantly pissed off, and so was Sheamus. I started thinking it was a rib, or maybe just something to amuse Vince: Every year, put Bryan and Sheamus on WrestleMania, then pull the rug out from under them at the last minute. I thought they were doing it to fuck with us.

Sometimes my narcissistic side gets the better of me and I think everyone's out to get me. Looking back, my thinking almost seems foolish. I'm sure they weren't doing it to mess with us, or to rib us,

or to amuse Vince. I'm sure they thought it was a good idea, a memorable way to coronate Sheamus as the new World Heavyweight Champion, and a great way to kick off WrestleMania. Arn didn't seem to like it any more than Sheamus or I did, but he also tried to look at the positive, given we couldn't change it. Arn thought it might end up working well for me, a "chickenshit champion." He saw the quick finish as giving my character something to gripe about before demanding a rematch. It would keep me in the main event picture another month, and another month in main events would put more equity in my character. Try as he might, it was hard to change my negative slant on the whole situation. Prolonging my main event run another month paled in comparison to the opportunity to have a killer WrestleMania match with a live audience of nearly eighty thousand people. Also, I didn't know if I'd ever be in a position to have a match like this again—a championship match against a friend, where we *knew* we'd have a great match. I needed to take my WrestleMania moment when I could get it.

I was bitter, and so was Sheamus, but he was also worried. He felt like there might be a backlash from the fans for the outcome and that they might turn on him. We had the main program on Smack-Down for the six weeks leading into WrestleMania, and it felt like fans were looking forward to the match. Wrestling in 2012 was different than it was in 1988, when Ultimate Warrior ran out and did essentially the same thing to the Honky Tonk Man. Wrestling had changed, and what wrestling fans wanted had changed. If they're looking forward to a match, sure, they want their guy to win. But rarely do they want to see it happen in under a minute.

The title bout that Sunday, April 1, in Sun Life Stadium is kind of a blur to me. In fact, the whole day is kind of a blur. The only thing I really remember is going down the ramp. I knew I wasn't doing anything in the match, so I put everything into "Yes!"-ing my way down the long ramp—and looked really good doing it with my new robe and gear. (A quick side note: I had this awesome gear made for Wrestle-Mania in anticipation of my big match. When the gear was delivered to me the week before the show, I put it on and it looked great—by far the nicest-looking gear I'd ever had. I've never worn it since, and not because of the bad memories, but because there were hard sequins on the kickpads. Had Sheamus and I *actually* had a match with me wearing those kickpads, every kick would have cut him to shreds.)

Everything went as planned: the kiss, then I turned around to get kicked in the face and pinned. Eighteen seconds was all it took. And it sounded like the crowd liked it, as they cheered because they couldn't believe what they'd just seen. Despite the audience's apparent enjoyment, I was discouraged afterward and thought WWE treating me like this would make it difficult to rebound back into the main event. Shows what I know. In hindsight, if we'd gone out and had a really good fifteen-minute match, I'm sure people would have liked it, but in terms of my career, it would have never had the same impact of the eighteen-second loss.

It turned out I wasn't the only one pissed about that eighteen-second loss. A bunch of guys came up to me backstage and said they couldn't believe the match. The funniest was the Great Khali, whose English is sometimes hard to understand. It wasn't this time. "Whuh happen, man? Thass bullshit, bruddah."

More importantly, the fans were angry. The people who attend WrestleMania travel from all over the world, and they are pretty hardcore into wrestling. If they don't like something, they'll let you know. The rest of the show, fans would randomly break out into "Yes!" chants or "Daniel Bryan!" chants. I didn't really notice because I wasn't paying much attention to the rest of the show, but the following night, the chants were impossible to ignore.

The night after WrestleMania at Miami's AmericanAirlines Arena, my only appearance on Raw was in a backstage interview with Matt Striker where I didn't say anything. That was it. I was only on the screen for about fifteen seconds. Still, somehow it became Daniel Bryan night. The Rock had an interview in the opening segment of the show, and throughout the whole thing there were *loud* "Yes!" chants. The Rock acknowledged it, and for a split second, I thought

he was going to use it and make it his own new thing. He's so witty and quick on his feet that I'm sure he could have done it. But he didn't. In fact, after the interview, on his way out he stopped and said to me, "Hey, man, the crowd is *really* hot for you out there."

At first I didn't quite understand what was going on with all the chants, and I assumed they would eventually die down. They didn't. The longer the show went on, the more it happened, and when Sheamus—the new World Heavyweight Champion—came out, they booed him mercilessly. I felt bad for him, because it wasn't his fault. "Daniel Bryan!" and "Yes!" rang out through the arena the entire night, even though I wasn't on the show.

Immediately after Raw went off the air, I performed in an untelevised six-man tag match—Sheamus, Big Show, and Randy Orton against me, Cody Rhodes, and Kane—and people were very, very excited to see me. Each time I got in, they cheered and "Yes!"-ed with every kick I did. Anytime I got hit, they yelled, "No!" and they booed when I tagged out of the match. It was crazy. Since I'd been in WWE, never had I felt like I was the guy the entire arena wanted to see. The finish was Sheamus hitting me in the face with his boot again and pinning me, and the crowd went crazy booing.

Sheamus, Randy, and Big Show semi-rushed to the back, and so did Cody and Kane, but I stayed out there. The crowd was giving me a great reception as I got to my feet, so I asked for a microphone, which the ringside production guy seemed hesitant to give to me, though he eventually did. I thanked the crowd for turning what had been the worst night of my career into something memorable and special. In a less important but mildly amusing addition to this story, I had been bothering the WWE merchandise guys on the road for about two months to make me a "Yes!" shirt. They tried to push it through, but someone in corporate thought it would never sell. Halfway through Raw, one of them told me if the chanting kept up, I had a lot better chance of getting the shirt made. Before they even told me they were going to make the shirt, I announced to the live crowd in my speech that thanks to them I was also getting a new shirt made. The "Yes!" shirts were available for sale the very next week.

Not only that, but most importantly, the crowd's reaction changed the direction WWE was headed. They really had no plan for what they were going to do with me, and they were going to put Sheamus in a story with Alberto Del Rio. But WWE couldn't ignore the people, and they extended my story with Sheamus for another month, keeping me in the main event picture.

I had a great time working with Sheamus. We did the two-week European tour shortly after WrestleMania, and we main-evented every show. The crowd reactions were a trip. Some nights they'd be intensely behind Sheamus; other nights the crowds were more like the one at Raw after 'Mania and were firmly behind me. Either way, we had great matches every night, and every night we did something different based on the audience's response.

That month, we did another World Heavyweight Championship match at the Extreme Rules pay-per-view, and we were given the time that we thought we should have had at WrestleMania. It was a two-out-of-three-falls match in front of a hot Chicago crowd, and though it was overshadowed by the excellent Brock Lesnar–John Cena main event, it's still one of my favorite matches in WWE.

After the Sheamus story played out, I wasn't sure what was next. I was in a weird position where I was a very popular bad guy. The fans kept cheering for me and chanting "Yes!" which made it a challenge for whichever good guy I was wrestling. That's why when WWE moved me into a story with CM Punk, I thought it was perfect.

I first met Punk in 2002 at a sixteen-man tournament called the Jersey J Cup. I'd heard about him and Colt Cabana because the two of them were tearing up the Midwest independent scene, but had yet to meet either of them. At the show, we exchanged a passing hello, but there were several different locker rooms, and Punk was changing in a different one than I was, so we never really got a chance to chat. All of a sudden, after his second-round match with Reckless Youth, I saw both Punk and Cabana rushing out of the building

in the middle of the show. It turned out that Punk had fractured his skull during the match and had to head to the hospital immediately. Fractured skulls, kids: That's one of the many reasons you don't try this stuff at home.

Punk later became a very important part of Ring of Honor, too. The company was in the doldrums after a scandal in 2004 involving owner Rob Feinstein, but a three-match rivalry between Punk and Samoa Joe that created great DVD sales almost single-handedly lifted ROH out of its funk. Punk and I did a lot of the same shows, but for some reason we didn't wrestle very much on the independents, though when we did, it was fun. We once wrestled for Full Impact Pro in Florida for nearly forty-five minutes in front of fewer than thirty people. That's why it was all the more special when we got to face each other several times on pay-per-view for the WWE Championship.

CM Punk wasn't just the perfect opponent because we'd known each other for so long. The hardcore fans sometimes turn against people they perceive to be pushed too hard by WWE, like what happened with Sheamus after WrestleMania. But Punk wasn't one of WWE's chosen ones. He had climbed his way to the top by consistently being the most entertaining person on the show with both his wrestling and his interviews. The same type of fans who were cheering for me liked cheering for him even more. When you're trying to be a bad guy, you absolutely need that.

At the time, Punk was in a strange position as well. Most of the top bad guys on the show were positioned to face John Cena, like Brock Lesnar was. Then, after John beat them, somewhere down the line, they'd wrestle Punk after they'd already lost momentum. Even though I'd lost to Sheamus, I was getting stronger and stronger reactions from the crowd and seemed to be coming in on an upswing, so I was a good fit and even better opponent for Punk at the time. WWE was comfortable putting us in championship matches on the pay-per-views but didn't think we could carry the main event position. Our first title match, for example, was at Over the Limit 2012;

we had a great match, but the show was main-evented by John Cena versus John Laurinaitis.

We were, however, entrusted with being the main event at non-televised live events—the first of which actually turned into a disaster. Prior to the match, I addressed the crowd and did my best to get them to boo me, but my promo just ended up getting goofy. Punk did a goofy bit after that, and though none of it was bad, our main event match was a street fight. We made the mistake of taking comedy too far, and it was impossible for people to get into the violence of this match. Unfortunately, we were never able to get them back. Afterward, John Cena asked me what I thought of my match with Punk, and I admitted we didn't get the reaction we needed. He responded, "That's right. That was not a main event." And he was a hundred percent correct. The crowd came to be entertained, and they enjoyed some of the comedic elements, but it took them away from the purpose of the match. I've always been confident in my ability to regain control of matches when they seem to be flying off the handle, but I'd let it go too far, and that was not a good thing, especially as a relatively new main event player.

Because our match was so bad, the next evening, Punk and I moved to the spot before intermission and Cena's match slid into the main event instead. Punk was furious. He knew we didn't have a good match, but also knew we could fix it. He fought for us to be in the main event, and he got it. We didn't do any goofing around that night and focused exclusively on tearing down the house, and we did. From then on, he and I were in the main event at the live events.

My last match with Punk was a no-disqualification WWE Championship match at the Money in the Bank 2012 pay-per-view event. We had what I thought was a really good match, but that's not what I remember most about it. When I found out about how short my WrestleMania match was going to be a few months earlier, I anticipated a need to change my character. I wanted to become unhinged by the loss and move toward a more crazy, militant, revolutionary type—like a crazy Che Guevara thing. So I talked to my friend Jill

Thompson, a comic artist , and she created this awesome gear that would match this mentality. It included a new logo with a "DB" placed within an anarchy symbol and ripped into the back of a green military jacket. Maroon paint came out of those rips and out of torn kickpads, creating an image of the gear bleeding. I loved it, but since the crowd changed everything, it never felt like the right moment to bust out the new gear. I thought a no-disqualification match might be the right moment.

I knew people within WWE wouldn't like the gear. It was too much of a departure from what I'd been wearing before. So I hid

the jacket all day and wore shorts over my trunks until right before I went out. (Keep in mind, this is about as rebellious as I get, wearing unapproved gear.) I passed through the curtain into the arena, and when I got to the ring, referee Chad Patton leaned in and told me to take the jacket off. I wasn't quite sure I heard him correctly, so I asked, "What?" Chad told me Vince himself had directed him to tell me, "Take that jacket off!" I did as I was told. Afterward, I felt bad because our producer Dean Malenko

Bryan's sole night in the "bleeding" logo ring jacket, 2012

was the one who really got yelled at for the whole thing, and he didn't even know about it. And, unfortunately, I've never been able to wear the gear since.

That was the last televised match I ever had against Punk. You can never say never, but I suspect I'll never get to wrestle him again. For some reason, I always thought that the two of us would someday have a WrestleMania match against each other, and it would be a modern version of the Bret Hart–Shawn Michaels 'Mania match that I loved when I was in high school. Some things just aren't meant to be.

Around the time the "Yes!" chants really started taking off, Bri and I decided to move in together, which stemmed from Bri and Nicole departing WWE in April of 2012. Their contracts were expiring, and they became frustrated when the writers told them they had run out of story ideas for twins. Bri and Nicole wanted to wrestle and be in good stories, not just be eye candy. I encouraged Bri to do what she needed to do to make her happy, but her leaving WWE put our relationship in a bit of a pickle. Since she was living in New York City and I was living in Las Vegas, we either had to accept that we would barely see each other, in which case our relationship would slowly dissipate, or we could take the next step and move in together. We, obviously, chose the latter and moved to Mission Bay in San Diego in a little apartment a couple of blocks away from the beach.

Initially it was very hard on me not seeing Bri on the road. I had gotten used to her being there with me in hotels and on long drives. She always makes a point to go to fun restaurants and do touristy stuff when she has a chance—stuff that makes life on the road a little bit more enjoyable. It was hard to convince the guys to do that kind of thing, and eventually I gave up.

That said, coming home to Bri in San Diego was wonderful. She's a bit obsessive when it comes to cleanliness, so our place was always spotless. She's a great cook, so there was always good, healthy food when I came home. With her doing all the housework, my days off became a true joy; we'd ride bikes together on the beach, go to the farmers' markets, and really, truly relax. You need that when you're on the road as much as we are. Most importantly, it allowed us to spend more time together in a nonwork environment, which made our relationship healthier.

19 "HELL" OF FAME
SATURDAY, APRIL 5, 2014—7:34 P.M.

Couples congregate backstage at a small cloaked booth with pictures plastered all over its exterior. A special WrestleMania photo booth gives all Hall of Fame guests the chance to snap four quick pics to commemorate this night to remember and bring home something for the front of their fridges. "Braniel" keeps the mood light with peace sign poses (Brie) and feigned mean mugs (Bryan), then takes the opportunity for a sweet lip connection. The couple collects their print, then gets prompted to the lineup for their arena entrance. But first, a certain seven-footer seeks his own photo-taking fun with his enemy-turned-tag-team-partner-turned-enemy. Unmasked and thus channeling a good deal less of his "Big Red Monster" side, Kane cuddles up with Bryan in a seat too small for the Superstars. The unlikely allies and real-life buddies pose for posterity—which just happens to be the foundation of their friendship.

After falling out of the WWE Title picture when my story with Punk was over, I was concerned about what was next. In an effort to be more of a bad guy, I stopped saying "Yes!" and told the fans to stop saying it as well. Of course they didn't, so I started saying "No!"

when the fans would say "Yes!" and I pretended the whole thing drove me crazy.

My music would hit, everyone would start "Yes!"-ing, and I would run out and make giant motions with my hands, screaming "No!" It was a lot of fun, actually, and a big part of the fun was getting in screaming matches with fans at ringside, where we'd be going back and forth with the "Yes!" and the "No!" These bursts of anger changed my character entirely and made me more entertaining, something I needed since I was no longer in the main event scene.

I soon found out that the plan for SummerSlam 2012 was for me to do a match with celebrity Charlie Sheen. He was going through a very public mental breakdown at the time, and somehow WWE brokered a deal for him to perform against me. He taped a couple of videos for Raw insulting me, and even though it was a goofy match to be in, it would have put me in one of the top matches at SummerSlam. Unfortunately, whoever brokered the Sheen deal never got him to sign any sort of contract to do the event, and in typical Charlie Sheen fashion, he bailed. What came about as a result ended up being the most fun period of time I've had with WWE.

During my story with Punk, WWE interjected veteran monster Kane, and we ended up doing a triple-threat match for the title in June at No Way Out; we ran the same triple-threat match on live events for a month or two afterward as well. This made Kane an easy person to start a story with on short notice heading into Summer-Slam, where I faced and beat him with a small package. At the time, I was doing my damnedest to become "Mr. Small Package"—a moniker I coined on the independents after claiming to have the "inescapable small package"—but it never caught on in WWE. Still, I used my flash win over Kane to get him more and more aggravated with me.

More important than our match at SummerSlam was a series of vignettes—filmed before SummerSlam, though they aired several weeks after the event—involving the two of us taking "anger management" classes, which was maybe not so ironically the name of

Charlie Sheen's television sitcom. We spent all day doing the shoot, and as we were filming the segments, I thought they would be rotten.

It was the first time I had done something with WWE that was filmed movie-style, where we shot the scene a few sentences at a time from a ton of different angles. Kane and I drew "anger collages," did a "trust fall," and essentially mimicked all the stereotypes you would think of about an anger management class. Although we thought they were awful when we filmed them, after they were put together, they turned out really well, and the fans liked them. Part of it was the entertaining dynamic between me, outrageously crazy and angry, and Kane, in his mask playing the more lucid, straightforward one. The funniest bit to me was Kane dryly recounting all the horrible things his character had done in the past, like electrocuting a man's testicles.

What also made the series work was "Dr. Shelby," an acting/drama teacher who played our therapist and was amazing in the role. He started off the vignettes as a therapist with infinite patience who saw the good side in everything, but just when Kane and I looked to have a "breakthrough," we instead started fighting, causing Dr. Shelby to lose it and throw the best fit ever. He was only supposed to be a one-time character, but he was so good that WWE kept bringing him back to shoot stuff with us on Raw. The only reason we eventually stopped using him was because he had a limited number of days off he could use as a teacher.

The vignettes turned Kane and me into a comedy duo of sorts. After they aired over the span of several weeks, the two of us were put in one of the weirdest segments I've ever been a part of. Occasionally on Raw, WWE gives the fans the power to vote on what they want to see. Usually it's choosing somebody's opponent or tag team partner, but in our case it was entirely different. The fans got to choose whether Kane and I would A) wrestle each other, B) team up together, or C) hug it out. As I walked to the ring, I didn't know which one the fans had voted for, so I had to prepare for each. Resoundingly, the fans voted for us to hug it out.

I was a little worried about that one option because we had a ten-minute segment to fill. How on earth were we going to fill a ten-minute segment hugging each other? I'm not quite sure how we did it, but not only did we fill the time, we went three minutes over. We stood there in the middle of the ring and made several attempts to hug each other. We just couldn't quite do it. The fans live in Chicago loved it and chanted, "Hug it out! Hug it out!" It was crazy. We were two grown men trying to hug each other not only in front of a packed arena but in front of millions of people on TV; one of us was in a full spandex leotard with a mask, and the other was in trunks as small as underwear and a T-shirt. When we finally did hug, the place went nuts. Of course we then started fighting—because, after all, it *is* pro wrestling—but when we walked back through the curtain, Vince was thrilled with it. Despite being worried the whole thing would bomb, I loved the segment, too. The "Hug it out!" chants followed us the entire time Kane and I teamed together.

WWE decided to do another fan vote to choose our name as a tag team, which is one time I wish they wouldn't have left a decision in the hands of the fans. The live interactive fan polls are, by nature, unpredictable. You can guess what the fans are going to want, but often you guess wrong. A good example of that was the night of the Nexus attack: They used an online poll to see who would wrestle John Cena, with the options being Rey Mysterio, Jack Swagger, and CM Punk. They thought it would be Rey because of his popularity, but the fans actually voted for Punk. As a performer, given you don't know about the results until the last minute, it can make things very challenging.

Kane and I didn't want a fan poll to determine our team name. We really liked the name Team Friendship and had already come up with a few ideas for awesome T-shirts, which included cartoon drawings of each of us with clouds and rainbows. I'm sure it would have been a real winner, but we never got to find out. In a poll between Team Friendship, Team Teamwork (a name I actually used on the independents when I teamed with Austin Aries and suggested as a throwaway option here, knowing fans wouldn't vote for it), and Team Hell No, the WWE Universe picked Team Hell No as the winner with 59 percent of the vote. I get why fans voted for it; Kane was supposedly a demon from hell, and I said "No!" a lot, so it would seem like a good fit. But from a merchandising perspective, we were a kid-friendly team, and very few parents will allow their kids to wear shirts that say "hell" on them. Sure enough, though we were a popular team, our shirts never sold as well as they should have, and I blame it on the name. Plus, how fun is "Team Friendship"?

Shortly after we started teaming, Kane and I won the WWE Tag Team Championship from R-Truth (whom I've known since he was thirty years old) and Kofi Kingston. At first we were just a comedy team who would argue a lot, and the idea was to break us up and have us feud shortly thereafter. Instead, since we clicked so well, we ended up teaming up for the next nine months. During that time I got to know Kane a lot better, but it was a slow process. Kane's real name is Glenn, and I'll refer to him as such from now on, because calling him Kane now feels really weird. Glenn is someone who is almost universally respected in the locker room. He debuted as the Undertaker's evil younger brother Kane in 1997, though he wrestled previously in WWE as the "fake" Diesel doppelganger of the original character portrayed by Kevin Nash, and Isaac Yankem even before that. I graduated from high school in 1999, so it was my junior year when Kane first appeared in WWE, and a veteran like Glenn could be intimidating to young new guys coming in, like me. He's also relatively quiet except with his closer friends, so I didn't get to know him very well until we started working together. Once we did, though, I was able to see a whole different side to him.

The two of us are a pretty absurd duo, and the first time we really started joking around was over a pretty absurd premise. I was reading a book by Mantak Chia called *Awaken Healing Energy Through the Tao: The Taoist Secret of Circulating Internal Power*. It's a long story, but I don't sleep well, and at the time I really lacked energy. I could feel it catching up to me in my body, so I was reading this book that

talked about taking your sexual energy up your chakras and then back down, circulating the energy to help you heal and be more vibrant. It's a very Eastern way of thinking. In order for it to work, you have to stop ejaculating, which, as you can imagine, makes most people stop reading right away. But not me; I plowed through the information, some of it interesting and some of it ridiculous. I was showing the book to someone in the locker room when Glenn came in, and we got him involved in the discussion. At first he was put off by the conversation entirely, but soon he started to enjoy the ridiculousness of it. He grabbed the book and started thumbing through it, then immediately stopped at a little drawing of a naked man lying down and a sun, along with an arrow that went from the sun to the man's perineum (otherwise known as the "taint"). The suggestion was essentially that to increase your sexual energy and, therefore, overall energy, you should expose your perineum to the sun. It was the most outlandish idea Glenn had heard in a long time, but for some reason he couldn't stop talking about it. And neither could I. The first bond I formed with this towering man who had participated in some of the most twisted scenes in WWE history was based on the idea of us tanning our taints.

Another time, in Spokane, Washington, there was a separate coach's office in the locker room. As the senior member of the locker room, Glenn claimed it and had his own little space. That day, for whatever reason, Cesaro and I had gotten the Petula Clark song "Downtown" stuck in our heads. While Glenn was sitting in his office, I blasted the song on my phone, tossed it into the office, and immediately closed the door. I hid underneath the window and slowly peeked my head up to watch as he picked up the phone, stared at it for a long time, confused, then looked up to see my stupid grin peering at him through the window. He shook his head in disgust. I had "Downtowned" him.

After our tag match on the show, I was the only person in the locker room. Earlier, I'd been ribbing Cesaro by stealing and hiding his chair every time he left the room, which would force him to go find a new chair. I decided to use all of those chairs to form a wall over six feet high in the middle of Glenn's office, creating an enormous barrier that separated his bags from the entrance. I turned off the lights to the office, slid my phone back in with "Downtown" blaring on repeat, and waited.

When Glenn got back to the dressing room, he looked a little confused when he saw that the lights were off. As he stepped through the door and turned the lights on, he saw the work I had done. This whole thing could have gone very wrong; Glenn was a veteran, and someone of his status isn't necessarily a person you should rib. But I didn't think about that before I started. When Glenn saw the chair wall, I saw a flash of anger cross his face. He dropped his head, looked at the phone (still playing "Downtown"), and then just shook his head. I popped out with a big "I gotcha, Glenn!" thinking I was the funniest man alive. At first he didn't think it was funny at all, but when he realized how much effort it took for me to build all the chairs so high, he came around and laughed at the ridiculousness of my hard work. Although it could have easily gone the other way, that was the moment when our bond became closer, from tag partners to friends.

The first several months of us teaming together was almost exclusively comedy stuff, the two of us being an odd couple who couldn't stand each other yet would ultimately be successful. Because I'd done some comedic stuff throughout my career, like at Butlins with All Star Wrestling and places like Pro Wrestling Guerrilla in Los Angeles, I felt very comfortable in the role and enjoyed it more and more by the week. I was actually grateful for all that time spent in England developing my humorous style because it gave me experience and really helped me embrace this new side of my character in WWE.

But we weren't always comedians. Kane and I got to do some really intense matches against the Shield, including the trio's WWE debut match: a Tables, Ladders, and Chairs match in which Glenn and I teamed with The Ryback. I also had my first good WrestleMania experience alongside Glenn in 2013. Our match against Dolph Ziggler and Big E was only a little over six minutes, but we really

entertained the fans. The entire MetLife Stadium was chanting "Yes!" at the end of it, and I was happy because I got to share that moment with Glenn.

On the European tour after WrestleMania 29, I teamed with the Brothers of Destruction, Glenn, and his storyline brother, the Under-taker, against the Shield. This was my first time being in the ring with the Undertaker, a wrestling legend I'd been watching since I was a kid. He is one of the most respected men in our industry because of his toughness, wrestling intelligence, and locker room leadership. It's weird for me to say this, because I normally don't get like this, but I really wanted to impress him.

Our generation of wrestlers has a reputation among the veterans of "not knowing how to work"—and that especially holds true for independent wrestlers, which, despite having been on the WWE roster for over three years, I still considered myself to be. I felt like I had to prove otherwise. That night, the Shield did a live event some-where else in England and took a helicopter to our building after their match. They got straight off the chopper and went directly to the ring to wrestle us. (Ironically, Shield's Dean Ambrose was the guy I did that with on the independents that one winter night, although I wasn't in a helicopter.) None of them had wrestled Undertaker before, but they were unfazed while doing their thing inside the ring. Ambrose, Seth Rollins, and Roman Reigns were wrestling machines that night, and they made us look like a million dollars. We had a great match, and the crowd was on fire for the entire thing.

Prior to the match, Vince told me he'd pay me several thousand dollars if I could get Undertaker to hug me. After we went off the air, I tried my damnedest. I grabbed the microphone and asked the crowd if they wanted to see me and the Undertaker "hug it out," and they all exploded with "Yes!" in response. As soon as I got the mic, though, 'Taker started moving toward the back, and even with the crowd reaction and me chasing him, he still escaped without me giving him that hug.

After the show I thanked Undertaker and told him it was a really cool experience teaming with him that night. He seemed physically sore but happy as he thanked me in return, then told me he thought I'd been doing a great job and he enjoyed watching me work. It was a really nice compliment coming from somebody like 'Taker.

With a WWE Tag Team Championship reign that lasted 245 days, Glenn and I finally lost the titles to Shield members Seth Rollins and Roman Reigns at the Extreme Rules pay-per-view in May 2013. We teamed for almost another month after that, but we ultimately "broke up," pretty much as if we were a couple. The period I spent with Glenn as Team Hell No was one of the most fun times of my career. The live events, the backstage skits, videos for the WWE app, photo shoots for *WWE Magazine*—all of it was fun. We even had a good time doing early morning media where I'd make outlandish claims about him being a Communist while he would tell everyone about my desire to have a composting toilet. I'm not sure we sold a single ticket, which is the purpose of the whole thing, but we had a good time. Not only that, but our partnership was a great learning experience for me as well, because throughout Glenn's long, successful career, he's seen what works and what doesn't.

He's one of the smartest people I've met in wrestling. He's turned me on to a bunch of his Libertarian craziness as well, which is an entirely different book, but I have to say that knowing him has made my life better.

One of the biggest compliments I've ever been paid was when Glenn told me that our teaming up was some of the most fun *he'd* had in his entire career as well, which says a lot. When he said that to me, I had to try really hard not to get too emotional. I responded by telling him I was going outside to tan my taint.

20 FAME AND FAMILY
SATURDAY, APRIL 5, 2014—8:42 P.M.

The front row alone at the WWE Hall of Fame Ceremony seats Hulk Hogan, "Stone Cold" Steve Austin, and John Cena. It's uncanny. Sharing that row is an individual whom many believe has the potential to be a star of similar proportion, Daniel Bryan.

It's not impossible to think that one day, years from now, Bryan may be among those distinctly honored at such an event. Yet the many matches and moments ahead—in the ring or otherwise—are not part of his present thoughts.

"I give very little thought to the future," he admits. "Even in wrestling, I've never really had these long-term plans. It's always been an incremental process, one thing after the next, doing things I'm inspired to do along the way."

Bryan elaborates, "I have loved my career. I know that this—wrestl... is something I love, but I also know it's not the only part that th... love in life. I guess it's my prayer to the universe to let me know... time to stop wrestling, because if it's left to me, I'll do it u... past when I should.

"Realistically, it'll either be children—two, ideally—...

tells me it's time that I will finally take my step back," he confesses. "When Bri and I are both done, we'd like to just disappear—not from the planet, just from the spotlight. It'll be just us and our family, living on a self-sufficient farm, if possible. I just want my place at the end of the world where my family can be safe."

In the present, beside him, the "Braniel" families watch intently as Mr. T gets a "Yes!" chant for so profoundly expressing his love for his momma. Bryan's mom subtly nudges him from his right side to acknowledge the crowd reaction and Mr. T's words for his mother. Yet another wave of "Yes!"-ing begins during "the most anticipated speech in the history of sports-entertainment," delivered by an icon who long ago widened the eyes of Bryan as a boy: the Ultimate Warrior.

The potent words selected by Warrior surely make an impression on those who isolate the spirit of the message. On the eve of WrestleMania 30, tonight has been a celebration of countless successes—from Warrior to fellow inductee Jake "the Snake" Roberts. In twenty-four hours, Daniel Bryan's quest for unparalleled success will continue beyond WrestleMania 30. The variable, however, will be whether or not he'll be taking two large golden prizes on the journey with him.

As the 2014 WWE Hall of Fame Ceremony concludes, the aspiring challenger and company—most notably, his mom, who's enjoying this rare firsthand experience at a WWE event—regroup with Brie Bella, who's spent the evening escorting the honorees. A body-to-body crowd of Superstars, Divas, friends, and family members like Betty Danielson marches ahead, with less than thirty minutes before WrestleMania Sunday is officially upon the WWE Universe.

In March 2013, Bri and Nicole came back to WWE after a ten-month break, and having Bri back on the road was fantastic. As traveling performers, we get to do and see a lot of incredible things. can tell people the stories, but it's not the same as a loved one there with us, living through the experience together. If s and I do something awesome, it's fun in that moment, but l Bri about it, it's just a story, not a shared experience. On the flip side, with her being back on the road, we have been able to do things we'll remember for the rest of our lives. Bri also breaks me out of the mold of airport, gym, show, sleep, and she is really good about forcing me to do fun stuff.

For example, I've been to Paris probably fifteen times, but never once had I seen the city's most famous attraction, the Eiffel Tower. On the April European tour after she came back, we did a show in Paris where we flew in that afternoon, had about an hour at the show, then got back to the hotel after the show around 11 P.M. and had another flight early the next morning. Normally I would've just gone to sleep, but Bri insisted we go out. Not only did I finally see the Eiffel Tower, but I got to see it just during the light show that happens immediately before they turn the lights off for the night. We also "locked our love" on the Lovers' Bridge and had a nice romantic dinner afterward. I was exhausted, but these are memories I'll never forget, and I wouldn't have done any of it without Bri there.

Bri coming back was also helpful in enduring all the frustrations that come with being in WWE. Before she took time off, she was there for the two Sheamus WrestleManias, and her support was invaluable. Likewise, when she came back, Bri and Nicole were promised a match at WrestleMania. Their match—the Bellas teaming up with Cody Rhodes and Damien Sandow to face the Funkadactyls (Naomi and Cameron), Brodus Clay, and Tensai—was scheduled to follow the CM Punk–Undertaker match, which went significantly over its allotted time. As a result, Bri's match got cut right at the very last minute. Her situation was more heartbreaking than either of my 'Mania fiascos because at least I knew ahead of time. She was in her gear, pumped up and ready to go out for the biggest show of the year, then never even got to walk out. In brutal situations like that, having someone who understands to comfort you is so important. I suppose I need more "comforting" than Bri typically does. She just gets mad as shit.

Bri's return to WWE and the road did, however, present one problem. A couple of months after we moved in together in San Diego,

we decided to get a dog. We debated back and forth on what type to get; I really wanted something that would protect her when I was gone, but the apartment we lived in was relatively small. I thought a beagle would be good because of their loud howls, the exact reason why Bri was nervous to get one in our apartment complex. Suddenly Bri started to really like French bulldogs, and when she found a picture online of a little white French bulldog puppy, she told me it was the one. Bri was so adamant about it and the puppy was so cute, I said yes without hesitation. Shortly thereafter, we brought Josie home and instantly fell in love with her.

We faced a big dilemma when Bri decided to come back to WWE: We had nobody to watch Josie! Considering our travel schedules, if we boarded Josie while we were gone, she would spend more time in boarding than she would with us, and that just wasn't acceptable. Bri even had friends who said they would watch her for us, but that would be a ton of work for them, plus, we also had the fear that Josie would start feeling more like their dog than ours.

Bri's mom, Kathy, lived in Phoenix and loved bulldogs, especially Josie. (If we treat Josie like she's our baby, Kathy legitimately treats her like her grandchild.) Weighing our options, we came to the conclusion that we had to move to Phoenix—an incredibly tough decision to make because, outside of Aberdeen, San Diego is my favorite place I've ever lived. My days off there were a joy, with the weather being so nice year-round and our proximity to the beach. Nonetheless, in May 2013, we moved from paradise to the desert, all for the love of our little French bulldog.

Back when she and Nicole first left WWE, shortly after Bri and I moved in together, a production company came forward to do a reality show on the two of them. I would be in it, if they could get it cleared by WWE, and so would Bri's entire family. The girls have a pretty big—and hilarious—family, who mostly live in the small town of Brawley, California, and work in the farming business. The filming they all did was supposedly really good, but Bri and Nicole decided against going forward with the show because they were afraid it would force unnecessary drama into their close-knit family. Seren-dipitously, when WWE called wanting to hire the girls back, one of the main reasons was so they could star in their new reality show called *Total Divas*. I didn't know much about reality television. For years, I didn't own a TV or have cable, so I don't watch much TV in general. What I did know was this: Reality shows are great for the networks because they are generally cheap to produce, they can film multiple seasons each year, and they don't have to pay the talent residuals when they replay the show because they are paid one sum per episode. The networks can reair the show as much as they want without having to pay the talent anything extra, as opposed to having to send Mr. Belding money every time a rerun of *Saved by the Bell* is played.

Total Divas premiered on July 28, 2013, on the E! Network, with the goal of gaining WWE exposure to a different market of viewers, and it's been very successful—even reaching an entirely new audience. One time, we were at a Chipotle near a live event and this very enthusiastic mother-daughter duo came up to us to say, "We. Love. Your. Show!" They didn't know we were in town for WWE, and when we told them about the event, they said, "Oh! That sounds fun!" as if they'd never thought of the idea of going to a wrestling show before. They were clearly *Total Divas* fans.

Naturally, being a part of the series and filming it has its drawbacks. The crew often comes and shoots us on our days off, which is somewhat problematic considering our WWE schedule. In 2013, for example, I did 227 matches on 213 shows. And that doesn't include travel days. When we film, they set up specific times for shooting, and given how very little free time we have, getting some necessary stuff done on our two days off per week can be nigh impossible—and I don't even have to film as much as Bri does. Luckily, I'm only on the periphery of *Total Divas*, while Bri has to deal with the pressure of being one of the main stars and filming all the time.

Still, Bri has also been able to do some really cool things on the show, like highlight certain issues we care about. For example, in one episode, she convinced E! and the producers to go on location to show the differences between factory chicken farms and organic chicken farms. Even though that episode may not have changed the world, it did help raise some awareness among people who'd never been exposed to that information. Generally speaking, the show has definitely allowed Bri and me to do things we would have never been able to do before, which I'll describe in more detail later. We have had some pretty amazing experiences thanks to *Total Divas,* and going through it all together—both good and bad—has brought us closer as a couple.

21 | THE HEAT IS ON
SUNDAY, APRIL 6, 2014—9:46 A.M.

The temperature feels immoderately warm in Daniel Bryan's hotel room this morning. With fiancée Brie across the city at Axxess's early session, Bryan sits in his quarters and describes the first thoughts of the day, WrestleMania Sunday.

"Once Brie left, I was able to go back to sleep, and when I woke up, I had a lot of energy," says a cool, relaxed Bryan. "And that's what you want: feeling excited as opposed to nervous. You think you'd be a little more nervous about something like this, but I'm not," he adds. "I woke up and feel really good."

Dual knocks at the door bring Bryan to his feet to welcome in this morning's visitors—two quite tiny. The chilled Superstar warmly greets his mom, plus his older sister, Billie Sue, and his pair of young, excited, and adorable nieces, ages four and two. They discuss logistics for the day and night ahead. During the pass-off of WrestleMania guest wristbands, the brief family banter results in smiles—Bryan and Billie Sue exposing their identical laugh—after cute cut-ins by Billie's adorable daughters.

"Awww, mannnn," the adults all say in unison, quoting a character from Dora the Explorer *whose adventure unfolds on one girl's iPad.*

Betty hugs and squeezes her son as he stretches on a piece of furniture midconversation. She then leaves him with a maternal kiss on the cheek, and the family heads out for now. The support is palpable.

"My sister has, by far, been to more shows than anybody else in my family, and she regularly comes to WWE shows when we're near her," Bryan says, beaming. "When I first started talking about becoming a wrestler, Billie Sue thought it was cool. My father was also thoroughly supportive of me; even when there were times that wrestling wasn't going well, he never once told me to stop wrestling. And when I made the decision to go to wrestling school instead of college, my mom was also unbelievably supportive."

He continues, "Overall, my family has always wanted what's best for me. It's something that makes me feel very, very fortunate."

The matches Glenn and I had with the Shield throughout 2013 really helped me gain momentum, even in defeat. We were wrestling them seemingly every week on TV, and every week the matches seemed to be great, getting the fans more and more behind me. After our tag team title loss to Rollins and Reigns, WWE.com wanted to record an interview with Glenn and me for the site, and they essentially wanted us to say something like, "Man, somebody needs to stop the Shield," which was a weird implication that somebody else needed to do it but we couldn't. Glenn and I just decided to do our own thing instead, going off the cuff. I got really passionate during the promo, going on this tangent about not being the "weak link" of our team—in fact, I think it ended with me screaming, "I am not the *goddamned* weak link!" The premise behind my statement was that I was the one who got pinned when we lost the titles and was the one who got pinned pretty much every time we lost. That was the way our team was designed: I was the beatable underdog and Kane was the monster. We needed to keep Kane the monster for our dynamic to work, so I would usually take the pins.

Somebody in charge must have seen my tirade on WWE.com and liked it, because the next night on Raw, we continued down this path of me crazily thinking everyone believed I was the weak link of Team

Hell No. My character's motivation changed and I became obsessed with proving to everyone that I was not the weak one, which led to a short television feud with Randy Orton.

On June 17, 2013, I wrestled Randy on Raw and was supposed to win. It would have been the biggest win in my career at that point and was going to really help me transition from the comedic figure I'd been for the last year and a half to someone who could be taken seriously as a main event performer. It didn't exactly go as planned. Randy and I had designed a spot where I missed my signature suicide dive through the ropes, and as I did it, my neck and shoulder crashed into the barricade. I felt a quick pain shoot down my right arm, but I didn't think anything of it. Minutes later, I did a dropkick off the top rope, and when I landed, I lost feeling in both of my arms. The left side came back pretty quickly, but the right side stayed numb for a while. I also couldn't stand up.

After an extended period, I heard Randy trying to talk to me. He had no idea I was hurt and asked, "Dan, what the fuck is going on?!" When I was finally able to get back to my feet, I still couldn't move my right arm and it was hanging limp. We kept going through the match, and after his draping DDT, Randy went to throw me over the top rope to the floor, but I held on. I was supposed to pull myself back into the ring, where Randy would boot me right back out, but at first I couldn't get my arm up to the rope. I finally used momentum to swing it up, and I was able to get partially upside down before Randy booted me to the floor.

While I was on the outside, Dr. Sampson, one of two WWE doctors at the time, came over to check on me. I told him I was fine, but he wouldn't listen. I insisted I was fine again, and he tried to call off the match, so I sprinted into the ring and started brawling with Randy to keep the match going. I saw this as my big opportunity, and I wasn't about to let it pass me by.

Randy still had no idea what was going on, so he threw me to the floor and gave me a backbreaker on the barricade. The referee pushed Randy aside, and Dr. Sampson came over once again, but

this time he directed the referee to stop it, and the ref waved off the match.

Usually I don't get superangry, and when I do it's barely visible. This time, I was furious and I let everyone know it. When I walked through the curtain, I yelled, "What the fuck is that all about?! That's fucking bullshit!"

"You need to calm down," responded Triple H, who had been communicating with the doctor over the headset and called for the match to be stopped.

"No, *you* need to calm the fuck down," I replied.

We were up in each other's faces and both ready to fight. I never had a match stopped in my entire career—not when I separated my shoulder five minutes into an hour draw and not when I detached my retina. Certainly not through any of my concussions. I'm sure I shouted all those things to him, but I was blackout mad so I don't necessarily remember. He was livid, too, and shouted back about stopping the match for my protection, but I wasn't having any of it. It felt hypocritical for Triple H—of all people—to do that, considering in 2001 Hunter himself tore his quad live on Raw and yet finished his match.

"How the fuck can you say that to me?" I asked. "You went out there and tore your quad and *you* continued to wrestle!" It was getting so heated that guys stepped in to separate us and I stormed off.

Bri was afraid I was about to start fighting people, so she took me into a room, which helped to calm me down. Soon after, Vince came to talk to me, and all of a sudden I was riled up again, yelling at him. I was a raving lunatic. He told me I needed to calm down, and I responded with something to the effect of "All these dumb motherfuckers are trying to calm me down and I have every right to be angry." Randy was one of the guys trying to get me to regain my cool. He was actually trying to help and on my side, but my statement pissed him off. He responded, "Don't call me a dumb motherfucker!"

It was kind of a big thing and the first time anybody in WWE had seen me like that.

Later on, after speaking with Bri and Regal, who found me back-stage, I started to find my composure. Regal advised me I needed to go apologize to both Vince and Hunter since they were only trying to protect me. I knew he was right. I blew up because I was frus-trated that the biggest win in my career was being taken away, some-thing I thought would help legitimize me to the WWE fans. Admittedly, I was also a little scared because I had never experienced anything like the numbness that happened to me.

By the time I went in to talk to Vince and Hunter (especially), I was embarrassed by how I had reacted. I told Hunter I was sorry and explained that I usually don't lose my cool like that, but I have so much pride in what I do. He apologized as well, and we buried the hatchet right there. We each understood where the other was com-ing from. He was trying to protect the talent, and I had the mindset of finishing the match—no matter what—which is a mindset he shares when he's in the ring.

The numbness went away in my right arm, but it became a signifi-cant problem going for-ward. When I got home on Wednesday, I went to go get an MRI, which showed that one of the discs in my neck was bulging into the nerve. Both WWE doctors

agreed that I was fine at the moment but it was likely I'd need surgery at some point. I was gaining momentum and didn't have time for that.

The next week on Raw, I wrestled Randy again in a street fight, and they gave me my win as Randy tapped out to the "Yes!" Lock while I pulled a kendo stick across his face. It worked out well be-cause this victory became much bigger than a win the week before would have been. Randy was the biggest star I'd ever beaten, and I

needed that win, especially because several weeks later, John Cena elected to face me for the WWE Championship in the main event of SummerSlam.

Originally I heard I might face John for the title at the Money in the Bank pay-per-view in July, right before SummerSlam. When that didn't happen, I was a little bothered because I anticipated that WWE couldn't possibly want me to face Cena at the second-most-important pay-per-view event of the year the following month. John told me he'd pushed for a match between us at Money in the Bank and when Vince asked him why, John said he felt like it was the biggest match WWE had at the time. Vince took a long pause—which he's notorious for—and then told John we weren't going to do it at Money in the Bank because if it was the biggest match WWE had, we needed to do it at SummerSlam.

They did a cool setup for our match in which Cena was going to get to select his own opponent and challenger on Raw, live in Brooklyn. When John came out to make his announcement, the audience in the Barclays Center was already fired up with "Yes!" and "Daniel Bryan" chants. John teased that his pick might have been a couple of other people: Chris Jericho . . . RVD . . . Sheamus . . . even Heath Slater. When he finally announced that he chose me, the place came unglued. It was the first time WWE fans actually voiced their opinion that they wanted me in the WWE Championship picture.

John Cena has helped me in a lot of ways. The first was back in 2003, when WWE used me as an extra. Typically, when extras had matches, they were just used as enhancement talent to make the WWE guys look good, and thus they would get very little offense. They booked me against John for their syndicated show Velocity on a night when he was starting a big championship program with Brock Lesnar. To set up his match with Brock, what he should have done was eat me alive in our match. But he didn't. We had a good 50/50 match that actually helped my independent career, as opposed to the squash matches that would typically hurt your career. When John got to the back, he got an earful. A championship contender should never give an extra that much offense, they told him. But he did anyway.

John also helped me in the buildup to our match ten years later, giving me some really good advice: "Just go out there and be genuine." It may not sound that complicated, but it is—especially when you have page-long scripts handed to you that don't sound anything like your voice. To be genuine, but still be the character that people want you to be, is a difficult thing.

We did a few back-and-forth promos heading into SummerSlam, and John encouraged me to hit below the belt a little bit, which we needed to build intrigue for a good-guy-against-good-guy match.

Earlier in the year during an overseas tour, I came to the realization that what we were doing in WWE was no longer pro wrestling. I know WWE uses the term "sports-entertainment" all the time, but it should still be the same thing. Instead, what most of WWE had become was actually a *parody* of wrestling. Yes, there were times to be a parody and entertain people, but I wanted something more. Cesaro and I were riding together at the time, and we talked about it at length. I didn't want to be a parody of wrestling anymore. And in my mind, being a wrestling parody was the worst possible thing a wrestler could be.

On the last Raw before SummerSlam, we needed a strong go-home segment between John and me to sell the pay-per-view. So as John stood there, decked out in his merchandise from head to toe, I stood face-to-face with the WWE Champion and called him a "parody of wrestling." John realized that there were a lot of people who did feel that way about him, but he let me do it anyhow. In fact, he encouraged it because it gave our story a little more bite. He responded as only John Cena can with an awesome promo talking about not being a parody to the kid in the front row, about being proud of who he is, and about how there was a long list of guys who don't respect him as a wrestler and yet he was still the top dog after more than ten years. When John fires up, he's the best talker in wrestling. But I wasn't finished yet. In my response, I made reference to a tradition

in Japan in which wrestlers would slap each other in the face to instill fighting spirit. I told John I'd love to slap him in the face right then and there, but he didn't deserve it—because he wasn't a wrestler. Between the match's significance and the intensity of the segment, I thought it was the best promo I'd done yet.

Words aside, the performance with John was one of my favorites. Just having the match—the main event of SummerSlam—meant WWE had a tremendous amount of trust in me. Plus, the match itself wasn't gimmicky; there were no ladders or table spots. On the contrary, it had a championship feel to it, and we went out and wrestled without it being a parody. I loved it.

On that night in Los Angeles on August 18, I debuted my new move, the flying knee, then pinned John Cena to win my first WWE Championship. Even though I lost the championship moments later when Triple H Pedigreed me and Randy Orton cashed in his Money in the Bank contract, it was still the biggest moment of my career up until then. Very few people beat John Cena clean in the middle of the ring, and I got to do it in the main event of SummerSlam.

Immediately after the big August pay-per-view, Cena needed triceps surgery and was going to be away from WWE for a couple of months, giving me the opportunity to be the lead protagonist driving stories forward. It didn't go very well, to say the least, at least not businesswise.

The basis for my main event story was that The Authority—Triple H and Stephanie McMahon—didn't want me as the WWE Champion because the WWE Champion is supposed to be the "Face of WWE," and I didn't fit that mold. Historically, the "Face of WWE" has been someone with a very good build, someone who's on the taller side; your Hogans, your Rocks, your Cenas—all people with these bodybuilder physiques. I don't fit in with that stereotype of what Vince sees as his top guy. This reality was the basis for a lot of the ideas for what became my rivalry with The Authority. They wanted a champion that could be put on magazine covers and pay-per-view posters, somebody who looked like a star and acted like one. I wasn't their type of guy. Randy Orton was, and thus Randy and I feuded over the WWE Championship for several months, with The Authority always stacking things in Randy's favor.

A lot of what played out on TV, I feel, stemmed from legitimate thoughts WWE has about me. They blended a bit of behind-the-scenes reality with on-air storytelling. I don't have the look WWE likes; nor am I overly charismatic the way Hulk Hogan, The Rock, and John Cena are. I'll never be on the cover of *Muscle & Fitness*; nor am I somebody Hollywood producers look at and want to give a role in a movie. Thus, I'm not the best-suited person to be the "Face of WWE."

The Authority also started calling me a "B+player," recognizing that I was popular, but also that my popularity was among a niche audience and wouldn't appeal to the masses. I was good to have around because people like me, but I wasn't going to move numbers. Here, story line met with reality once again. Despite what I thought was good buildup, SummerSlam main-evented by me against John Cena did disappointing numbers, as did the subsequent two months of live events headlined by me and Randy.

Despite recognizing that the entire premise was partially legitimate, I thought it was a good story, especially in today's world where people are sick of homogenized, shoved-down-their-throat celebrities. It seemed as if the stories we were doing on television were drawing anger from the fans, but in a good way, in a way that made them want to see me stick it up The Authority's ass. Unfortunately, when it came to delivering, we ultimately failed in that two-month run.

Randy Orton is one of the best guys I've been in the ring with, and we've had some great matches. Regrettably, none of them were during the three times we main-evented pay-per-views in late 2013. Don't get me wrong; I don't think great matches are absolutely necessary in successful stories. Satisfying conclusions, however, are. And none of the pay-per-view main events we had gave those. At Night of Champions, I beat Randy, but crooked referee Scott Armstrong counted fast, and the title was taken away from me the next night

on Raw. That would seem fine, but because Scott was doing the fast count on my pin, I wasn't allowed to make any pinfall covers during the match, which killed some of the drama. At the next pay-per-view, WWE Battleground, there was no finish to the match; Big Show came out, knocked out both me and Randy, and walked off. The show went off the air like that—no announcement of who won or lost. All of that would have been fine had it been on a Raw on free TV, but to pay $50 and have a show end like that had a lot of fans giving up.

My final main event pay-per-view performance with Orton was at Hell in a Cell, in the event's signature match in which most of the ringside area is enclosed in a giant, roofed cage. Shawn Michaels was made the special guest referee—an interesting plot twist since he was my original trainer and is also Triple H's best friend. This was probably the best of the three major matches Randy and I had, but again, it ended in a strange finish. Shawn got knocked down somehow, prompting Triple H to come into the cage to check on him, along with a doctor. I went over to check on Shawn as well, but Triple H threw me down. When I got up, I charged and hit him with the running knee, just as Shawn recovered in time to see it. Though he was the ref, Shawn himself superkicked me, then counted as Randy covered me for the win.

When I initially heard the finish, I thought maybe WWE had convinced Shawn to come back and face me at WrestleMania months later, which would've given meaning to the closing moments of my match with Randy. Shawn had done a retirement match with the Undertaker at WrestleMania XXVI, but wrestlers rarely stay retired. If such was to be the case for me and Shawn, the whole finish would have been amazing. Performing against Shawn Michaels at Wrestle-Mania is my ultimate dream match because not only was he my original trainer, he's also known as "Mr. WrestleMania," boasting more show-stealing matches at the big show than anybody in history.

After speaking with Shawn, however, it became clear he had no intention of ever wrestling again, and the finish was constructed the way it was just to get out of the situation while still protecting me from losing. I appreciated the fact that WWE bothered with protecting me, but again, the fans left feeling dissatisfied in a way that didn't help business going forward.

Though I did not get a WrestleMania match with Shawn, I still got to experience a cool moment with him the following night on Raw. I was in the ring, and he came out to explain himself to me, asking me to shake his hand, which I refused. Shawn then slowly turned into an arrogant asshole, demanding that I shake his hand, which I did, then immediately turned the handshake into the "Yes!" Lock as retribution for the previous night's incident on pay-per-view. Shawn is a master storyteller, both with his wrestling and his promos, and being able to do that with him was a lot of fun.

Later in the night, I was attacked by the Wyatt Family (Bray Wyatt, Luke Harper, and Erick Rowan), which essentially ended my two-month run as a main-eventer. I feel like I did well in terms of performance, more so with my ability to carry multiple segments

on Raw—wrestling and talking—and I got vastly more comfortable on the microphone during this time. But when you're in the top position, it's your responsibility to draw in the fans. It doesn't matter how well you wrestle or how well you talk if fans don't pay to see it. In that regard, I failed, and I didn't think I convinced the higher-ups in WWE that I was anything more than a "B+ player."

In the middle of my main event run with Randy and The Authority, something in my personal life overshadowed what was going on at work. On September 25, 2013, I asked Bri to marry me.

I originally planned on proposing to Bri a couple of months later when we returned to Boston. My intent was to go back to the Isabella Stewart Gardner Museum (where we had our first date), take her to the third floor (which we didn't make it to on our first visit), and propose to her there. I know it's kind of cliché to propose where you had your first date, but for good reason: Your first date is an important milestone in your life, and thus it's a return to where the whole thing started.

But in late August, Russell, the lead producer of *Total Divas*, asked me if I'd be willing to have the proposal take place on the show. I was OK with it, but they needed it to happen soon to make the season-two midseason finale. I already had the ring, custom-made from an awesome jeweler in New York who specializes in environmentally friendly and socially responsible jewelry. Most importantly, I wanted to make sure the moment was special and not thrown together, so together with Russell and Nicole, Bri's sister, we formulated a game plan: Bri and I would go on a vacation to Big Sur, where *Total Divas* would film us staying in a handmade dome house in the woods. Bri would think it was because they just wanted to film us in a zany eco-retreat episode with beautiful scenery.

I hoped she wouldn't suspect anything, but my big concern was Nicole. Being twins, the two of them tell each other *everything*. I was worried Nicole would let the cat out of the bag, but, luckily, she didn't. Or if she did, Bri kept the secret so safe that she's never told me.

My new plan was to propose to Bri somewhere along a five-mile hike at Big Sur. I didn't know when or precisely where it would happen, because it was my first time on this hike that I only researched on the Internet beforehand. I figured I would just feel when it was right. But, in order for the crew trailing us to be prepared to get good footage of the proposal, we agreed to have me say a code word or phrase, something like "Boy, the sky sure does look blue." In the meantime, for the sake of the surprise, the camera guys filmed most of the hike simply because it would seem strange to Bri if they didn't.

Even though it wasn't *that* steep a hike, it's much more difficult when you're loaded down with equipment. The crew's sound guy never made it to the top, which made me feel a little bad but also made me laugh. *Everyone* was sweating by the time we made it to the top of the ridge with this beautiful view overlooking the Pacific Ocean. I knew immediately that this was the place and the time.

I was really nervous, and my hand started shaking. I knew Bri would say yes because A) we went ring shopping together in New York before WrestleMania 29, just so I could see the kind of style she liked, and B) from that moment on, she gave me grief about when I was going to propose. To add to my anxiety, I kept recalling how Bri once told me the only thing she cared about was the words I would say when I proposed. If the moment weren't being filmed, that wouldn't have been such a big thing, but if I messed it up on camera and it aired on *Total Divas,* I would never hear the end of it. I was so nervous that I forgot to say the code word. The cameraman wasn't ready, and neither was whoever was handling the sound.

I was vaguely aware of scuttling going on around me as everyone rushed into position when they realized I was getting down on one knee. I looked at Bri and said, "It's been two years, seven months, and ten days since the very first time we kissed. And it's not enough. I want it to be forever, like all this," referring to the endless-looking ocean. Then, for the very first time, I said, "I love you," followed by asking her to marry me. Oddly enough, Bri was so excited in the moment that she couldn't even process the words she previously said

would be so important. Still, as you know, she said yes. It felt like the perfect moment.

Afterward, sitting on the cliff overlooking the ocean, we ate the peanut butter and jelly sandwiches we'd packed . It was an incredible moment of calm and happiness. Our trip to the top of the mountain felt like an accomplishment of sorts, the end of one journey. When we got back to the bottom, it felt like a new journey had begun.

Bryan and Bri celebrate their engagement, September 2013

One of the things that made the proposal so special was that immediately afterward, we had a surprise engagement dinner that *Total Divas* had our families flown in to attend. They set up a beautiful area in the woods, and for the first time, our families got to meet each other. The cameras were rolling, but nobody even seemed to notice because we were all having so much fun enjoying the special moment.

There are certainly times when filming the show can feel invasive, but then there are moments like that—with elaborate and thoughtful planning—that *Total Divas* creates to demonstrate their appreciation, and it makes it all worthwhile.

I'd been dealing with a little bit of pain after the stinger I got in the match with Randy back in June, but all of a sudden it got substantially worse. The bulging disc was pinching on the ulnar nerve—which runs from your neck to your shoulder, through your triceps, past your elbow, and into your hand—driving pain down my entire right arm. The pain made the two-week November European tour miserable as it started shooting at random, making it nearly impossible for me to sleep more than an hour or two at a time.

When we returned to the United States, I was sent to get my first epidural steroid injection: They use a long, thin needle to inject cortisone into the space surrounding the nerve, helping to reduce the nerve's inflammation. That first shot helped a great deal, giving me my first relief from the pain in months, and I was finally able to sleep through the night. I was scheduled to get a total of three injections, spaced about a month apart, but during the second treatment, something went wrong.

They numb your entire upper back and neck area before the injection, so you're not really supposed to feel much of anything. Given the amount of sensitive material around your neck and spinal column, they use X-ray guidance to direct the needle exactly where it needs to go. Somehow, on the second injection, the doctor hit the nerve with the needle and I screamed out "FUCK!" as an intense pain shot through what felt like my entire body. I was shaken up, and so was the doctor, yet when they asked me if I wanted to do it again, I agreed because I figured it couldn't get much worse than that. The next attempt went fine, but didn't end up giving me any relief from my existing pain.

Since the second treatment went so poorly and did very little for my pain, I chose not to get the third injection. I couldn't do any heavy lifting, but acupuncture and massages helped minimize the discomfort. Fortunately, it wasn't really affecting my wrestling. When my adrenaline is flowing, I tend to not feel much pain anyway. I was getting weaker, but luckily I designed my entire WWE offense around *not* lifting people up. And moves I do execute that involve moving my opponent's body, like a snap or German suplex, are all about hip movement. The rest of my offense is comprised of high-impact strikes,

submissions, and flying around. I continued to perform and finished up a tumultuous 2013, which ended with what will probably go down as my favorite show I've ever done.

My family has only been able to come to very few of my shows, either on the independents or in WWE. There just aren't that many events that emanate from Washington State every year. One time, I performed in a crappy independent show in a flea market in our neighboring state of Oregon, just so my dad could come see me wrestle. It was a horrible show, but my dad had a great time.

On December 9, 2013, the annual Slammy Awards show emanated from Seattle, and my dad was able to get off work and go. Before the event, my dad and a couple of guests he brought with him to the show went to eat at a restaurant, and some people in Daniel Bryan T-shirts entered. His boss's wife stopped them and told them he was my father. Just like me, my dad was a naturally shy person, so of course he got really embarrassed being pointed out like that, but the fans thought it was the coolest thing to meet my dad, and they asked for his autograph. This naturally made him even a little more shy, but he still signed for them, inscribing "Buddy Danielson, Daniel Bryan's dad" on their tees.

Later that night, this Slammys edition of Raw started off with me wrestling Fandango, and the hometown crowd was going crazy for me from the very beginning. I could tell it was going to be a fun night. The Slammy Awards are voted on by the fans, and I went on to win multiple, including the ludicrous Beard of the Year award. Since Bri and I also won Couple of the Year, I went in to talk to Vince earlier in the night to ask about the two of us going out together for my match. He didn't want that, but while I was there in his office, I also asked if there was anything he wanted me to say if I won the Slammy for Superstar of the Year. Vince just kind of laughed, almost in disbelief that I thought I could win, and told me I could say whatever I wanted.

Well, I did win—by probably the smallest margin in the history of the award, narrowly beating out John Cena. The Seattle crowd cheered wildly when I came out to accept the award, and at the end of my acceptance speech, I gave them a loud "Go Seahawks!," a nod to Seattle's favorite sports team. It was all actually pretty neat, because even though I don't see winning Slammys as overly important, it was fun that Bri and Nicole won Diva(s) of the Year, I won Superstar of the Year, and together Bri and I won Couple of the Year. After I accepted my award, WWE took a bunch of pictures

Bryan accepts the 2014 Slammy Award for Superstar of the Year

of us together holding the Slammys, which is nice because they were cute pictures (well, as cute as I get) that we can show our kids someday.

The end of the night featured the Championship Ascension, a symbolic hoisting of WWE's two top titles, the WWE Title and the World Heavyweight Championship, above the ring days before they were to be unified at WWE TLC. In the ring for the ceremony stood past champions, including myself, as well as the current title holders, Randy Orton and John Cena. WWE was trying to bill the unification match as the biggest match in WWE history, given the significance the two titles previously had, but as soon as the segment started, the Seattle fans starting chanting for me. I was only out there because I was a previous champion, that's it. In no way was I involved in the upcoming match, but the crowd didn't care. As Triple H tried to speak, the entire crowd drowned him out in a sea of "Yes!" and "Daniel Bryan!" chants. I couldn't do anything but laugh in the background, and I was almost concerned that somehow the whole thing would be blamed on me. Another former champion, Mark Henry, was standing next to me, and he raised my arm to huge applause, hoping that would help the crowd let it out and then they'd simmer down a little and get back to focusing on the segment. But that only made it worse. As Randy started to speak, the crowd just got louder and louder, cheering for me. Situations like this are why John Cena has been the top guy in WWE for the last ten years. Thinking quickly on his feet, he asked me to come forward, then asked a series of questions.

"What's your name?"

"My name is Daniel Bryan," I replied. Huge cheer.

"Where are you from?"

"I'm from Aberdeen, Washington." Even louder cheer.

"Were either your mom or dad a past WWE Superstar?"

"Nope, my dad is actually a log scaler." Another loud cheer, as logging is a huge industry in Washington.

And that's where Cena turned it around. He said guys like me and him had to get to the top on our own, while Randy came in with everyone expecting him to succeed because his dad was a WWE Hall of Famer. John got the segment right back on track and focused on the title unification match. At the conclusion, a brawl broke out, and the show ended with—you guessed it—"Daniel Bryan!" chants. For the first time, what we later called the "Yes! Movement" essentially hijacked Raw.

After the segment, as the show was ending, my dad came up to the rail elated, as proud as he could be. I gave him a big hug and told him how happy I was he could come. My father later told my sister about the amazing time he had, about how loud the crowd was cheering for me and that people had even wanted *his* autograph, just for being my dad. He'd had a great time.

What made it my favorite show wasn't winning the Slammys. Nor was it the amazing crowd reaction. It was that my dad got to see all that and got to be in the crowd while everyone was going crazy for me; he got to enjoy it, to stand back and be *proud*. I am incredibly thankful for that, because it was the last live show he would ever see.

For a few months after Hell in a Cell, I was in a story with the Wyatt Family, who'd been trying to get me to join their clan, led by cult leader Bray Wyatt. The Wyatts and I seemed like a natural fit.

They all have huge beards (much bigger than mine), and they are pretty out-there characters. I had been pitching to join them and do some vignettes showing Bray brainwashing me, which we thought would be really cool. It was taken under consideration by WWE writers but was seemingly dropped until, randomly, on the final Raw of 2013, I actually did join the Wyatts.

It was weird because the story changed from Bray brainwashing me to me deceiving the Wyatts. It was all a part of my plot to destroy the group from the inside. Our connection wasn't supposed to last very long, but I pushed and pushed and pushed to get the whole story extended. Bray was on tap to begin a feud with John Cena leading into WrestleMania 30. I figured with me joining the Wyatts, it would add to their credibility, and as a result, I would be a part of one of the main stories heading into the biggest show of the year. Since there were really no plans for me for WrestleMania at the time, I thought being a part of this would at least give me something big to do, especially if I turned on them after 'Mania, when there is kind of a lull following the excitement of the big show.

But the week after I joined them, I ended up getting quite a bit of mainstream attention. I was in my hotel room when Titus O'Neil texted me and told me to put on ESPN's *SportsCenter*. I never turn on the TV in my hotel rooms, but I did, and, much to my surprise, they were showing a whole arena at a basketball game chanting "Yes!" I had no idea what to make of it. The Michigan State college football team had just won the Rose Bowl the week before, and after a touchdown, Travis Jackson, one of the players, started "Yes!"-ing. The team was doing a huge celebration of their Rose Bowl win during the halftime of a Michigan State–Ohio State basketball game, and Travis got on the microphone to get the whole arena to start "Yes!"-ing as well. It caught on. The fans at the basketball game kept doing it throughout the rest of the game, especially when the other team was at the free throw line. Instead of the usual noodle things or wiggly balloons that basketball fans use to distract the other team, they used the "Yes!" chant. It was an amazing visual. Not only did

SportsCenter pick up on it, but so did media sources around the country, and they all credited me as the inspiration. The whole thing blew my mind.

I'm not sure if it's because the basketball game got so much mainstream attention or if it was the plan all along, but the following week, I turned on the Wyatts. Bray and I were doing a tag match against the Usos inside a steel cage and after the Usos won, Bray wanted me to submit to him by allowing him to hit his "Sister Abigail" signature move on me. I refused, and the crowd that had been dead for the last ninety minutes of the show all of a sudden came alive. Bray charged at me and I dodged it, lighting him up, knocking the other two Wyatt Family members off the cage, and then at the end, hitting Bray with the flying knee. I climbed to the top of the cage and sat there, leading the entire arena in "Yes!" chants. It was another really cool visual.

Somewhere around this time, I was speaking with Vince in his office, and though I forget what we were originally talking about, he suddenly changed topics; he wanted to talk about his plans for me for WrestleMania 30. Prior to this discussion, I had been talking to Triple H about possibly doing a match with him, but also, in the back of my mind, I was still hoping they had convinced Shawn Michaels to come back to wrestle me. But Vince's idea was neither of those. He wanted me to wrestle Sheamus.

Let me say right now that I love working with Sheamus. We have great matches, we get along really well, and, with the exception of the two WrestleManias we'd already wrestled, we always had fun together. However, given that I was, at worst, the third most popular wrestler in WWE—and on some shows the most popular—it was a pretty low-positioned match for WrestleMania. We would be lucky if we were the fifth biggest match, given WWE had already planned to have Randy Orton–Batista for the title, Brock Lesnar–Undertaker, Triple H–CM Punk, and John Cena–Bray Wyatt. With those four matches, it would be difficult for anything else to get much time.

Though demoralized, I thanked him for the opportunity and was determined to do the best with what I was given.

But the road in life is uncertain and nothing is set in stone, even what Vince tells you—maybe *especially* what Vince tells you. Things can always change, which is what happened to my WrestleMania plans at the 2014 Royal Rumble in January.

Royal Rumble is when WrestleMania season starts, and the winner of the event's headline thirty-man Rumble match goes on to compete for the championship at WrestleMania, presumably in the main event. Next to 'Mania, the Royal Rumble crowd usually has the most hardcore fans in attendance. People fly in from all over the world for the annual event, and those people are very vocal. That year they also happened to be pretty big Daniel Bryan fans. I knew I wasn't going to be in the Rumble match, and I hadn't been advertised for it, but nobody specifically said I wouldn't be in it, either.

I didn't mind that I wasn't involved in the Rumble, because I had a match with Bray Wyatt earlier in the show and I was able to just focus on that. We wrestled in the second bout on the show and had a great match, fueled by an amazing crowd in Pittsburgh that was overwhelming in their support for me. The only times I had seen anything like that audience was the night after WrestleMania XXVIII and shows in my home city, Seattle. And just like at those shows, the fans continued to chant "Yes!" and "Daniel Bryan!" long after my match was over.

It's interesting that wrestling has moved into this postmodern era where fans understand that what they're watching is entertainment. They choose to cheer for what entertains them, whether the character is good or bad, and they reject things they don't want to see by booing, chanting "Boring," or creating their own entertainment among themselves. One crowd might start the wave; another might start chanting for an announcer or the local hockey team. I don't know where this idea came from to start having your own fun and stop paying attention to what's being presented, but it has its pluses and minuses.

Fortunately for me, it's been mostly positive. For instance, in the title match for the unified WWE World Heavyweight Championship featuring John Cena against Randy Orton, the crowd initially rejected it. They were chanting "Boring!" and "Yes!" and "This is awful!" The thing was, it *wasn't* awful. It was an actively good match, so much so that the same crowd that wanted to reject it at first actually got into it by the end.

I sat in the back in Pittsburgh during the main event Royal Rumble match, watching and wondering if there would be any discernible negativity toward me not being in the Rumble. At first there wasn't; there were "Daniel Bryan!" chants, but they dispersed pretty quickly. Generally speaking, the fans were just enjoying the Rumble. But they didn't know I wasn't going to be in the match. Not yet.

When Batista—the guy WWE wanted to be the headlining hero going into WrestleMania—came out, the crowd booed because they figured that if I didn't win, he would. Shortly after he entered, the chants for me increased, and the closer the match drew to its final entrant, the louder those chants got. When the countdown to the thirtieth entrant started, the fans were on their feet in anticipation. However, once the countdown was completed and the buzzer sounded, instead of hearing "Ride of the Valkyries," they heard Rey Mysterio's music. This was the moment when the fans finally realized I wasn't going to be in the match, and they started booing—loudly.

As I watched, I instantly felt bad for Rey. He's the last person to deserve that kind of reaction, and I've looked up to him since I was in high school. Rey has worked through more injuries than one could count, and he has always done his best to entertain the fans with his high-flying style, despite the toll it might take on his body. And yet the fans booed him because he wasn't me, and I was what they wanted. It's weird for me to be typing that now. It sounds egotistical, but I don't know how else to say it. The fans turned on the whole match. They booed pretty much everyone except for CM Punk and Roman Reigns. When Batista won, the crowd mercilessly booed him, the man who was going to main-event WrestleMania. Then they followed with a loud "Daniel Bryan!" chant. They were directly telling WWE what they wanted.

You have to keep in mind that this was one crowd on one night. All crowds weren't like that, and Batista got some amazing positive reactions after he'd come back. WWE knew that the WrestleMania crowd would be very similar to this crowd, and I wondered if WWE would listen to what the crowd told them. Truthfully, part of me was already resigned to just hoping that maybe I could build up enough momentum for the following year's 'Mania.

The next night, another bizarre incident occurred. CM Punk left WWE. I don't know why, and it's not my place to guess. That side of it is his to tell, should he choose to tell it. All I know is he left and he didn't come back, and all I can tell you is how that affected me. As for WWE, Punk's departure put the company in a strange place for WrestleMania; two of the big four matches they planned were going to be much different than they thought. One, the Punk–Triple H match at WrestleMania, was not even going to happen. And two, if they moved forward with the WWE World Heavyweight Championship match between Randy Orton and Batista, the fans were going to turn on it just like they turned on the Rumble match.

For a couple of weeks, I didn't hear of anything changing. I knew Hunter wanted to face me at WrestleMania. Unfortunately, even in his position, Hunter doesn't always get what he wants. I've seen him come out of the TV production meetings on the road to discuss stories looking like he's been in a battle and lost. I think Vince was still hoping that Punk would come back or that Batista would win back the crowd. Neither of those things happened, but then WWE came up with a solution to both of those problems: me.

Not only did the fans want me in that spot, but it made sense storywise. The Authority had kept me from being champion since SummerSlam the year before, and every time I got close, they took it away. They ignored my popularity and didn't even put me in the Rumble match to get an opportunity to compete for the title at WrestleMania. It was a very legitimate story that could easily be told about a

corporate machine (The Authority) holding the little man (me) down. All they had to figure out was how to get us there.

WWE came up with a very creative idea based on the "Occupy" movements that protested against social and economic inequality, which were happening all over the world. It was called "Occupy Raw," and I, along with a bunch of "fans" wearing Daniel Bryan T-shirts, hijacked the ring and did not leave until we got what we wanted. Most of the fans that were in the ring were actually production or catering people that work for WWE, though the people on the floor surrounding the ring were real fans. I'm not sure how those individuals were picked, but they sure were enthusiastic, which helped. One of the real fans actually jumped in the ring and stood right next to me as I sat on the turnbuckle, and you could see him taking a bunch of selfies during the entire segment.

Our seizing control of the ring threatened to ruin the show, and after putting up as much resistance as they could, The Authority finally gave us what we wanted: I got a match with Triple H, and if I won, on that very same night, I would be entered into the WWE World Heavyweight Championship match and main-event Wrestle-Mania 30.

22 TIME FOR CHANGE
SUNDAY, APRIL 6, 2014—11:12 A.M.

The first Superstar on the coach bus headed to the Mercedes-Benz Super-dome, Bryan receives the genuine support of all who step aboard and shuffle down the aisle for the biggest day in WWE—Arn Anderson ("DB! This is your week," he exclaims), the Miz, Mark Henry, and others. Once he's arrived and inside the massive stadium, Bryan rolls his suitcase and the modest "Makin' Groceries" Whole Foods bag he'd picked up earlier in the week toward the Superstars' quarters. He finds his spot among his fellow warriors in the locker room and carves out his niche.

As he's expressed this week and for the past several months of his devel-oping Movement, a sea change feels imminent. Should he succeed tonight, WWE may never be the same .

"Things will change because expectations have to change," Bryan declares, addressing Triple H and The Authority. "What 'they' think someone needs in order to be a successful Superstar has to change. Whether I win or not, my popularity has spoken for itself."

Tonight at WrestleMania 30, the "People's Couple" has a rare opportu-nity to emerge as a power couple (though they'd likely prefer never to be given such a moniker). Daniel Bryan and Brie Bella could emerge from

277

the Show of Shows with the top prizes in their divisions—not unlike Triple H and Stephanie McMahon themselves had done in 2000. To Bryan, it's not about the grandeur, however.

Midday inside the Superdome, near the foot of the entrance ramp of the WrestleMania set, "Braniel" reconnects after their morning apart. As much as this night means to Bryan, it's also a significant event for Brie, who's vying for the ladies' top title in the Divas Championship Invitational. It could very well come down to sister against sister, among several other possible outcomes weighing on the Total Divas *star's mind. She—like Bryan—needs to be prepared for anything.*

"I just try to tell her to go out there and do what you do," Bryan encourages. "Last year, [Brie and Nikki's] match got cut from WrestleMania, and that's hard because that's one of the reasons they came back. They wanted to wrestle at WrestleMania. [Brie has to] try not to get caught up in the distractions and drama that are inevitable."

Their ringside huddle shifts elsewhere, much like the "Yes!" Man's face, which is slowly changing. The jocular Goat, as the bearded star is likened to, starts to resemble an American Dragon as he internally prepares for the battle (or battles) beyond at WrestleMania.

As you can imagine, I was ecstatic about the opportunity to main-event WrestleMania. There is no higher mountaintop in professional wrestling. I was also a little overwhelmed because not only did I have the biggest matches of my career, but also Bri and I had bought our very first house together the week before and we were getting married a mere five days after 'Mania. The logistics of everything that needed to be done that week to make sure everything would go off without a hitch were very stressful, as you can imagine.

The timing of our wedding ceremony was based purely on the filming needs for the season two finale of *Total Divas*. Originally Bri and I wanted to have our wedding outdoors in Washington State, which meant we would need to wait until summer for ideal weather. *Total Divas* offered to pay for our wedding if they could shoot it, and, though hesitant, we said yes. Weddings are expensive, and ours

My sister, Billie Sue, happily sits with her little
brother, Bryan, the fattest baby ever.

My mom, Billie Sue, and I pose with one of many
family pets over the years, our dog Mikey.

Out on a fishing trip with my sister and my dad.

Me, carrying the Ring of Honor World Championship, which I held for 462 days. (Photo by George Tahinos)

Hanging out with Lance Cade and sporting my "American Dragon" mask on our first tour of Japan.

Celebrating on the ramp after winning the Global Honored Crown Junior Heavyweight Championship title in 2008.

Choked with a chain by Takeshi Morishima. I didn't get fired for this one.

(Photo by George Tahinos)

Streamers rain down inside the Hammerstein Ballroom in New York City for my emotional farewell to ROH on September 26, 2009. (Photo by Scott Finkelstein)

Our symbolic "changing of the guard" photo, taken backstage after WWE, TLC, 2011 in Baltimore. The change did not quite pan out the way we had thought, but it remains a proud moment.

The WWE medical staff stops my match with Randy Orton in June of 2013. Cooler heads would prevail, but for a moment my temper got the best of me, a rare occasion.

A long way from our Velocity match ten years earlier, I face John Cena in the main event of SummerSlam 2013.

. . . And so begins the most dominant tag team run of the modern era! Glenn and I had incredible chemistry in and out of the ring, making Team Hell No one of the most enjoyable times in my career.

Bri says "Yes!" to my proposal at the top of Big Sur, in front of an ocean view and an exhausted *Total Divas* camera crew.

Dad, Billie Sue, and me, rocking our 12th Man jerseys, Christmas 2013.

The "Yes!" Movement makes history in March 2014 during an "Occupy Raw" stunt that leads to me fulfilling my childhood dream at WrestleMania 30.

More than 75,000 people in New Orleans celebrate my WWE World Heavyweight Championship win in the main event of WrestleMania 30. "Yes!"ing with those two titles is harder than you'd think.

Just a few days after WrestleMania 30, I marry Bri on Friday,
April 11, 2014. Our outdoor ceremony and celebration takes
place in the beautiful nature of Sedona, Arizona.

would be especially, because Bri has such a large family. We still wanted to have it in Washington, but when the producers told us the second week of April was the last possible weekend they could shoot it, we realized an outdoor wedding at that time of year would be too risky in the Northwest. We talked about it and decided to get married in Sedona, Arizona, a beautiful desert area about an hour and a half north of Phoenix. We wanted to get married outside surrounded by nature; plus, Sedona was where we spent Valentine's Day the year before, so it seemed like the perfect place. And it was.

Bri did most of the planning for the wedding—not "our" wedding, "her" wedding, as she referred to it—which was very helpful, but I was still put in charge of managing some things. Most importantly, I was completely responsible for our honeymoon. So, while preparing for this huge moment in my career—wrestling in two matches in front of seventy-five thousand people and so many more watching around the world—I was also managing the details of our honeymoon trip. Getting all that in order was fun, just stressful given the timing.

Closing on our new house was just circumstantial as well. We'd been kind of looking at houses after renting for so long, but were content to wait to buy anything until after the wedding. There was one specific street we always walked down whenever we'd take Josie on walks, where people greeted one another and neighbors seemed to know each other. All of a sudden, I stumbled upon a perfectly sized and inexpensive house that had opened up on it. I was really excited about it and wanted Bri to take a look at it. Unfortunately, she was on the road doing media for *Total Divas* and within days of going on the market, before Bri even got home, someone apparently bought it. No big deal, we thought; if it wasn't meant to be, it wasn't meant to be. Two days before we left for WrestleMania week, our real estate agent—who was Matt Bloom's (a.k.a. Tensai's) wife, Sarah—called and told us the previous buyers' financials fell through and, if we wanted to, we could take a look at it. This was just three hours before we were leaving for Sedona to check on the wedding venue and a couple of other things. We couldn't pass up the chance, so right before we left, we swung by the house to check it out. Bri loved it. It was small and cozy, and she envisioned ways we could remodel it to make it our own. As we were leaving the place, two more potential buyers were coming in to look at it. By the next morning, we put in an offer that was ultimately accepted. It was a very opportune thing.

It obviously wasn't ideal to have all of these things going on while preparing for the biggest matches of my career. I would have liked to be a hundred percent focused on WrestleMania during that week. But life is rarely ideal, and these were all good things, so I rolled with the tide.

23 WARRIORS
SUNDAY, APRIL 6, 2014—4:23 P.M.

Twenty-four years ago, WrestleMania VI's Ultimate Challenge altered the landscape of the WWE Universe and forged a new breed of fan that rallied behind a behemoth named Ultimate Warrior. Among them was Daniel Bryan. Long before he discovered technicians like Shawn Michaels and Bret "Hit Man" Hart, the submission specialist was an enthralled young Warrior himself.

In the wide halls of the Mercedes-Benz Superdome, Bryan encounters the grayed yet ever-intense Ultimate Warrior, mere hours prior to WrestleMania. He shakes hands with the presently neon-fringe-free legend for the first time and fulfills a moment little Daniel Bryan only dreamt of years back.

"I'm looking forward to your match," Warrior bellows at the five-foot-eight Superstar as they break.

Ironically, tonight, Bryan takes aim at breaking the mold Warrior once propagated as a successor to "the Immortal" Hulk Hogan. An industry that once flourished on the backs of big men is about to change forever.

When I was walking down the hall the day of WrestleMania and saw the Ultimate Warrior backstage, I had to take the opportunity to say something to him. I don't see myself as someone the old-school wrestlers and WWE Legends would recognize, but Warrior was certainly very nice and, to me, quite sincere. He said, "You're doing a great job with what you're doing." I don't even know if he watched what I did closely, but it was an honor and pleasure to get the chance to go up to him and tell him that I was a huge fan of his as a kid.

This first live wrestling show I ever went to took place in the summer of 1990 at the Tacoma Dome, about ninety minutes from our house in Aberdeen. My parents surprised me with the tickets when I came home from school one day after I'd heard an ad for the show on the radio and, for weeks, begged my mom and dad for us to go. I would have wanted to attend *any* wrestling show at the time, but what made me feel like I *needed* to go to this one in particular was the DJ's announcement of one person competing that night: the Ultimate Warrior.

When the first notes of Warrior's entrance music hit, the entire Tacoma Dome erupted. I cheered as loud as my little nine-year-old voice would permit, while standing on my chair to get a better glimpse of my hero. He sprinted to the ring, his face painted and his huge, muscular arms made even more vascular by the vibrant string tied around his upper biceps. He shook the ropes like a maniac as soon as he got to the ring and the crowd roared with approval. The Ultimate Warrior looked like a superhero on television, but in person, he looked like a deity.

That's all I remember from the show—that entrance, that energy. It transcended the visual and auditory excitement I'd previously only gotten from seeing it on a TV screen. Live, you could *feel* it. That excitement struck a chord in me that I've never forgotten.

Nobody else in my family who was there that night remembers Ultimate Warrior's entrance. They remember his opponent, "Ravishing"

Rick Rude. In the middle of their match, Warrior attempted to give Rude a sunset flip. Rude stood his ground—with his back to us—and he would not go down. In order to gain more leverage, Warrior reached up and pulled at the top of his tights. Still Rick Rude would not go down . . . but his tights sure did. His bare ass was directed right toward us.

My dad loved telling this story and howled laughing every time, mostly because of my sister's reaction. Her mouth went agape and her eyes opened wide. She stared in shock for what seemed like an eternity, and then dropped her head down in embarrassment. It was the first adult male butt she had ever seen. Embarrassingly enough, there've been many times in my career when I, too, have been sunset flipped and had my pants pulled down. I wonder if there were any mouths agape and eyes widened. I wonder if mine could be the first adult male butt some kid has ever seen. (My dad always howled laughing at that thought as well.)

Meeting Ultimate Warrior was cool, yet the best part was seeing how much he loved his little girls and his wife. Bri was one of the Divas who walked the Hall of Famers out to the stage that weekend, and she told me that Warrior didn't want anyone but his daughters to walk him out. I'm a big softy, and it always nearly makes me cry at the Hall of Fame when guys talk about their wives putting up with them over the years and how family got them through so much. With his passing, it was hard to lose one of the guys I adored as a child, but what really made it heart-wrenchingly sad for me was how much he loved his family.

One year, I dressed up as Ultimate Warrior for Halloween. My mom got me face paint and sewed me a costume—a stuffed bodybuilder-type bodysuit with neon spandex-covered strings stitched on the arms. Years later in 2010, I worked a show with NWA after I'd been fired by WWE. A fan had won the opportunity to announce the main event of the show, which was me against Adam Pearce. The guest announcer was incredibly nervous and when the guy announced me, he mistakenly presented me not as the American Dragon but the *Ultimate* Dragon. So I came out and decided to do a full-on Ultimate Warrior entrance, sprinting to the ring, shaking the ropes, and all that.

24 THE MOVEMENT MEETS THE AUTHORITY
SUNDAY, APRIL 6, 2014—5:59 P.M.

It's the final countdown, and Daniel Bryan is suiting up for his clash with "the King of Kings," Triple H. In the locker room, Bryan slides on his new fur-lined kickpads. "Bruiser Brody," he plainly proclaims, hinting at the homage to the similarly feral-bearded former WWE Superstar. While changing into his unique battle armor, the Beard finds a moment to converse with his one-time mentor, the rugged William Regal. Another supporter of the "Yes!" Movement, the English grappler is elated to see Daniel Bryan take to the Grandest Stage of Them All against one of the ring's greatest competitors, the Game. It's probably one of the most important prematch talks Bryan will have this evening. So much history and so much respect fuel his conversation with Regal.

Beyond the dressing room, Superstars are huddled around monitors in the backstage area watching what is a WWE fan's dream sequence with Hulk Hogan, "Stone Cold" Steve Austin, and The Rock inside the middle of the ring. Mere yards away, Daniel Bryan is warming up with kicks that would make Craig Wilson proud. The air takes a beating from the Beard prior to what's in store for the Cerebral Assassin.

Match time finally falls upon him, and in anticipation the huge crowd musters the loudest "Yes!" chant you've ever heard. In heavy contrast to his rival, the theatrical entrance and gold armor accentuating Triple H's wealth of power is an unforgettable image, but it's instantly rivaled and topped by Bryan's simple, full-heartened gallop down the ramp to the ring. Daniel Bryan emerges on the Grandest Stage of Them All to 75,167 voices shouting in his favor. Tonight, they seek the fall of The Authority and the triumph of the "Yes!" Movement.

As they'd so desperately hoped, he does it. Bryan wins. Any other year, this victory would be any other Superstar's WrestleMania moment. Dethroning Triple H—the Game, a thirteen-time World Champion and WWE's quintessential competitor—at WrestleMania is something few men can claim. And Daniel Bryan does it with skill and tenacity, securing an indisputable pinfall over The Authority's leader. But before Bryan can celebrate and move on to a triple-threat match against Randy Orton and Batista, the Cerebral Assassin deploys a brutal attack, sabotaging the underdog with a deck already stacked against Bryan. It's "business" as usual for WWE's nefarious villain, Triple H.

Craig and the crew from WWE.com did an excellent job chronicling my WrestleMania week. They followed me around, snapping pictures and asking questions. So did producers from WWE Network, as I was a focus for one of their short documentaries. They captured all the major moments of the week, so I feel like I don't have to say much about it. The only thing I will mention is that I'm probably the only person to main-event WrestleMania who flew there economy class. I didn't mind, though, because I had my future wife right next to me in the middle seat.

Despite everything going on—finalizing wedding plans, multiple crews documenting my days, and, of course, two hugely important main event matches—I was relatively calm and confident all week. I had stuff to do and my body to take care of; plus, the Superstars usually have a million signings, meet-and-greets, and media days. Truthfully, you get so swept up in the whirlwind that is WrestleMania week that you don't have time to be nervous. The only things

I was really anxious about were, first, the pain running down my arm and, second, my gear. There was nothing more I could do about the pain, but the gear I wore on WrestleMania was a very important and conscious decision I was going to have to make.

Since 2004, I've worn maroon in my ring attire. At the time, Dave Taylor was running a wrestling camp, and William Regal was there not just helping out, but also getting himself back into ring shape. On a trip to India, he had gotten a heart parasite, had to have his heart stopped, then started again, and couldn't wrestle for a year. But he was finally ready to come back. I went out to Atlanta and stayed with him to help him get ready, and it became an awesome, week-long learning experience. At the end of the week, Regal gave me a brand-new pair of maroon boots, maroon kneepads, and maroon trunks. Maroon was Regal's signature color for a long time, and from then on, it became the dominant color in my gear. It's a small nod of appreciation to the man who's been the biggest influence on my career.

Even though he hadn't ever talked to us about it back at his Academy, Shawn Michaels had some of the best ring gear ever. He also had some of the worst ring gear ever, like when he returned to WWE in 2002 after his back surgery and wore brown tights. With that notable exception and the times when he refereed in bike shorts, Shawn looked the part. My ring attire was never something I put a huge emphasis on early in my career, so when I started in WWE, I really had to step up my game as far as ring gear went.

What I wore when I debuted on NXT was just a basic, design-free maroon, which is what I liked when I was in Ring of Honor: plain. A few years later, I was reading a Jill Thompson comic called "Beasts of Burden," which was about a group of dogs (clearly something I'd be into). Through social media, Jill saw a photo of me reading her comic and reached out to say she thought it was awesome that I liked her book. I thought it was awesome that she liked wrestling and I asked her if she had any interest in making my ring attire because I always figured comic book artists would be the best at designing ring gear. Her first design was what I wore at Money in the Bank 2011; she viewed me as the classic wrestler, so she integrated the stripe from the design of a classic Ford Mustang into the gear she made. There was so much more thought put into it than I'd ever imagined would go into something like my ring attire.

When I was involved with the Wyatts a few months before WrestleMania 30, I knew I didn't want to wear exactly what they wore, even though that's what I ended up doing for the short, two-week run. What I originally envisioned, long term, was appearing more like one of my favorite bearded wrestlers, Bruiser Brody. When he competed, Brody wore furry boots and a fur jacket, and he wrestled like a wild man. When I explained the idea to Jill, she immediately drew up something awesome that I had never seen before: kickpads with fur on the back. I didn't know if it was possible, but I sent the design to my gear maker in Japan. He said he thought it was really cool and that he'd find a way to make it work. Within a month's time, he had it complete and in my hands, but it was far too late for me to use it as a Wyatt. Unsure of my direction for WrestleMania 30 and beyond, all I knew was that, at some point, I was going to have to wear this new gear.

WrestleMania is usually the time when all the top stars bust out their most elaborate gear. Heading into WrestleMania 30, I didn't want an extravagant robe like I had at WrestleMania XXVIII. That wasn't me, nor was it the character fans saw on TV every week. I did have some new gear designed that looked really nice, but I kept going back and looking at my unused Brody gear, which I loved. I recognized it was a radical departure from what I had been wearing, so I just wasn't confident it would work, yet I brought it for the trip, just in case.

On the Sunday of WrestleMania, I still didn't know what I was going to wear, so I brought both sets of gear to the stadium. I asked Bri for her opinion, and she liked the Brody gear, but, like me, she was indecisive about it. So that day, I just put it on and asked the one person whose advice on wrestling I trust more than anyone else's:

William Regal. He liked that it was different, though he couldn't tell if it was different *good* or different *bad*. His advice was that it was probably not the time to try something radically different. This might have been the first time ever I didn't take his advice.

I tried on my other new gear, and it looked good. However, the Brody gear had my heart, and at the last minute I decided to take the chance. It ended up not making a difference one way or the other, but besides the pain in my arm, that decision was the biggest stressor on the biggest day of my career.

Once the gear issue had been solved, I was focused exclusively on my matches. First up was the one-on-one match with Triple H, who had this awesome entrance. He emerged out of smoke, and the lights shone on a massive throne where he was seated with three scantily clad ladies by his side. Hunter was wearing a robe and a crown, but the robe had golden football-esque shoulder pads on it with enormous spikes sticking out of each side. The crown connected to a golden skull mask that covered his face, and as he stood up from the throne, the women unclasped the robe. He slowly took off the crown, and then his ring music hit for his walk down the ramp. The decadence and splendor of the whole thing fit him well. Likewise, the simplicity of my entrance fit me. I just came out in my Brody gear, wearing my usual shirt with my usual music doing my usual entrance. What made it special was that seventy-five thousand people were "Yes!"-ing on my entrance along with me.

When you're wrestling Hunter, regardless of when it is, you're in a main attraction with a guy who only wrestles a couple of times a year. I've never been looked at by WWE as the guy to wrestle any of the iconic Superstars who come back. It was neat because a moment before the match, I was able to take a step back from the situation and think about how I'd been watching Hunter wrestle since I was a teenager. The irony was not lost on me that Triple H's first 'Mania match, at WrestleMania XII, was the first WrestleMania I'd ever ordered. Nor was the coincidence that his first WrestleMania match was a supershort squash match against Ultimate Warrior, and my first WrestleMania match was a supershort squash match against Sheamus.

On top of that, Triple H was the first guy I'd ever been in the ring with who wrestles with an Attitude-era, heavyweight, main event style. My style in WWE is completely different, more of a fast-paced, cruiserweight style. One of the things I'd always loved about being an independent wrestler was the opportunity to wrestle so many different people with so many different styles, and this was a chance to do that on a much grander scale than I had ever done before. The match itself was a blast. It wasn't a Triple H match and it wasn't a Daniel Bryan match; it was a blend of both. I did things I hadn't done in WWE before, like the front flip dive I used to do on the independents, just without doing it *into* the fans and without the springboard. (The last thing I wanted to do was slip while trying to spring up to the top rope on the biggest night of my career.) Triple H was great to work with, and I learned a lot from him in that one match. It's nearly impossible to explain to nonwrestlers this learning that happens as you wrestle someone, but afterward, it made me even more disappointed that I didn't get the experience of wrestling him and Shawn Michaels on a nightly basis the way guys like Randy Orton, Batista, and John Cena did.

Hunter and I took the crowd on a roller coaster, and when I hit the flying knee and pinned him, the crowd jumped up and down in excitement. With that win, I would, in fact, be going on to the final match of the night and contending for the WWE World Heavyweight Title. Making the moment even more dramatic, Stephanie got in the ring and repeatedly slapped me in the face, and then Hunter attacked me from behind to go after the shoulder that was "injured" in a beatdown he gave me two weeks prior to the show. As he slammed my shoulder into the ring post and whacked it really hard with a chair, the cheers instantly turned to boos.

25 HEALING KISS
SUNDAY, APRIL 6, 2014—7:09 P.M.

Wounded yet victorious, Bryan hobbles up the ramp in a condition that appears to signify that his greatest hope of winning the WWE World Heavyweight Title is in heavy jeopardy. The "Yes!" Man finds his fiancée waiting for him to pass through the curtain. She's overjoyed for her husband-to-be and proud of the "Yes!" Movement. So much yet lies ahead for both competitors, and so their exchange is short and is sealed with a kiss.

Due to Triple H's postmatch assault (which is methodically consistent with the one he'd levied on WWE programming weeks ago), Bryan receives attention from WWE medical trainers. The new "co"–No. 1 contender for the WWE World Heavyweight Title winces each time he raises his left arm farther during the assessment. Meanwhile, time ticks away before his triple-threat match against both Batista and Randy Orton. Some might stop right there. Quit. But the Animal and the Viper will have no choice but to face an unwavering American Dragon.

"I've got one more match," Bryan asserts. "I've fought through worse and I'll fight through this."

Soon after, jaws remain agape in the audience and around the world following the greatest upset in the history of WrestleMania. Brock Lesnar has rendered a blemish on the Undertaker's streak, and now that it's time for his second match of the night, Daniel Bryan aims to rally the Mercedes-Benz Superdome back into an optimistic frenzy by sustaining a one-armed "Yes!" chant. The WWE Universe was already pulling for the underdog warrior, but now, with the fall of a Phenom, Bryan has become the last hope for WWE fans this night.

After the opening encounter with Hunter, I went into near isolation in order to prepare for the second match. The first match was good and physical—the way I like it—but that also comes with repercussions. I had to allow my body to come down from that first high, then get ready to repeat it just a few hours later. I'd done this before, but never at such a high level—and as I get older, the harder it becomes. It's not as easy now as it was when I was twenty years old doing the Super 8 and King of Indies tournaments, especially with my neck issue.

I was so focused on getting ready that I didn't even see it when Brock Lesnar pinned the Undertaker, ending his WrestleMania winning streak at 21-1. I heard the bell, turned over and looked at the monitor, then stood in shock as I saw Brock with his hand raised, while the Undertaker was down. This was the one match that everybody *knew* the finish of, and we were all wrong. Myself included. As a performer, the first thing I recognized was that with Brock's win, the life and energy were suddenly gone inside the Superdome. On trons around the venue, there were amazing shots of the audience's reactions and people standing with their mouths wide open, as if they had just witnessed the impossible. I'm sure if they had filmed the Superstars and Divas backstage, there would have been even better stunned reactions. My concern instantly went to Bri. Her match was next, and the silence that permeated the Superdome was eerie. The ending of the Undertaker's streak was one of the most shocking, monumental events in WrestleMania history. And now Bri and the other Divas had to follow it. I kept my eyes glued to the screen to see how she would do.

Throughout the week, I could tell how eager Bri was for her match at 'Mania—a fourteen-woman match for the Divas Championship. After the disappointment the year before of having their match pulled right before they went out, this time the Bella Twins had to go out in front of a crowd completely deflated by the Undertaker loss. But Bri wouldn't be deterred. Even though it was a short match, she did her best. She and Nicole were able to get the crowd back into it when the two of them did a double-suicide dive to the floor, rarely seen from the Divas, and then came back and had the first Bella face-off in a long time. When they went at it, fighting back and forth until Nicole hit Bri with her Rack Attack, the crowd came up for it. She did a great job with the opportunity she had, and I was very proud of my soon-to-be-wife.

I was getting ready to go on next, and as I was getting ready to walk out, I saw Undertaker just outside of the Gorilla position, lying down in a heap on the floor. He'd suffered a serious concussion, and a doctor and a trainer were checking on him, among other people. I walked past the scene as I went out and couldn't help but think of how much Undertaker had given of his body and of himself to make WrestleMania special. Our main event needed to keep it special. For the first time, I felt the pressure of the moment. All I could do was focus on my performance.

26 YES! HE DID!
SUNDAY, APRIL 6, 2014—9:51 P.M.

Hurting but unrelenting, Daniel Bryan manages to keep Batista and Randy Orton at bay until the three-way dance starts to resemble more of a handicap scenario, not in Bryan's favor. He's explosive despite an exhausting exhibition with the Game merely two hours earlier; the fight in Daniel Bryan is inconceivable.

The rapt audience only grows louder with each passing moment. The collective voice of seventy-five thousand individuals in New Orleans seems to suggest there's not a soul in the crowd who's not pulling for the "Yes!" Man . . . except two deplorable souls named Triple H and Stephanie McMahon.

They try everything to intervene, even coming equipped with their own crooked referee, a returning Scott Armstrong (last seen cheating Bryan out of the championship seven months before). Bryan persists. He forces the Game to eat sledgehammer, then performs an Authority-crippling Flying Goa" dive to the outside. In the midst of his fury, his opponents strike hard. Their vile innovation to take out the bearded hero? A Batista Bomb–RKO combo through an announce table—a lethal result of an Evolution reunion, as if it's 2004.

The WWE Universe refuses to give up on Daniel Bryan, and he does the same. Midtransport on a stretcher, the grizzled grappler rolls off the gurney and treads back into action against Batista and Orton as they decimate one another. Charging knee strikes fell both foes; then it's the faithful maneuver sharing its name with his Movement that renders a new WWE World Heavyweight Champion. At last, the Animal, Batista, is tamed by submission. He taps out to the "Yes!" Lock, and a brilliant new era begins in WWE.

Confetti pours from all corners of the Mercedes-Benz Superdome and envelops the entire ringside area, including WWE's newly christened champion. "Ride of the Valkyries" never sounded so good.

The euphoria is infectious inside the stadium. Swathed in purple and gold confetti, WWE fans are taking photos to capture the moment when the "Yes!" Movement—their crusade—reached the Promised Land. In the ring, the indie star turned WrestleMania history-maker implores his sister and family to cherish and savor this emotional triumph inside the ring. Billie Sue's younger brother has come a long way from sleeping on her sofa on wrestling tours. Tonight, this humble family from Aberdeen, Washington, sits at the epicenter of the entire WWE Universe.

Walking out, I could tell the crowd was different than during the first match a few hours earlier. The whole atmosphere had changed after Undertaker's defeat, and even though Bri, Nicole, and the rest of the Divas did a good job, the crowd was back to an eerie silence, still stunned and distracted. I came out last, after Randy Orton and Batista. As I "Yes!"-ed down the ramp, some people joined in, but it was nowhere near like it was in the beginning. The first seven or eight minutes of the match, the audience was still relatively quiet, despite all three of us working our asses off. The longer we went, however, the more the crowd got into it. When I hooked Randy in the "Yes!" Lock and Triple H came out to pull the referee out of the ring, the fans truly came alive. We had them after that. They were sucked into the story, the underdog with everything stacked against him while trying to achieve his dream. Finally the audience came back to enjoying what they were watching.

We tied in events that happened months before, like bringing in Scott Armstrong as Triple H's personal referee, since he was the ref that screwed me at Night of Champions. But I kicked Scott in the head as I was down and he fell out of the ring; then I dove onto him and Triple H. Next, Hunter tried to hit me with a sledgehammer, his weapon of choice for years, but I stopped it and hit him with it. Just when it looked like I might beat The Authority, Randy and Batista were back in control and started beating the crap out of me.

The scariest thing we did all night was a spot where Batista stood on one announce table, powerbombed me onto the other, and Randy jumped off some steps and gave me his RKO on my way down. The spacing of it was difficult, because Batista couldn't see with the powerbomb, and tables are always unpredictable at best. Luckily, we escaped with none of us getting hurt, although Randy came the closest, landing atop a television monitor on the way down. The crowd erupted at the spectacle. After that, medical staff strapped me to a stretcher and started taking me to the back, but shortly after we passed the ring, I started fighting my way off the stretcher. It was like a movie scene with the hero being nearly beaten to death but refusing to give up. Just when it looked like Batista was going to beat Randy, I ran in and hit him with the flying knee and trapped him in the "Yes!" Lock. There was this moment in time, in between me putting Batista in the hold and him actually tapping out, where there was this incredible energy emanating all around us. It's the energy of expectation, that what you'd hoped would happen might actually *be* happening in that exact moment. I don't know if that was my own internal energy or the energy of the audience, or maybe even it was all in my head.

When Batista tapped out, all of a sudden, a dream became a reality. Not only had I main-evented WrestleMania 30, I won the WWE World Heavyweight Championship. I was fulfilled that the match had come out as good as we had hoped and that the crowd reacted to it as such. As purple and gold streamers came down, I started hoisting the two heavy titles up in the air, yelling "Yes!" I went down to ringside and hugged my mom, my two little nieces, and my sister, Billie Sue, then told her to come into the ring with my oldest niece. A majority of the stadium was still on their feet and chanting with me.

The whole thing didn't feel real. It was like being in somebody else's body, living somebody else's life. The only thing that kept taking me out of this moment was the producers relaying the instruction to "keep 'Yes!'-ing." After two long, hard matches and my right arm being weak as it was, lifting each of the twenty-pound titles again and again was exhausting. Soon I just tried to ignore them telling me to "Yes!" as much as possible, and instead, I simply enjoyed the moment. This was everything I had wanted since the time I was a little kid.

When you experience a moment like that, there are always things you think of that could have made it better. In this case, I wish Bri had come down to the ring to join in the celebration. (She wanted to, but was stopped in Gorilla and told she couldn't.) We don't have any pictures in our house that would indicate to anybody that either of us wrestled at all. I would've liked a picture of Bri and me with my sister and my niece in the ring filled with confetti for the biggest moment of my career. My only other wish was that my dad could have been there in New Orleans to see that live as well, but he wasn't able to make it down to WrestleMania.

27 THE JOURNEY CONTINUES
SUNDAY, APRIL 6, 2014–10:18 P.M.

"'Yes!'-ing with those titles is a lot harder than you would imagine," jokes Bryan, still catching his breath on the other side of the curtain. "We had seventy-five thousand people out there tonight, and they were amazing. They made this moment happen, and they made this moment special. And for that, I can never thank them enough."

Just ahead of him is a diverse but committed crew of familiar faces waiting for the man of the hour when his ticker-tape-dusted frame crosses through the curtain. WWE Superstars, indie alumni, and Bret "Hit Man" Hart—one of Bryan's wrestling muses—are among those on hand to applaud the individual who refused to be told he couldn't be WWE World Heavyweight Champion. The Celtic Warrior, Sheamus, who made his own World Title WrestleMania moment at Bryan's expense two years ago, shares a strong embrace with his friend.

Yet it's a beautiful friend, confidante, fan, and lover who offers the warmest arms to Bryan. Though titleless herself despite her best efforts in the Divas Championship Invitational earlier, Brie smiles ear-to-ear at her fiancé's accomplishment. They exchange I-love-yous, and Bryan drapes his good arm over her. They exit the backstage ramp and walk on toward a brilliant future as husband and wife.

From here, they'll return to their lives in a brand-new dream home. They'll pick up their French bulldog, Josie, from doggy daycare. They'll finalize their plans for the (unofficially titled) "Yes!" Wedding and say "I do" five days from now. Plus, there's always Raw.

The World Champion "Face of WWE"—more appropriately, "Sweet Face," as Brie likes to identify her fiancé—just grew a beard.

She might not have been allowed to come down to the ring, but Bri was the first person I saw as I came through the curtain, and I gave her a big hug. She was beaming and seemed so proud of me. I thanked Randy and Batista, who worked their asses off and, in truth, worked around me. Randy kind of knew I was in bad shape, and they did their best to make me look as good as possible. I thanked Hunter, both for the match earlier and for helping make the main event so special. Then I thanked Vince. He gave me a big hug and congratulated me on the performance. None of this would have been possible without the opportunities he'd given me.

One of the special things about this moment was being able to share it with friends I had known throughout my career. Seth Rollins and Cesaro. Sheamus and Cody Rhodes. Glenn. Jamie Noble, whom I hugged since he'd done so much to get me to that point.

And then there was William Regal. It's impossible for me to overstate how much he has been there for me, ever since I was nineteen years old. He was there through it all, and I would never have gotten anywhere near WrestleMania without him. Seeing him after the match, there was no way I could ever thank him enough for all he's done for me. I could see in his eyes how proud he was of me, in the way a father is proud of a son, and it touched my heart.

I got to the dressing room, and for a while I sat there by myself, immersed in a powerful moment of solitude. So many things in my life don't feel real. When I gallop down to the ramp with thousands of people screaming "Yes!" with me, it doesn't feel real. This amazing, beautiful woman loves me, and sometimes that doesn't feel real. What I had just done was not real; it was fiction. I fictionally bucked The Authority. I fictionally won a championship. I was surrounded by fiction, but succeeding in the fiction felt like a real accomplishment, and everyone around me was treating my success in the fiction as if it were a real accomplishment.

I wondered if the movie heroes ever felt like that after shooting an action movie, feeling as if they had really somehow saved the day. I would imagine not. I couldn't help but laugh at the ridiculousness of it all. Still, I was proud. I rested there, holding this fictional, symbolic championship, seizing the opportunity to reflect on what had happened. This wrestling thing is strange. It blends fiction with reality in a way that makes them sometimes hard to separate, even when you're on the inside. Regardless, it took my breath away, the scope of it—not for the destination, which was fiction, but rather for the incredible, *real* journey.

EPILOGUE

Five days after the biggest moment of my professional wrestling career, I stood next to a gorgeous stream, on a beautiful sunny day, surrounded by friends and family. When "Here Comes the Bride" started playing, emotion welled up inside me. After I hadn't seen her all day, when Bri turned the corner and slowly walked up the aisle of roses with her father, tears ran down my face. I was so happy. We vowed to love each other for the rest of our lives, a very powerful agreement, and one that neither of us takes lightly.

The rest of the night was magic, like a dream. We ate, we danced, and we laughed, surrounded by the people who had loved us throughout our lives. Before we went to bed, we consummated our marriage in rather spectacular fashion. Despite all the pomp and circumstance of WrestleMania 30, *that* day was the greatest day of my life.

If this were a movie, this is where the story would end. The protagonist accomplished his dream, then celebrated by marrying the love of his life. The viewer would turn off the TV feeling good, as if from then on, they lived happily ever after. But again, that would be fiction.

Bri and I left for our honeymoon in Hawaii—the first time I had ever been there—two days after our wedding. We stayed at an eco retreat and spent the week in a beautiful bamboo hut, where on one night we were able to watch a lunar eclipse directly from our bed. We woke every morning to the sun rising and went to bed shortly after it got dark. We hiked, we explored, we swam under waterfalls, and we bodysurfed in the Pacific Ocean. When we returned, I truly felt as if life had started anew, better and more vivid than it was before.

Two days later, I was in Baltimore, the city where I first won the World Heavyweight Championship. Bri and I were leisurely preparing to go to Raw, when I got a phone call. My dad had died, completely unexpected, at the age of fifty-seven. I went from an unequivocal high to an unequivocal low. If our wedding day was the best day of my life, the day my father died was the worst.

I cried and cried and cried and cried. I cry now as I write this. I did the opening segment of Raw that night, mostly because I didn't know what else to do. The next day, I flew to Washington, went to the funeral parlor, and saw my dad's face for the very last time. I hugged him, trying to say good-bye, but nothing felt good enough.

My dad had not been able to come to our wedding. He and his wife, Darby, were going to come; however, shortly before the wedding, Darby got bad pneumonia and was hospitalized. My dad told me he wished he could come, but if anything happened to Darby while he was gone, he would never forgive himself. Not only did I understand, I knew he was doing the right thing, and I told him as much. He stayed with his wife, the woman who had stood by him for over twenty years. After the wedding, I called him and told him how well it went and how happy I was. He loved hearing about it and was happy for me. For us.

Whenever anyone has asked me if wrestling is "worth it," meaning is the reward worth the pain, worth the travel, worth the being away from your family, I've always answered yes. And it always felt like it was. But I naïvely assumed that when I was done wrestling, I could always go home and make up for all the time I've missed with my family and friends. Now, going home isn't the same, and there is nothing I can do to make up for all the time I've spent away from my father. Instead of being proud of my accomplishments, all I feel is regret about not being there for the most important people in my life, the people who have loved me in a way that had nothing to do with wrestling. If you were to ask me today if all the reward was worth the sacrifices, I would say no. Yet I keep on because I'm not quite sure what else to do with myself and because stopping now won't give me any more time with my father.

The last time I saw my dad was Christmas of 2013. My sister came over to spend the holiday with us, along with her two daughters and her husband. My dad came over, and he was so excited that he was going to be able to play Santa for the girls. We had a nice Christmas dinner, and shortly afterward my dad went in to get dressed. We were all in the living room, where we have a sliding glass door, and all of a sudden we heard bells ringing. My oldest niece's ears perked up, and she turned to my sister to say, "Mom, it's Santa!" My dad came out in his Santa suit, saying, "Ho, ho, ho! Merry Christmas!" He played the part well, and his eyes were beaming as his two grand-daughters came to sit on his lap. When he left, we gave each other a big hug, and he told my sister and me how happy that night had made him. I will never forget that night.

While I was at the funeral home, seeing my father for the final time, one of Darby's daughters gave me a box my dad left for me. When I opened it, it contained a silver bracelet, presumably a gift he'd gotten me for the wedding. Inscribed on the front were my initials, and as I looked at the back of the bracelet, I started crying even harder. My dad had inscribed, "To the man that you've become, and the son you'll always be."

The last time I saw my dad, Christmas, 2013